BLACKS AND THE MILITARY
IN AMERICAN HISTORY

NEW PERSPECTIVES IN AMERICAN HISTORY

UNDER THE EDITORSHIP OF
James P. Shenton

John M. Dobson, POLITICS IN THE GILDED AGE:
A New Perspective on Reform

Gerald Sorin, ABOLITIONISM: *A New Perspective*

William L. Barney, THE ROAD TO SECESSION:
A New Perspective on the Old South

George Dargo, ROOTS OF THE REPUBLIC:
A New Perspective on Early American Constitutionalism

Blacks and the Military in American History

A New Perspective

Jack D. Foner

FOREWORD AND CONCLUSION
BY JAMES P. SHENTON

PRAEGER PUBLISHERS
New York • Washington

To my brother, Henry Foner

Published in the United States of America in 1974
by Praeger Publishers, Inc.
111 Fourth Avenue, New York, N.Y. 10003

© 1974 by Praeger Publishers, Inc.

Library of Congress Cataloging in Publication Data
Foner, Jack D.
　Blacks and the military in American history.
　(New perspectives in American history)
　Bibliography: p. 263.
　1. United States—Armed Forces—Negroes.
I. Title.
E185.63.F64　1974　355'.00973　70-151952
ISBN 0-275-50180-8
ISBN 0-275-84640-X (pbk.)

Printed in the United States of America

Contents

Foreword

by James P. Shenton

When W. E. B. Du Bois observed that the central question of the twentieth century would be the color line, he might well have added that it had been the central question of the previous three centuries. From the moment in 1619 when whites and blacks first met in the future United States, the blacks were consigned to a subordinate relationship. Over time the condition of the blacks worsened as the system of slavery pervaded all aspects of black life. Blacks, both free and slave, lived in a world in which their humanity was superseded by the fact that they were viewed by whites as commodities to be bought and sold in slave markets. It was a process that Abraham Lincoln succinctly described as "dehumanizing."

Emancipation established the legal fiction of black equality. More to the point, custom, mores, and traditional practice, as well as economic exploitation, combined to legitimize the imprisonment of blacks in the caste system of segregation. The response of the black was an amalgam of conflicting strains. Some struggled to prove their humanity by striking back through violent protest and, more often, covert resistance, only to have the white react with savage suppression. With greater frequency, blacks struggled to prove their worth by seeking to share with whites the risks and benefits of American society. If nothing else, their effort was to prove time and again that whites were ready to share the risks, while stubbornly blocking access to the benefits.

Nowhere has this experience been more fully demonstrated than in the black experience in the armed forces. Blacks have fought in every American war except for the one fought with Mexico. Free and enslaved blacks fought in all the colonial wars; they helped secure American independence; their blood was shed on both land and sea during the War of 1812; and their massive participation in the Civil War, according to Lincoln, insured the Northern triumph and the preservation of the Union. Nonetheless, whites persisted in believing that blacks were only passive onlookers in wartime. As recently as 1928, one historian could write: "The American Negroes are the only people in history who became free without any effort on their own behalf."

The black military experience since Appomattox has until recently been similarly characterized. Four black regiments fought in the Spanish-American War, but their achievements were belittled by white Americans determined to uphold and enforce an all-pervasive, expanding code of segregation. The ghastly incongruity of mocking black men who were ready to die for their country moved Paul Lawrence Dunbar, the black poet, to write in late 1898:

> The new attitude may be interpreted as saying: "Negroes you may fight for us, but you may not vote for us. You may prove a strong bulwark when the bullets are flying, but you must stand from the line when the ballots are in the air. You may be heroes in war, but you must be cravens in peace."

No less revealing was the recurrent white response to black participation in wartime. At first, whites refused to allow blacks to join the war effort, but as the struggle deepened whites were ready for the duration to have them as allies. And no less surely, blacks seeking to prove their worth would join the fight only to be thrust aside when peace returned. And even in wartime they were subject to indignities and humiliations. Rayford Logan, the black historian, remembered that being an officer gave no safety. It was a period in which "he was seared with the 'Mark of Oppression' more grievously than at any time in his civilian life."

The war to make the world safe for democracy had no sooner ended than the screws of segregation were further tightened. Blacks detected a less than subtle irony to the rising American concern over the dynamic growth of Nazi racism. As the United States mobilized to meet the danger, they were aware that the Air Corps excluded them, the Marine Corps barred them entirely, the Navy confined them to the mess crew, and the Army detailed them largely to menial tasks. It was a condition that Roy Wilkins summarized in these words: "At the beginning of World War II Negro Americans in uniform were virtually pariahs in their native land and its armed services."

Despite the humiliation and discrimination, blacks accepted World War II service. Whites faced with a struggle for survival once again permitted blacks in the hundreds of thousands to serve and die. A handful of them rose to military posts never before held by their race. But the overshadowing reality was the segregation that pervaded all the armed forces. Americans still served and died in a Jim Crow military establishment. But unlike the aftermath of previous wars, blacks refused upon its conclusion to return to the old ways. Instead, they insisted that their dues were fully and finally paid. They would either be full citizens or become domestic dissidents.

With the collapse of empire after World War II, increasing numbers of blacks came to see parallels between their condition in the larger American society and that of other non-white people in the former colonial areas of the world. They would mount their challenge to caste and segregation in the courts, in classrooms, at lunch counters, aboard public transportation, in the streets, and in the military. The armed forces, which have always been a microcosm of American society, have provided a faithful reflection of the larger society. The old forms of segregation and discrimination within the military have eroded and collapsed, but the disintegration of Jim Crow has brought the American into a final confrontation with a deeply rooted racism. The struggle to rid American society of ancient prejudices, and the no less bitter struggle to undo centuries of discrimination, remain the unfinished task. The color line has been breached but not eradicated.

In the remarkable account of the black military experience in America that Professor Jack Foner has written, he has traced a history that has been brutal, exploitative, and agonizing, but it was one that the black can face with pride. It is a history infused with black suffering and endurance. More importantly, it suggests that people who have borne such heavy burdens, and with transcendent dignity throughout, are bound to overcome.

Acknowledgments

It is a pleasure to acknowledge the cooperation of numerous persons and institutions in this project. I am particularly indebted to James P. Shenton of Columbia University, editor of the series, and to Gladys Topkis and Vivien Fauerbach of Praeger for their careful reading and invaluable assistance in preparing the manuscript for publication. I also owe thanks to my son, Eric Foner of the City University of New York, for a number of insightful suggestions; to Stanley Faulkner for generously placing his files at my disposal, including the manuscript "Racism and Discrimination in the Berlin Brigade"; and to Edward M. Coffman of the University of Wisconsin for permitting me to examine his paper, "The Blacks in American Military History." For cooperation in obtaining essential materials, gratitude is also expressed to the library staffs of Atlanta University Library, the Schomburg Collection of the New York Public Library, the Manuscript Division of the Library of Congress, the U.S. Army Military Research Collection, the Franklin D. Roosevelt and Harry S. Truman Libraries, the Yale University Library, the U.S. Military Academy Library, the Wisconsin State Historical Library, the National Archives, the Defense Department Race Relations Institute Library, and numerous others. I am grateful to Earla B. Robertson, of the Colby College Library staff, for her assistance in obtaining interlibrary loans. I owe a special debt of gratitude to the Leopold Schepp Foundation and the Humanities Grant Committee of Colby College for grants that facilitated the course of the research. Finally, my thanks to my wife, Liza, for her patience and encouragement.

BLACKS AND THE MILITARY
IN AMERICAN HISTORY

1

Black Soldiers and Seamen in the War for Independence

In the years before the Revolution, each colony raised its own militia to maintain domestic order and defend its frontiers against Indians and Europeans. Originally, every available man, slave and free black as well as white, was included in the militia. But colonial leaders soon developed misgivings about the presence of blacks in military units intended to maintain slavery by force if necessary. In addition, apprehension grew that slaves trained in the use of arms might revolt, stage joint uprisings of Indians and blacks, and defect to the Spanish or French. A group of Carolina patentees summed up these fears when they wrote that in arming blacks "there must be great caution used, lest our slaves when armed might become our masters."

Free blacks presented a special problem to colonial leaders of militias, for they were often viewed as potential leaders or instigators of slave revolts. Such fears persuaded the colonists to alter drastically the recruitment system for the militia. Blacks, both slave and free, were totally barred from bearing arms. In 1639, the first discriminatory provision in American history was passed. All Virginians, except blacks, were required to arm themselves. In 1656, Massachusetts reversed its previous position and excluded blacks from military service. In 1661, four years after an uprising of blacks and Indians in Hartford, Connecticut also barred blacks from military service. The other colonies soon followed suit.

Their mandatory exemption from military service appeared to place blacks in a privileged category, which led the colonists to alter their policy again. The militias continued to bar slaves, but new regulations now stipulated that free blacks must accept limited assignments in the militia. They were forbidden to bear arms but were required to serve as drummers, fifers, and trumpeters, as road and highway laborers, or on guard duty. Refusal to perform assigned duties was punishable by fine or imprisonment.

Wartime exigencies forced the colonists to rescind their restrictions, for the white population alone was not a sufficient source of troops to wage war against the Indians and then the French. The colonists therefore were compelled to accept blacks into military service and even offered slaves freedom as a reward for outstanding performance. When South Carolina faced an Indian attack in 1703, for example, it authorized masters to arm their slaves and promised freedom "at the charge of the publick" to any slave who killed or captured "one or more of our enemies." In 1715, several hundred South Carolinian slaves fought alongside their masters against the Yamassee Indians. Twenty-four years later, threatened by the Spaniards in Florida, the South Carolina Assembly authorized the governor to empower militia captains to enlist "recommended" slaves. But they were to receive arms only in times of general alarm and invasion. The law again promised freedom to slaves who killed or captured an enemy in battle. But a serious slave insurrection at Stono in September 1739, and the slave conspiracy in Charleston nine months later, led the Assembly to a "fearful re-examination of the militia question," which ended with the repeal of the law in 1740. Carolinians had become so fearful of slave revolts that, as John W. Shy has noted, they "no longer dared to arm Negroes; in fact, they hardly dared to leave their plantations in time of emergency."

In the French colony of Louisiana slaves were enlisted to help fight the Chickasaw and Natchez Indians. Many of these slave soldiers were freed and organized into a company under their own officers. Indeed, from the earliest times, among the French and Spanish in the New World freedom was obtained by service in black regiments.

During the four American wars against the French, laws excluding blacks from military service were again overlooked. Many towns, unable otherwise to furnish their quotas, gladly accepted all blacks. To slaves, the prospect of freedom made enlistment in the colonial forces attractive; for free blacks, the hope of elevating their low social status was the prime inducement.

Blacks served most extensively during the French and Indian conflict as soldiers, scouts, wagoners, laborers, and servants. As in previous colonial wars, they served in unsegregated units and received equal pay with whites. However, a slave had to surrender all or part of his wages to his master, and some slaves were compelled to return to slavery at war's end. But in a number of cases military service in the colonial cause brought freedom. Jeremy Belknap, a distinguished contemporary, explained the decline in the number of slaves in Massachusetts by 1763 by the fact that, in the two preceding wars, many of them were enlisted either into the army or on board with a view to procuring their freedom.

As Belknap indicated, military service of blacks included employment "on board" ships. Throughout the colonial era, the intolerable conditions aboard vessels frequently led white sailors to desert; ship captains were therefore often forced to rely on free blacks and slaves to man the ships, whether local fishing vessels, freighters, privateers, or even pirate vessels. Many ambitious slaves gained freedom by running away to join the crews of privateers.

Blacks played a significant role in the events leading to the American Revolution. In 1776, the total population of the rebellious colonies approached 3 million, of whom 600,000 were black. Most blacks were slaves, who were concentrated most heavily on the tobacco and rice plantations of the Southern colonies. In South Carolina black actually outnumbered whites, and in Georgia blacks constituted more than 40 per cent of the population.

On the night of March 5, 1770, five years before the outbreak of hostilities, Crispus Attucks, a runaway slave, became the first American killed while resisting British authority in the Boston Massacre. Attucks, whom John Adams held responsible for leading the charge of the patriots protesting the presence of British soldiers, was buried in a common grave with four of his white companions.

Blacks were active as Massachusetts took the lead in preparing for armed resistance. In March 1774, the Continental Congress designated certain units of the Massachusetts militia as "Minutemen," and, since the Congress had not placed a color bar on enlistments, the Massachusetts Committee of Safety permitted blacks to join town and village companies. Several promptly enlisted.

When the military phase of the Revolutionary War opened on April 19, 1775, blacks were among those who responded to the call to arms issued by Paul Revere and William Dawes. Blacks fought with the patriot forces at the Battle of Lexington and at Concord and were among the casualties in the battles.

After Lexington and Concord, white and black patriots entered the ranks of the provincial New England army. A black named Salem Poor enlisted in the 5th Massachusetts Regiment on April 24, 1775, directly from his service as a Minuteman; with two other blacks, Lemuel Haynes became one of Ethan Allen's Green Mountain Boys. Blacks participated in the first aggressive action of the American forces, on May 11, 1775, when Fort Ticonderoga was captured. Not long after, blacks participated extensively in the savage fighting at Bunker Hill. A black by the name of Peter Salem is reputed to have fired the shot that mortally wounded Major John Pitcairn, the leader of the British forces, and Salem Poor fought so bravely at Bunker Hill that fourteen Massachusetts officers signed a petition addressed to the Massachusetts legislature, requesting official recognition of Poor. "In the person of this said Negro" read the petition, "centers a brave and gallant soldier."

Although blacks had proved themselves brave and competent soldiers in the opening phases of the war, objections were soon raised, particularly by slaveholders, to their presence in the patriot army, and steps were taken to exclude them from service. On May 29, 1775, the Massachusetts Committee of Safety issued an order prohibiting the enlistment of slaves as "inconsistent with the principles that are to be supported, and reflect dishonor on this colony."

Other colonies followed the example of Massachusetts. On June 17, 1775, the Continental Congress assumed jurisdiction over the patriot army around Boston and appointed George Washington Commander-in-Chief. Washington viewed with distaste the use of black soldiers, and shortly after he took command his headquarters prohibited the enlistment of blacks. The order, dated July 9, 1775, instructed recruiting officers not to enroll "any stroller, Negro, or vagabond." It said nothing about blacks who were already in the service.

When the Continental Congress reconvened, an attempt was made to remove blacks already serving in the army. Edward Rutledge, delegate from South Carolina, introduced a resolution requiring that Washington discharge all blacks, free as well as slave. But the Congress refused its assent, even though the resolution was strongly supported by many of the Southern delegates.

On October 8, Washington and his staff met at Cambridge to consider, among other things, whether blacks should be enrolled in the new army and whether a distinction should be made between "such as are slaves and those that are free." They unanimously agreed to exclude slave and, by a large majority, to prohibit the enlistment of free blacks. An official delegation from the Congress that conferred with Washington later in the month endorsed the action, agreeing that blacks, bond and free, should be "rejected altogether" from military service. In accordance with these several decisions, Washington, on November 12, 1775, issued an order from Cambridge specifically forbidding the enlistment of blacks, although those already enlisted were to be allowed to finish their tours. State and local authorities quickly followed Washington's lead.

Thus, at the very outset of the struggle against Great Britain, the question of black troops exposed a basic and perennial contradiction in American democracy. The fears, prejudices, and vested interests implicit in slavery prevented the colonists from fully living up to the egalitarian creed with which they justified their rebellion.

The cessation of black recruitment had been dictated by several factors. Most colonials were averse to depriving a master of his property. Colonial leaders who were themselves slaveholders were determined to close the road to freedom that the army had opened to slaves either as a refuge for runaways or as a reward for military service. Many leaders of the Revolution, including Washington, were unwilling to countenance the use of blacks as soldiers, for they considered them cowardly, servile, and distinctly inferior by nature. Also, although "many Northern blacks were excellent soldiers," according to Samuel Swet, a contemporary, "Southern troops would not brook an equality with whites." Above all, the possibility that arming bondsmen and training them would lead to insurrection stirred anxious fears. Many of those who did not share these fears and racist views nevertheless felt that it was both incongruous and morally wrong to expect slaves and free blacks, whose status was

severely limited, to share in the defense of freedom. Indeed, they
deeply resented such jingles as the following, which went the
rounds of the British and Tory soldiers early in the war:

> The rebel clowns, oh! what a sight
> Too awkward was their figure
> 'Twas yonder stood a pious wight
> And here and there a nigger.

But the decision to halt black recruitment did not meet with
universal approval. Blacks in and out of the army protested their
exclusion, and they were joined by not a few others. For example,
General John Thomas, writing to John Adams on October 24, 1775,
insisted that it was unwise to close the ranks of the patriot army to
blacks, many of whom in action "have proved themselves brave."

Soon events once again impelled a partial reversal of the exclusionary policy. At the very time that the American Army ended the
practice of recruiting blacks, the British adopted it, hoping in this
way to overcome their acute manpower shortage, to cripple the
rebellious colonies economically by inducing slaves to desert their
rebel masters and seek refuge within the British lines, and to convince the blacks, by offering them liberty in exchange for military
service, that their freedom depended on the success of British arms.
"Things are now come to that crisis," wrote General Thomas Gage
to Lord Barrington, the British Secretary-at-War, "that we must
avail ourselves of every resource, even to raise Negroes in our
cause." On November 7, 1775, Lord Dunmore, the Royal Governor
of Virginia, issued a proclamation promising freedom to slaves of
rebel owners who would join the British and bear arms against the
American colonists. Slaves eagerly responded to Dunmore's proclamation, forcing Southerners to mount guards to deter their slaves
from entering British lines. Nevertheless, by December 1775, three
hundred slaves had joined Lord Dunmore's special unit, officially
designated the Ethiopian Regiment, to fight for their freedom in
uniforms bearing the inscription "Liberty to Slaves." Understandably, slaves in British uniforms generated alarm in the American
command.

Coupled with this new threat from the British was the problem
of holding the Continental Army together as enlistments expired at
the end of 1775. Despite appeals from Washington, few of those

whose time was up were willing to sign for another year, and new enlistments were also discouragingly slow. Washington dealt with the urgent need for manpower by utilizing the Congressional authority granted him to requisition short-term militiamen from several colonies. On December 30, 1775, "in a reversal of policy," he authorized recruiting officers to accept free blacks who wished to enlist. He informed John Hancock, President of the Congress, that the free black soldiers had expressed extreme displeasure at being discarded and that, if discharged and not allowed to re-enlist, they might "seek employment in the ministerial army." Washington explained that he intended to re-enlist free black soldiers unless the Congress ordered otherwise. On January 17, 1776, the Congress accepted the general's recommendation and agreed to the re-enlistment of free blacks "who have served faithfully in the army at Cambridge" but insisted that no others should be accepted. Thus the British action had forced the leaders of the Revolution to modify their initial policy.

Early in 1776, British officers on the coast of Georgia promised freedom to defecting slaves, and soon many slaves joined the British forces. Indeed, so many slaves were said to be deserting their masters for the British Army that in April South Carolina passed an act authorizing the death penalty for blacks found guilty of fleeing to the British or persuading others to do so. At that time the Reverend Dr. Samuel Hopkinson of Rhode Island, "the most influential theologian of the American Revolutionary period," appealed to the Continental Congress for speedy action to prevent black bondsmen from seeking liberty in the British service. The only meaningful deterrent, he insisted, was to offer freedom to slaves who fought for the American cause. "This would at once be doing them some degree of justice, and defeat our enemy in the scheme they are prosecuting." The Congress, reluctant to antagonize the slaveholders, refused to respond to this appeal. However, events were once again to compel a reversal of the exclusion policy.

As the war progressed, a critical manpower shortage plagued the American effort. In September 1776 the Congress ordered the states to raise eighty-eight battalions of Continentals to serve for three years or the duration of the war. Three months later, Washington was authorized to enlist sixteen more battalions. By January 1777, all states were requested "forthwith to fill up by drafts, from their militia or in any other way . . . their respective battalions of Continental troops."

The imposition of state quotas and the passage of the draft facilitated black enlistments. Despite inducements of bounties of money and land, white men were still reluctant to sign up for extended service. As a consequence, without Congressional sanction, the Northern and Middle-Atlantic states authorized the enlistment of free blacks to meet their quotas. As the war continued, these states eventually were obliged to authorize the enlistment of slaves, the owners to receive compensation and the blacks their freedom at war's end.

The most radical step was taken by Rhode Island, which early in 1778, with two-thirds of the state occupied, was experiencing grave difficulty in raising its quota of two battalions. In January 1778, General James Varnum proposed to Washington that the two seriously depleted Rhode Island battalions encamped at Valley Forge be united and their officers sent home to raise a new battalion, to be composed of blacks. Governor Nicholas Cooke of Rhode Island approved Varnum's proposal and a month later the Rhode Island assembly authorized the enlistment of blacks and the formation of a black battalion, offering freedom to those who enlisted for the duration of the war, granting them the same pay and bounties as whites, and compensating their masters for the value of the slaves up to $400. The preamble to this measure stated that "history affords us frequent precedents of the wisest, freest and bravest nations having liberated their slaves and enlisted them as soldiers to fight in defence of their country." Governor Cooke, notifying Washington of the legislature's favorable action, added that the measure had been adopted because it was "impossible to recruit our battalions in any other way."

Rhode Island's "black battalion" was ultimately composed of five companies numbering 226 officers and men and was headed by Colonel Christopher Greene, a white. Similar proposals for the enlistment of all-black units of slaves failed to pass the Massachusetts and Maryland legislatures. However, Connecticut organized a black company consisting of fifty-two enlisted men, which fought as a separate unit between June 1780 and November 1782, when it was disbanded and its members were distributed among the white companies of a battalion.

The substitution system further advanced the recruitment of blacks. A draftee could avoid service by supplying someone to take his place, and many slaveholders in the North, who wished to avoid field service, sent their slaves as substitutes. An entry in the journal of a Hessian officer as early as October 23, 1777, read: "The Negro can take the field instead of his master, and therefore no regiment is to be seen in which there are not Negroes in abundance, and among them are able-bodied and strong fellows."

In 1777 Connecticut allowed masters to free slaves who served as substitutes for white citizens. New Hampshire permitted slaves and free blacks to meet the state levies, and those who signed up for three years received freedom and the same bounties as whites. Massachusetts authorized black enlistments in 1778, and three years later New York passed a law emancipating blacks whose masters allowed them to enlist.

Once the decision to use black soldiers had been made, many positive aspects were discovered. As Donald L. Robinson states:

> Negroes were less reluctant than whites to sign up for long enlistments, and readier to go wherever their commanders ordered them. Typically, they had fewer reasons for clinging to civilian life and were thus less likely to desert their regiments to go home. Thus they made better Continental soldiers. Furthermore, when blacks served in the Continental regiments, whites could be given shorter enlistments and be saved for local defense.

Among the Southern states only Maryland officially permitted slave enlistments. In October 1780 the legislature authorized the recruitment of slaves with the consent of their masters. Seven months later it decreed that free blacks "were . . . subject to the draft."

In July 1775 Virginia opened the militia to "all free male persons." Soon slaves were deserting their masters for the army, pretending to be free blacks, or were being passed off as such by masters eager for them to serve as substitutes for themselves or their sons. Two years later a supplementary act required "recruiting officers to take only those Negroes or mulattoes who could produce a certificate of freedom issued by a justice of peace." It left in service those blacks already enrolled.

The Lower South consistently opposed black enlistments despite repeated efforts in the Congress and the army to persuade South Carolina and Georgia to permit black enrollment. Early in 1778, the British shifted their major offensive operations southward, anticipating aid from large numbers of loyalists and blacks. Within the year Savannah and Augusta, Georgia, had fallen. From Georgia the British Army invaded South Carolina. The march of the British Army through the South sent thousands of slaves pouring into the British lines, especially after word spread that Sir Henry Clinton had officially promised freedom to all slaves who deserted rebel masters for British service.

As the situation grew more desperate, Governor John Rutledge of South Carolina asked the Congress for help. A committee of five was immediately appointed to study the critical situation in the Southern states and to find "ways and means for their safety and defense." The committee report submitted on March 25, 1779, stated that more soldiers were badly needed for the defense of South Carolina and Georgia; that no forces were available from the Continental Army; that the Continental battalions of the two states were inadequate for their defense; and that the militia could not effectively defend the states because so many citizens had to remain at home to prevent their slaves from revolting or deserting to the enemy. The committee therefore proposed to meet the emergency by having South Carolina and Georgia immediately raise a force of three thousand black troops and organize them into separate battalions commanded by white officers and noncommissioned officers, appointed by the two states. For each slave who enlisted and passed muster, the committee recommended that the Congress pay his master up to $1,000. The black soldiers themselves would receive no bounty or pay but would be fed and clothed at the expense of the federal government. Those who survived and served "well and faithfully" to the end of the war, and then turned in their arms, would be freed with a fifty-dollar bonus. The committee assured the Congress that blacks would make good soldiers because they were easy to discipline and, once trained, would reduce the danger of revolts and desertions by drawing off "the most vigorous and enterprising" of the slaves, at the same time pacifying the others by holding open the door of possible freedom. Finally, they urged that, since the proposal might "involve inconveniences" to South Carolina and Georgia, the Congress should meet the cost of the project.

On March 29, the Continental Congress unanimously endorsed

the proposal but stipulated that it be put into effect only with the consent of the two states concerned. On the same day, John Laurens, who had suggested the proposal to his father, a member of the committee, was commissioned by the Congress as a lieutenant colonel to head the black battalion. He was instructed to present the proposal to the state legislatures of South Carolina and Georgia. Henry Laurens doubted the likelihood of his son's success in trying "to persuade rich men to part with the very source of their wealth, and, as they suppose, tranquillity."

Henry Laurens's doubts proved justified. Fear of black insurrection bordered on panic in the Lower South, and it was inevitable that the Congressional proposal should be viewed as a serious threat to the social and economic order. "Many in South Carolina and Georgia," one historian notes, "regarded arming the slaves as an unpleasant way to commit suicide." "We are much disgusted here," wrote Christopher Gadsden, aristocrat and politician, from Charleston, "at the Congress recommending us to arm our slaves, it was received with great resentment, as a very dangerous and impolitic step." In spite of Laurens's pleas in its behalf, the measure was rejected overwhelmingly "with contemptuous huzzahs" by the South Carolina legislature. Indeed, the proposal impelled the privy council to recommend that South Carolina withdraw from the conflict, a proposal that failed of acceptance.

While John Laurens was absent abroad on a special mission to seek aid from France, General Benjamin Lincoln, commander of the Southern army, repeatedly pointed out the need to enlist black troops, but South Carolina remained adamant in its opposition to the arming of slaves. One thousand slaves, however, were ordered enrolled as pioneers, fatiguemen, oarsmen, and mariners. In 1781, General Nathaniel Greene, who had replaced Lincoln, warmly supported the proposal that South Carolina and Georgia arm the slaves. "That they would make good soldiers," he assured Governor Rutledge, "I have not the least doubt." Greene was no more successful than Lincoln.

In 1782, after his return from France, John Laurens made a second and a third attempt to win the support of the South Carolina legislature for black troops, a proposal that also proved futile, even though he proposed to take only slaves of confiscated Tory estates. Donald Robinson says, "The South Carolinians were determined not to arm the blacks, however helpless they might be without them." Instead, in order to induce whites to enlist in the Continental Army, the legislature on February 25, 1782, offered "a slave as bounty to each new recruit." The Georgia legislature delayed action on the Congressional proposal until June 1782, and then quickly rejected it. "So," writes the historian John R. Alden, "ventures which might have given a powerful impulse toward gradual destruction of slavery failed."

The specter of a slave insurrection also haunted loyalist slaveowners in America and West Indian sugar planters. They successfully prevented the British from mobilizing significant numbers of slaves with the promise of emancipation. Thus, a common fear of the repercussions that would flow from the arming of slaves effectively limited the number of black soldiers used by both sides to meet chronic manpower shortages in the War for Independence. Both sides apparently were far less apprehensive about employing blacks aboard ships. During the war blacks were common in the Continental Navy, in the state navies, and on privateers. They served on the ships as gunners, seamen, and cooks and performed their duties well. Blacks were present at John Paul Jones's engagement with the British ship *Serapis*.

More black sailors served on state naval vessels than on Continental ships, for the pay was usually better and the term of enlistment shorter. Even in the South, blacks were commonly used as ordinary seamen or pilots to meet manpower needs. Black sailors in the South were mostly slaves. Caesar, a slave pilot from Virginia, fought in two naval engagements, receiving praise from his superiors on both occasions.

Blacks, many of them runaway slaves, found widest employment during the Revolution on privateers whose captains rarely bothered to inquire about the status of their black crewmen. James Forten, serving at the age of fourteen on a Pennsylvanian privateer, was captured, imprisoned for refusing to change sides, and consigned to a prison ship for seven months. After the war he acquired wealth and fame as the inventor of an improved sail and as an abolitionist.

Blacks also served in the British Navy, mainly as pilots leading British raiding expeditions up the narrow and tortuous bayous of the Southern tidewaters.

By the end of the war some 5,000 blacks had seen service with the American forces. The New England states furnished more black soldiers than any other region. Underlying the slaves' willingness to serve was their desire to escape slavery. The names the slaves gave themselves reflected their hopes: Dick Freedom, Jeffrey Liberty, Jube Freeman. According to the historian Benjamin Quarles, the black's loyalty was not to a people but to a principle. "Insofar as he had freedom of choice, he was likely to join the side that made him the best offer in terms of those 'inalienable rights' of which Mr. Jefferson had spoken." Quarles suggests several other reasons that free blacks volunteered in the patriot army, including the desire for adventure, belief in the goals of the Revolution or in the justice of the American cause, and the enticement of the bounty.

Most free blacks were subjected to the draft since few could afford a substitute. The typical black was an infantryman, invariably a private, and usually unarmed. A small number served in artillery regiments. The black soldier was likely to serve in the Continental Army for three years or more, often through the entire war. Rhode Island's "black battalion" fought for five consecutive years.

Blacks participated in almost every military engagement from Lexington and Concord to the siege of Yorktown. At the Battle of Rhode Island, where the newly recruited black troops confronted two Hessian regiments reinforced by British regulars, an observer who took part in the battle noted:

> Had they been unfaithful or even given away before the enemy all would have been lost. Three times in succession they were attacked with more desperate valor and fury by well-disciplined and veteran troops and three times did they successfully repel the assault and thus preserved our army from capture.

On May 4, 1781, during an engagement at Points Bridge, Croton River, New York, Rhode Island's black battalion suffered heavy casualties in a futile attempt to save the life of its commander, Colonel Greene. The survivors continued to serve until the end of the war, fighting courageously at the battles of Red Bank and Yorktown. Baron von Closen, describing the Continental Army passing in review at Yorktown, wrote: "Three-quarters of the Rhode Island regiment consists of Negroes, and that regiment is the most neatly dressed, the best under arms, and the most precise in its maneuvers."

A contingent of 545 free coloreds plus slaves from the French West Indies fought in the allied French forces with courage and skill during the unsuccessful 1779 siege of Savannah. Among those who took part in this and other campaigns on the American continent were several, including Henri Christophe, who later played important military and political roles in the liberation of Haiti. When Spain joined France as an ally of the American cause, black troops from Louisiana also saw service in the war. The Spanish organized militia companies of free blacks and slaves commanded by black officers of the line. In 1779, Governor Bernardo Galvez of Louisiana led "a half-white and half-black army" in a successful campaign to drive the British from Louisiana and the Mississippi Valley. Later that year, "with more slaves and free coloreds added to his force," Galvez took possession of Mobile and Pensacola. Six black officers were cited for bravery in this campaign and were rewarded with medals of honor from the King of Spain. Professor Ronald C. McConnell says of the Louisiana blacks in the American Revolutionary War:

> Not only had these troops performed creditably against the British, their first experience against trained European soldiers, ... but they ... contributed to America's winning of independence by helping to close the gateways to the American West and South through which the British planned to strike at the western flank of the colonies. In so doing they engaged British troops that might have been used elsewhere.

Most blacks in the American forces served in racially integrated units. The Continental Army from its inception included fifers and drummers in each company, typically blacks. Other blacks made valuable contributions by gathering intelligence about enemy troop movements, as military laborers employed in manufacturing the supplies of war, as drivers and guides, and as laborers repairing roads and building redoubts and outworks. As Quarles has said, the black was often, then as in subsequent struggles, the man "behind the man behind the gun."

Many blacks received commendations from their commanding officers, and several emerged as war heroes, including Jack Sisson, who facilitated the capture of Major General Richard Prescott, commander of British troops in Rhode Island, in July 1777 at Newport, apparently by breaking down a door with his head; and Jordan Freeman, who, armed only with a spear, fought the British at Fort Griswold in May 1779 and was slaughtered following the fort's seizure. On September 26, 1863, the *Army and Navy Journal*, in an article entitled "Negro Soldiers in the Revolution," declared:

> The record is clear, that from the beginning to the conclusion of the war of the Revolution, Negroes served in the Continental armies with intelligence, courage, and steadfastness; and that important results in several instances are directly traceable to their good conduct.

Quarles estimates that no more than a thousand blacks bore arms for the British, the bulk of them in the South. In the British Army as in the American, blacks served more as guides, spies, informers, and pilots than as combat soldiers. Blacks were also employed by the British as buglers, musicians, laborers, foragers, servants, and orderlies. The historian Sylvia Frey says:

> Negroes were perhaps the least fortunate members of the army. . . . They occupied the last rung in the British military caste. When provisions were short, the Negro was not victualled as a soldier, but was fed Indian corn. He was marked, like a piece of military equipment, with the number of the regiment or the initials of the department to which he was attached. Those not so designated were flogged out of camp on the orders of Cornwallis.

One corps, the Black Pioneers, was formed entirely of free blacks who fought for the Crown in anticipation of receiving grants of land. Another contingent, serving the British as "the King of England's soldiers," effected such harassment along the Savannah River that Georgia feared a general insurrection of blacks.

The American Revolution brought some specific gains for blacks. Some slaves in fact obtained the freedom promised in return for military service. However, not all slaves who fought for the patriot cause were freed. In 1782 Virginia sold almost all the state-owned slaves in its navy. Blacks elsewhere had to resist attempts by their masters to re-enslave them upon the expiration of their term of enlistment. Even the Virginia legislature found the efforts of former masters too much to accept and on October 20, 1783, passed a law forbidding the re-enslavement of veterans who had been promised their freedom in exchange for service and declaring that all slaves enlisted as substitutes "should enjoy the blessings of freedom as a reward" for their service. However, not all states legislated freedom for slave substitutes, and while some masters kept their promises, others failed to do so. In any event, many black veterans simply took off for freedom without waiting to find out whether their masters would honor their promises.

Ironically, it appears that more blacks obtained their freedom by serving with the British than with the patriots. During the final days of the war, the ports of Charlestown, Savannah, and New York were filled with blacks who had sought refuge behind the British lines and who were waiting to be evacuated by sea. Prior to the surrender at Yorktown, the British carried off 5,000 of them. When the war ended, the British, in spite of protests by American slaveowners, set sail with more than 15,000 additional blacks. While the British refused to compensate the slaveowners for the loss of their property, the slaves did not always realize their expectations of freedom. Instead, many escaped slaves were carried off by loyalist slaveholders, and others were taken by British officers to the West Indies, where they were resold into captivity. The greatest number, however, were freed, and most of these liberated blacks settled eventually in the West Indies, Florida, or Canada. About 3,000 blacks settled for a time in Nova Scotia, and in 1792, led by Thomas Peters, a black loyalist ex-sergeant, approximately 1,200 black Nova Scotians, disappointed and disillusioned over their failure to receive the land pledged to them, crossed the Atlantic to take up land in the recently founded colony of Sierra Leone on the west coast of Africa.

The American Revolution, then, did produce an improvement in the status of black people. Out of military necessity, many were permitted to serve in the American or British forces and thereby secured their freedom. Invoking the ideology and rhetoric of the Revolution, individual slaves petitioned for manumission, and in groups they memorialized the legislatures to abolish human bondage. In the flood of revolutionary idealism during the war and in the immediate postwar years, some masters freed their slaves, a number of states prohibited the slave trade, and Southern states such as Virginia and Maryland liberalized their manumission laws, opening a door through which thousands of slaves ultimately passed to freedom. In the North, Vermont, New Hampshire, and Massachusetts abolished slavery outright, while other states made provision for gradual emancipation. Former black soldiers and seamen such as the founder of black Masonry, Prince Hall, and the wealthy Philadelphia sailmaker and abolitionist James Forten emerged as leaders of the developing free black community of the North. The Reverend Lemuel Haynes became a preacher to white congregations in southern New England and Vermont.

Still, one should not magnify the impact of the antislavery and antiprejudice impulses growing out of the revolutionary ideology. In the South, where the vast majority of slaves were located, only a relative few gained their freedom as compared with the great number still held in bondage. And in the North, even where freedom was achieved, social, political, and economic equality for blacks remained strikingly absent. Moreover, the services of the blacks in the Revolutionary War were soon forgotten. There are no national heroes and hardly a monument to remind us that blacks fought in the American Revolution and that, in the face of frequent prejudice, they compiled a record of honorable service. In February 1831 Forten pointed this out in a communication expressing his opposition to the proposal of the American Colonization Society calling for the removal of free blacks to the west coast of Africa:

> I well remember that when the New England Regiment marched through this city [Philadelphia] on their way to attack the English Army under the command of Lord Cornwallis, there was several companies of coloured people, as brave men as ever fought, and I saw these brave men who fought at the Battle of Red Bank, under Col. Breen, where . . . the Hessians were defeated. All this appears to be forgotten now, and the descendants of these men, to whom we are indebted for the part they took in the struggle for independence, are intended to be removed to a distant and inhospitable country.

2

From the Revolution to the Civil War

Between the end of the Revolution and the outbreak of the Civil War, the social, political, and economic conditions of all blacks steadily deteriorated. In the South, the post-Revolution liberalization movement came to a halt in the early nineteenth century, and subsequently controls on the slave population steadily tightened. In the North, blacks lost the right to vote, faced increasing discrimination and segregation, and surrendered even their menial jobs to Irish and German immigrants. The policy of excluding blacks from military service, except for some individuals relegated to menial positions, was an early indication of their deteriorating condition.

The Constitution vests the power to regulate military forces in both the national and the state governments. Nowhere does it restrict membership in the regular army or the militia to individuals of any particular race. Nor did the act of April 30, 1790, which simply defined recruits competent to enter the service as "able-bodied men," deny blacks a place in the regular army. Yet, although black veterans of the War for Independence would have become part of an experienced nucleus for the new nation's armed forces, blacks were largely barred from military service by the racial policies of the regular army as well as the state militia. It is true that the Militia Act of May 8, 1792, called for the enrollment of "each and every able-bodied white male citizen between the ages of 18 and 45," although it is unclear whether the act forbade the enlistment of blacks or merely required whites to enroll. In any case, all the Northern states and Maryland and Virginia interpreted the law as excluding blacks from military service, and in their own militia laws they barred blacks. Paradoxically, South Carolina and Georgia utilized free blacks as fatigue men, pioneers, and musicians. North Carolina actually included free blacks in the militia as late as 1812; thereafter they served as "musicians only."

Several factors account for the exclusion of blacks from combat roles. The "low manpower demands" after 1792 lessened the need for them. Moreover, the militia quickly took on importance as a social and political institution. As Robert J. Gough notes:

> Drill day, the quarterly occasion when an entire company mustered, was often an opportunity for community gathering and festivities. For politically ambitious individuals, leadership in the militia was a useful stepping stone to state office. Understandably, white militiamen would not wish to have blacks involved in such political and social matters.

An unstated factor was the fear generated by the Haitian Revolution. During the 1790's and the early years of the nineteenth century, the greatest slave rebellion of modern history racked the island of Haiti. Led by Toussaint L'Ouverture, a black slave army utilizing guerrilla tactics effectively defeated a series of French and British expeditionary forces, and finally, in 1802, defeated a powerful army dispatched by Napoleon under the generalship of Victor Leclerc. Defeat ended Napoleon's dreams of reviving France's American empire and led directly to the sale of Louisiana to the United States, which, ironically, opened vast new areas for the expansion of slavery. "The United States," Winthrop Jordan writes, "was not then or afterward overwhelmed with gratitude for Haitian assistance." Instead, stories of racial warfare and atrocities in Haiti led to the tightening of Southern slave codes, the exclusion of blacks from the militias, and the barring in 1798 of blacks from the Marines and naval forces. Not until World War II would blacks again serve in the Marines, but the restriction in the navy proved difficult to enforce. Naval officers unable to recruit sufficient numbers of white sailors continued to enlist free blacks, and blacks were among those impressed by the British in the years leading up to the War of 1812. Thus, in 1807, a British warship stopped the American warship *Chesapeake* and took from the crew at gunpoint several men—including three blacks.

Finally, on June 12, 1812, the United States declared war on Great Britain. The Congressional acts of 1811, 1812, and 1814 contained no racial restrictions; they referred simply to "able-bodied, effective men," or "free, effective, able-bodied men." But despite the absence of Congressional prohibition, blacks were still excluded. During the first two years of the war blacks tried to volunteer, but despite the acute troop shortage their efforts were generally futile, except when individual captains, contrary to regulations, accepted blacks. Secretary of War John Armstrong received several appeals urging the recruitment of black units. For example, Alexander Bill, a white infantry officer, wrote Armstrong from Vermont, "The Negroes of New England are actuated by principles equally honorable with those of the whites, and differ from them in nothing but the tincture of the skin." Such appeals proved unproductive.

Blacks had participated in the undeclared naval war with France, and since the Act of March 3, 1813, permitted the enlistment of free blacks, they flocked into the navy. They formed between 10 and 20 per cent of the crews and played a conspicuous role in American naval victories. Nathaniel Shafer, of the schooner *Governor Tompkins*, described the heroism of a black sailor who was mortally wounded during an Atlantic engagement:

> The name of one of my poor fellows who was killed ought to be registered in the book of fame, and remembered with reverence as long as bravery is considered a virtue; he was a black man by the name of John Johnson; a 24 lb. shot struck him in the hip and took away the lower part of his body; in this state the poor brave fellow lay on the deck and several times exclaimed to his shipmates, "Fire away, my boys, do not haul a color down."

Oliver Hazard Perry initially raised serious objections to the sailors assigned to him, describing a group of replacements as "a motley set—blacks, soldiers, boys," but added that he was satisfied to get "anything in the shape of a man." His commander, Isaac Chauncey, advised Perry that he had "fifty blacks" on his own ship and that "many of them are among my best men," adding: "I have yet to learn that the color of a man's skin or the cut and trimmings of the coat can affect a man's qualifications or usefulness." After his victory Perry spoke of his numerous black crewmen as "among my best men."

During 1813, large numbers of slaves again fled to the British, serving them as spies, guides, messengers, and laborers. The number of slaves escaping to the British increased sharply in the spring and summer of 1814, after Vice Admiral Sir Alexander Cochrane assumed command of British land and naval forces in the American theater and encouraged slaves to desert with the aim of "weakening the American economy and disrupting American society." On April 2, 1814, Cochrane issued a proclamation promising all those who were "disposed to emigrate" from the United States that they would be welcomed aboard British ships or at British military posts and given "their choice of either entering into His Majesty's sea or land forces, or of being sent as FREE settlers to the British possessions in North America or the West Indies, where they will meet with all due encouragement."

Cochrane did not mention slaves specifically, but the proclamation was given to raiding parties to distribute among the slave population, and many hundreds of slaves, largely from the Chesapeake region of Virginia and Maryland, came over to the British side in anticipation of freedom. About 200 former slaves were organized into a unit of black marines, which participated in the major Chesapeake campaigns of 1814. These black marines were part of the British forces that in late August defeated the Americans at Bladensburg, seized and burned Washington, and attacked Baltimore.

Following the fall of Washington, blacks loyal to the American cause joined whites in erecting breastworks and fortifications at Baltimore, Philadelphia, and New York. In October, the New York legislature authorized the enlistment of 2,000 black troops, including slaves whose masters would receive their pay and bounty while the blacks would receive their freedom.

After their Chesapeake campaign the British turned their attention to New Orleans. When the United States acquired Louisiana, it inherited "an organized and disciplined colored militia," composed of free blacks who wore an eagle on their caps. Although they had provided invaluable services to the French and Spanish authorities by their forays against runaway slaves in the swamps, many white inhabitants opposed their continued use, fearing collaboration between rebellious slaves and the militiamen. The Haitian rebellion intensified their fears, and in 1804 the black militia was dissolved. An unsuccessful attempt was made to reactivate it in

1807. Ironically, when a 500-man slave force was marching toward New Orleans, free blacks responded to the call for volunteers and were gladly accepted by territorial Governor William C. C. Claiborne. He later reported that they performed their mission "with great exactitude and propriety."

In April 1812, Louisiana achieved statehood, and nine weeks later war broke out with England, creating a serious need for troops to bolster the defenses of New Orleans. In August, the legislature, after a bitter struggle, authorized the governor to enroll free black landholders in the militia. Claiborne organized the four authorized companies of sixty-four men each into a unit known as the Battalion of Free Men of Color, commanded by a white, Major Fortir. At the same time, Claiborne commissioned three black second lieutenants—the first black commissioned officers in the militia of any state.

During August 1814, reports circulated that a large British expedition including the 1st West Indian Regiment, made up of black enlisted men and white officers, was proceeding to New Orleans and that upon arrival off the coast the British forces would seek to rally the blacks to their cause by offering to free and arm those who joined them. In this situation, the members of the Free Black Battalion offered their services against the British and proposed an increase in the size of their corps to include all 800 free men of color in and about New Orleans. White citizens, eager to dispense with the black unit entirely, rejected the proposal. On August 14, Governor Claiborne informed General Andrew Jackson of the offer of the black battalion and of white opposition. The governor feared that the British would "tamper" with the black troops unless the government demonstrated its confidence in them. On September 21, Jackson responded from his headquarters in Mobile, Alabama, noting the need for soldiers to defend New Orleans and insisting that the offer of the blacks be accepted. By so doing "you engage them by every dear and honorable tie to the interest of the country who extends them equal rights and privileges with the white man." Jackson explained to Claiborne that there was no risk involved in the recruitment of the blacks, adding: "No objections can be raised by the citizens of New Orleans on account of their engagement as they will be removed from amongst them, if fears of their infidelity are entertained."

At the end of October, Jackson issued an address "To the Free Colored Inhabitants of Louisiana" in which he referred to blacks as "brave fellow citizens . . . sons of freedom." He exhorted them to unite with other Americans "to rally around the standard of the eagle, to defend all which is dear in existence." Simultaneously he denounced as mistaken the previous denial of their participation in the "glorious struggle for national rights." He promised blacks the same pay, rations, clothing, bounty money, and 160 acres of land as white soldiers received.

Jackson effectively dashed any hope the British might have had of rallying the free people of color to their side. Two black-led volunteer battalions under Major Pierre Lacoste and Major Louis Daquin were organized, equipped, and trained for battle. At a review in New Orleans on December 18, 1814, Jackson informed the black volunteers that, while he had expected much from them, they had surpassed his hopes.

On the morning of January 8, 1815, the British attacked. At least 600 black troops effectively aided in inflicting the worst defeat a British Army had suffered in years. Among the last troops mustered out, the black volunteers received, as promised, the same pay and bounties as the white soldiers and were highly commended by General Jackson. But not long afterward, Jackson reported to President Monroe that the inclusion of free blacks had been a choice between having them "in our ranks or . . . in the ranks of the enemy."

The federal pensions, bounties, and land warrants promised the black volunteers of New Orleans were endlessly delayed. The black militia's refusal, in February 1815, to work on the levees, a chore usually performed by slaves and considered demeaning, raised white resentment and suspicion. In succeeding years, the black veterans were not permitted to march in the annual celebration of the Battle of New Orleans. The black militia was allowed to deteriorate until, by 1834, it was nonexistent. As Rodolphe L. Desdunes, the historian of the free blacks of New Orleans, wrote: "They were forced to be content with honeyed words and stately phrases, lavished upon them before action, but which became empty phrases after the victory." The other states followed the same course as Louisiana and excluded blacks from their militias. In 1821, South Carolina's Senator William S. Smith cited as proof that blacks lacked federal citizenship the fact that "there is no state that admits them into the militia," an argument Chief Justice Roger Taney revived in the Dred Scott decision.

In the two decades after the War of 1812, Northern blacks were increasingly denied the right of suffrage. Ironically, while new state constitutions eliminated white property qualifications, black suffrage was being either severely restricted or altogether eliminated. In convention debates, defenders of the black franchise cited black military service to oppose revocation of black suffrage. One Federalist delegate to the New York convention declared: "In the War of the Revolution, these people helped to fight your battles by land and by sea. Some of your states were glad to turn out corps of colored men, and to stand 'shoulder to shoulder' with them. In your late war, they contributed largely towards some of your most splendid victories. . . . They were volunteers . . . to defend that very country . . . which had treated them with insult, degradation, and slavery." All such appeals failed except in Rhode Island, where black service in suppressing the Dorr Rebellion of 1842 led to a reinstatement of the suffrage lost two decades earlier.

Blacks not only lost their suffrage but were segregated in housing, religion, transportation, and public institutions. When Lafayette visited in 1824 for the first time since the Revolution, he was amazed to find that prejudice seemed much greater than in the revolutionary days, when, as he recalled, "black and white soldiers messed together without hesitation."

Under the Act of March 3, 1813, free blacks continued for several years to make up to 10 to 20 per cent of those in the navy. One naval surgeon, noting that segregation rarely occurred on board vessels during those years, wrote: "The white and colored seamen mess together. . . . There seems to be an entire absence of prejudice against the blacks as messmates among the crew."

In 1839, a former naval gunner charged that officers enlisted their slaves in the crews of numerous naval ships in order to draw their pay themselves. As a result of these charges, a new set of regulations was promulgated, which decreed that no slave was "to be entered for the naval service or to form a part of the complement of any vessel of war of the United States."

By 1839, the proportion of black to white naval enlistments had grown so large that Southerners complained. The Secretary of the Navy reacted by fixing black enrollment at 5 per cent, a level that remained fairly constant until the Civil War. The critics were not satisfied, and in 1842 South Carolina Senator John C. Calhoun attempted to restrict blacks in the navy to cooks, stewards, and servants. Calhoun added that "those who have to sustain the honor and glory of the country" should not be "degraded by being mingled and mixed up with that inferior race." The Senate passed Calhoun's measure, but the House never voted on it.

Despite Calhoun's feeling, there was probably less racial prejudice and tension on naval craft than anywhere else in the society of the 1840's. A recent study has found much more evidence of "warm comradeship" and "a relaxed relationship" between blacks and whites aboard ship than of racial prejudice. The word "nigger" was almost never used by enlisted men except in quoting an officer. Blacks, however, seem to have had more of their share of punishments in some cases, especially floggings. However, officers' servants were exempt from such punishment.

Racist policies remained unchanged in the army. Although Congress authorized an army of 10,000 men, far greater than the previous peacetime military establishment, no blacks entered the military service. An example of prevailing sentiment is to be found in an undated memorandum in the War Department records, evidently issued in the spring of 1815, which, among other things, quotes the register of discharges in Boston as observing that "a Negro is deemed unfit to associate with the American soldier."

On February 18, 1820, the army issued a general order that read: "No Negro or Mulatto will be received as a recruit of the Army." A year later the General Regulations of 1821 limited enlistment to "all free white male persons." Thereafter blacks were excluded from the regular army, not by any Congressional edict but by army regulations.

Attorney General Edward Bates noted in 1864 that Congress had never "prohibited the enlistment of free, colored men into either branch of the national military service." In his classic study of American military law, Colonel William Winthrop observed that the insertion of the restrictive word "white" into the army regulations was a "striking instance of legislation by an executive department."

Despite these restrictions, the War Department permitted blacks to serve as mechanics, laborers, or servants. In 1842, the Quartermaster Department employed 106 slaves, "mostly in Florida." During the same year, the Engineers Department used 570 blacks, of whom 545 "were designated as slaves," on public works, and the Ordnance Department employed twenty-eight slaves.

Blacks played a significant role in the first and second Seminole wars—but they fought against the federal troops. For years, Florida's Seminole Indians had given refuge to slaves escaping from the plantations of South Carolina and Georgia. The Seminoles had incorporated them as equals into the tribe. Many black Seminoles married Indians. Blacks often lived in their own villages, with each family operating its own farm. Many of them achieved the status of chief counselors and tribal war leaders, and in wartime even conducted negotiations with whites. They and the Seminoles together fought to prevent the federal government from wiping out the slave haven in Florida and from returning fugitive slaves and their offspring to the plantations of the Lower South. The First Seminole War has been described by the foremost authority on the subject as "almost as much a slave-hunting as it was a punitive expedition," whose objectives were to deprive "the slaves of neighboring states of a refuge by destroying the Negro towns of Florida and eventually bringing the province under United States rule."

In 1813, three hundred blacks and a small group of Indians occupied a newly constructed fort abandoned by the British some sixty miles south of the Florida border. The settlement, known as Negro Fort, was equipped with cannon, small arms, and a large store of ammunition. Offering a haven for fugitive slaves from Georgia, Negro Fort, in the eyes of Georgia slaveholders, endangered their property rights. In 1816 Andrew Jackson directed Colonel (later General) Edmund P. Gaines to destroy the fort and "return the stolen Negroes and property to their rightful owners." A cannonball fired by Gaines's troops hit the fort's ammunition supply, which exploded and killed 270 blacks. The survivors were returned to their Georgia owners. Two years later, Jackson continued the struggle by marching into Florida, ostensibly because the British were arming the blacks and Indians against the United States. In reality, as Jackson himself admitted, the First Seminole War was a "Negro war."

In 1819 the United States purchased Florida from Spain, and eleven years later Jackson, now President, ordered the removal of all Indians in the Southeastern states, among them the Seminoles, to the Arkansas Territory. The decision to remove the Seminoles stemmed partly from the continued presence among them of fugitive slaves. Rather than accept expulsion, the fugitives united with the Indians in a renewed struggle. The Second Seminole War, which began as "an attempt to remove the Seminole Indians from Florida and simultaneously re-enslave the Negroes living among them," lasted from December 1835 to August 1842. Federal troops finally achieved a victory of sorts, but at a cost of 1,500 lives and $40 million.

At the war's height, more than half of the regular army and large numbers of volunteers were engaged. At first the war went badly for the American forces. General Winfield Scott believed, as another officer remarked, that "a sergeant's guard might drive the whole nation from the Floridas." Scott employed conventional military tactics, which were no match for his adversaries, who were "masters of guerrilla warfare in the swampy Everglades." Only after Scott's replacement by General Thomas Jesup did the military situation change, and then only because Jesup adopted a policy of "no quarter"—the destruction of Indian villages and the burning of crops —which left the Indians no choice but starvation or surrender. In reward for successfully carrying out this policy, Lieutenant Colonel William J. Worth was promoted to brigadier general.

Blacks played a major part in the fighting, and one general worried that "if this war is not speedily put down the South will feel the effects of it in their slave population before the end of the next season." Throughout the war black Seminoles liberated hundreds of slaves from Florida plantations, and at its conclusion army officers sold hundreds of black Seminoles into slavery. With the removal of the Seminoles from Florida, the slaves, in the words of one officer, "no longer had a place to fly to." But Professor Charles Crowe cites the postwar experience of several of the black Seminoles as a classic example of "stubborn black resistance":

> When peace came to Florida, some blacks made an incredible "long trek" to northern Mexico where they waged guerrilla warfare for many years against Texas planters who were so skeptical about black courage that they invented fanciful stories about refugee "Marmeluke" soldiers from the remote Ottoman Empire to explain the presence of the troublesome dark-skinned fighters.

Among the many American military leaders who emerged from the Seminole wars with a heightened respect for the fighting ability of blacks was General Rufus Saxton, who commented to a fellow officer:

> I have never had any doubts, Colonel, since my services in the Seminole Wars. There were many fugitive slaves among the Indians who fought us in the Everglades; in fact, I realized that was why we had been ordered to attack. The Negroes would stand and fight back, even with their bare hands.

When Saxton made this comment he commanded black troops. For the most part, the lesson of the Seminole wars was quickly forgotten, especially because blacks served in the Mexican War only as body servants. Pre–Civil War America saw the black as cowardly and childlike, with little fighting ability. By the 1850's, the deeds of black soldiers had been effectively erased from both the pages of American history and the memory of most Americans.

Nevertheless, black writers and journalists in the 1850's mounted a campaign to remind their people and the rest of the country of their forgotten military achievements. It was an effort designed to prove blacks were entitled to equal rights in a land they had helped to defend. William Cooper Nell, a black historian and abolitionist, launched the effort in an 1851 pamphlet on the role of blacks in the Revolution and in the War of 1812. His preface explained why he chose to emphasize black military accomplishment: "A combination of circumstances have veiled from the public eye a narration of those military services which are generally conceded as passports to the honorable and lasting notice of Americans." No less a man than William Lloyd Garrison judged this work of great historical interest and value:

> It proves how ready have been the colored Americans to shed their blood in defense even of the country in which they have been most atrociously treated from the beginning.

Two years later, delegates to the National Colored Convention in Rochester, New York, demanded an end to the policy of exclusion of blacks from the militia. In the same year, blacks supported the antislavery delegates to the Masssachusetts Constitutional Convention who attempted to open the state militia to blacks. Nell and other blacks vainly petitioned the convention, whereupon William Watkins wrote to Garrison's *Liberator*:

> Why is it that we colored people are thus treated? In the days of the Revolution our fathers stood side by side with your fathers and perilled alike their lives for a common liberty. Yet now, when we petition for the right to be enrolled in the military companies of the State of Massachusetts, we are told our complexion is "unconstitutional."

In 1858, the Republican-controlled Massachusetts legislature passed a bill opening the militia to blacks, only to have it vetoed by Governor Nathaniel Banks. In that same year the militant black abolitionist John S. Rock, at an Attucks Day celebration in Boston, predicted that "sooner or later the clashing of arms will be heard in this country and the black man's services will be needed."

3

Blacks in the Civil War

On April 12, 1861, secessionists opened fire on Fort Sumter. The Civil War had begun. President Lincoln issued a call for 75,000 volunteers, and Northerners, including free blacks, flocked to the recruiting centers. New York City blacks formed a military club, while in Cleveland a newly organized military corps of blacks declared that they were ready to do battle "as in times of '76 and the days of 1812."

The War Department had no intention of enlisting black troops. Recruiting centers turned blacks away, and state and local authorities rejected, often insultingly, their efforts to form military units. The Lincoln Administration feared that black enlistments would drive the slaveholding border states into the Confederacy. Lincoln's original policy of fighting solely to preserve the Union and leaving slavery alone precluded the use of black troops. Many observers predicted a conflict of short duration, which would be won without black troops. Whites seemed ready to fight to save the Union but not to free the slaves, and many flatly refused to fight alongside blacks. Governor David Tod of Ohio, rejecting a request to raise a black regiment, asked: "Do you know that this is a white man's government; that the white men are able to defend and protect it; and that to enlist a Negro soldier would be to drive every white man out of the service?"

From its outset, abolitionists and radical Republicans insisted the war was both a struggle to preserve the Union and the instrument to abolish slavery and racial discrimination. They insisted that, without the abolition of slavery and the use of black fighting men, the Union could not be saved. The most persistent advocate of arming the blacks was the outspoken black abolitionist Frederick Douglass. "Colored men," he complained, "were good enough to fight under Washington, but they are not good enough to fight under McClellan." He added: "The side which first summons the Negro to its aid will conquer."

Some military commanders, such as John C. Frémont, James H. Lane, Thomas Wentworth Higginson, David Hunter, John W. Phelps, and Rufus Saxton, pressed hard for abolition and the utilization of the black as a soldier. But blacks themselves initiated much of the action that culminated in abolition and their admission into the armed forces. Thousands of fugitive slaves flooded the Union lines wherever federal forces penetrated new areas of the South. Without a general governmental policy toward fugitives, field commanders were obliged to make their own decisions on the question. Some commanders tried to send the fugitives back to their masters, forbade them to enter the Union lines, or permitted masters and their agents to enter Union lines to retrieve their property.

The first move to utilize the fugitive slaves in the military effort was made by General Benjamin Butler in May 1861. When blacks from neighboring plantations took refuge within the federal lines near Fortress Monroe in Virginia, Butler learned they had previously been employed in building Confederate fortifications. He declared them "contrabands of war"—a phrase that stuck, and put them to work in nonmilitary capacities, mostly building fortifications for wages. By the end of 1861, large numbers of blacks were constructing Union fortifications, working as cooks or carpenters, or working in other service areas.

Meanwhile, the debate over using blacks in combat intensified. Some predicted that employing blacks as soldiers would lead to racial equality; that whites would be insulted if blacks wore the same uniform and received the same pay; and that white soldiers would react by deserting, as other whites refused to volunteer. Some whites charged that blacks were too submissive to prove effective in combat. Others contended that, once armed, they would go wild, killing whites indiscriminately. And some held that arming blacks would stir up slave insurrections throughout the South.

These arguments proved less compelling as Northern volunteering waned, setbacks beset the Union cause, and the realization grew that the war would be long and bloody.

Early in the fall of 1861, Governor John Andrew of Massachusetts, convinced that the nation was in for a protracted conflict, told a New York audience:

> It is not my opinion that our generals, when any man comes to the standard and desires to defend the flag, will find it important to light a candle, and see what his complexion is, or to consult the family Bible to ascertain whether his grandfather came from the banks of the Thames or the banks of the Senegal.

Andrew was known as a radical, but by the middle of 1862 even conservative Northern newspapers were urging recruitment of black troops, inverting the racist argument and asking why blacks should be exempt from the right to die. The Philadelphia *North American* said, "A white man is of as much consequence as a Negro," and went on to insist that "the lives of white men can and ought to be spared by the employment of Blacks as soldiers."

In July, 1862, Lincoln's call for 300,000 volunteers met with a disheartening response. In the same month, Congress revoked the provision in the militia law that excluded blacks and authorized the President to use blacks in the army as laborers or in other capacities. But Lincoln, although willing to use blacks as laborers, still refused to sanction their employment as combat soldiers lest he alienate the border states, whose loyalties, he was still convinced, were crucial to the Union cause. Arming the blacks, he argued, "would turn 50,000 bayonets from the loyal Border states against us."

Lincoln, however, steadily altered his view of the war and moved closer to emancipation. When he finally issued the preliminary Emancipation Proclamation in September 1862, his motives were varied. He intended partly to forestall European intervention on the side of the Confederacy, partly to undermine the Southern economy, partly to reassert his own control over the Republican Party, and partly to furnish a prelude to the enlistment of black troops. Already some steps were being taken in this direction. Several commanders, acting on their own initiative, employed small units of blacks. In May 1862 General Hunter, commanding the Department of the South, began recruiting blacks from the Sea Islands without permission for formation into the 1st Regiment of

South Carolina Volunteers. The troops were used mainly to build bridges and trenches. War Department opposition forced their disbandment early in August, with the exception of one company that continued on active duty. However, the regiment attracted much attention and helped prepare the country to accept black troops.

In August 1862, General Lane, over the opposition of Secretary of War Edwin Stanton, set about raising a black regiment in Kansas. Lane recruited more than 500 black troops in Kansas. On January 13, 1863, the Kansas Colored Volunteer Regiment was mustered into federal service, the first blacks raised in a free state and the first to take part in combat, skirmishing with Missouri guerrillas.

In July 1862 Brigadier General Phelps, an ardent abolitionist, resigned when permission to raise three regiments from among black refugees in Louisiana was denied by General B. F. Butler.

In August General Butler reversed his position and agreed to recruit free blacks, but in practice no one asked prospective recruits whether they had been free or slave before the war. By September 1 Butler expected shortly to have a 1,000-strong regiment. Although the War Department withheld specific approval of Butler's action, he quickly mustered in the 1st, 2d, and 3d Native Guards with their own officers.

Late in August 1862, in a radical shift in War Department policy, Stanton officially sanctioned the recruitment of blacks. He directed General Saxton of the Department of the South to arm and equip up to 5,000 black volunteers. All black slaves admitted into military service, together with their wives and children, were declared "forever free." Saxton, using Hunter's disbanded troops as a nucleus, organized at Port Royal, South Carolina, an all-black regiment with white officers, the 1st South Carolina Volunteers, and appointed Thomas Wentworth Higginson, an abolitionist from Boston and a friend of John Brown, as commander. In January 1863 the regiment was formally mustered into federal service.

From the beginning, national attention was focused upon the 1st South Carolina Volunteers. Higginson later wrote:

> There is no doubt that for many months the fate of the whole movement for colored soldiers rested on the behavior of this one regiment. A mutiny, an extensive desertion, an act of severe discipline, a Bull Run panic, a simple defeat, might have blasted the whole movement for arming the blacks.

Although Higginson was inclined toward paternalism, referring to his black soldiers as "docile, gay, and lovable," nevertheless he was convinced that enrolling blacks in the army would contribute toward eliminating prejudice and ending slavery. One officer, an associate of Higginson, commented on his first encounter with black volunteers: "The average plantation Negro was a hard-looking specimen, with about as much of the soldier to be seen in him as there was in the angel in Michelangelo's block of marble before he applied his chisel." But, after drilling and teaching, "the plantation manners, the awkward bowing and scraping . . . with hat under arm and with averted look," were exchanged for "the upright form, the open face, the gentlemanly address, and soldierly salute."

After the 1st South Carolina Volunteers saw action in Florida and South Carolina early in 1863, Colonel Higginson commented:

> No officer in the regiment now doubts that the key to the successful prosecution of this war lies in the unlimited employment of black troops. . . . Instead of leaving their homes and families to fight they are fighting for their homes and families. . . . It would have been madness to attempt with the bravest white troops what I have successfully accomplished with the black ones.

Only after the issuance of the Emancipation Proclamation, on January 1, 1863, did the enlistment of black troops begin in earnest. The proclamation transformed the nature of the war in innumerable ways. Thereafter the Union army was a liberating army in every section of the South it entered. All hope of compromise, of negotiated peace, of "the Union as it was" had ended. As Allan Nevins has summarized it, war became revolution. And among the revolutionary effects of the proclamation was its provision for the induction of blacks into the armed forces. The first fully authorized enlistment effort occurred in the North. Previously, the only military use of Northern blacks had occurred in Cincinnati in September 1862, when the city seemed threatened by Confederate attack. Blacks were impressed to work for three weeks on the city's fortifications.

On January 26, 1863, Governor Andrew of Massachusetts received permission from Secretary of War Stanton to establish the 54th Massachusetts Infantry, a black volunteer regiment with white commissioned officers. Early in February the following advertisement appeared in a Boston newspaper:

To Colored Men

Wanted. Good men for the 54th Regiment of Massachusetts Volunteers of African Descent, Col. Robert G. Shaw. $100 bounty at the expiration of term of service. Pay $13.00 a month and State Aid to families. All necessary information can be obtained at the office, corner of Cambridge and North Russell Streets.

Lieut. J. W. M. APPLETON
Recruiting Officer

Enlistments, however, proceeded slowly. Massachusetts had fewer than 2,000 free blacks of military age, and many of these had been absorbed into wartime employment at wages far greater than those before the war. They were not eager to leave these new jobs, and Governor Andrew was compelled to seek volunteers elsewhere. A recruiting committee made up of Frederick Douglass, Martin Delany, Henry Highland Garnet, Charles Lenox Redmond, and other black abolitionists toured the North urging volunteers to fill the ranks of the first all-black Northern regiment. Douglass added stirring editorials in his Rochester newspaper urging blacks to enlist. On March 2, 1863, he issued his historic appeal "Men of Color, to Arms," in which he argued that "liberty won only by white men would lose half its luster." On another occasion he insisted that military service offered the blacks a genuine opportunity to achieve first-class citizenship.

Douglass and his fellow recruiters found some Northern blacks reluctant to enlist. But Douglass insisted that the war was now a black man's fight. The arming of blacks, he argued, would prove a calamity to pro-slavery forces; blacks needed to learn the use of firearms; their participation would prevent any compromise of the policy of emancipation; and it would enhance both their self-respect and white respect for them. Soon, the ranks of the 54th Massachusetts were filled with 1,000 men under the command of the aristocratic Boston abolitionist Robert Gould Shaw. Their departure from Boston on May 28, 1863, was a great civic occasion. Governor Andrew hoped the regiment would be a model for all future ones. "Its success or failure," he wrote, "will go far to elevate or depress the estimation in which the character of Colored Americans will be held throughout the World."

A second black regiment, the 55th, soon followed. Connecticut, Pennsylvania, Ohio (where Governor Tod employed John M.

Langston, a black abolitionist, as a recruiting agent), Illinois, Indiana, and Michigan also raised one or more regiments composed of black soldiers.

But most blacks resided in the South, and that was where the largest number of troops was to be raised. On March 26, 1863, Stanton issued an order directing Adjutant General Lorenzo Thomas to raise black regiments in the Mississippi Valley. General Grant gave Thomas active assistance in carrying out the new policy, calling upon the officers to subordinate their prejudices. "It is expected," he said, "that all commanders will especially exert themselves in carrying out the policy of the administration, not only in organizing colored regiments and rendering them efficient, but also in removing prejudice against them."

In May, General Thomas, having successfully recruited black volunteers, concluded his mission. After his return, the War Department, on May 22, 1863, established a Bureau of Colored Troops to handle the recruitment, organization, and service of black regiments. In the fall recruiting stations were established in several states, and by December more than 50,000 men had been organized and were in actual service, with the total number swelling daily. With the exception of the two Massachusetts regiments, the 54th and 55th, black military organizations were mustered directly into the federal service and eventually became known as the United States Colored Troops (USCT). On July 4, 1864, Congress authorized the Northern states to send agents into the South to recruit blacks to meet their draft quotas.

The first major engagement in which black troops participated took place in May 1863 at Port Hudson, a Confederate stronghold on the lower Mississippi. Against a strongly entrenched force, the 1st and 3d regiments of Louisiana engaged in several assaults in which they lost one-fifth of their number.

Many in the North and South were surprised to find that blacks, especially those who had been slaves, made good soldiers. *Harper's Weekly* summed up its reaction to their performance in the early battles in these words: "Wherever the Negroes have had a chance, they have given evidence of the most exalted gallantry." And Henry Allen, Governor of Louisiana, said: "we have learned from dear bought experience the Negroes can be taught to fight." Allan Nevins stated it most cogently: "The year 1863 was definitely a year of apprenticeship for the colored soldier in which he proved himself. . . . By 1864 the army was ready to accept them as invaluable fighting reinforcements." White officers, including General Banks the former Massachusetts governor, and General Samuel Ullmann, declared that the blacks had "behaved magnificently, and fought splendidly," and that their conduct was decisive in the victory. A soldier concurred, writing from Port Hudson: "Let no one speak against the colored soldiers. They have mingled their blood with ours on the battlefield. They have done some of the best fighting of the campaign, and have lost fearfully."

In June, at Milliken's Bend, Louisiana, black troops faced an attacking force twice the size of their own. Though recently inducted into the army and largely untrained, the black troops defended their position ably. Indeed, their conduct in this battle convinced General Grant that "they will make good troops." In midsummer 1863, the 54th Massachusetts Regiment, in its first engagement, attacked an entrenched Confederate position at Fort Wagner, a key position in the defense of Charleston, South Carolina. Driven back, the black unit suffered severe losses. Of the 600 men who launched the attack, 247 were killed, including Colonel Shaw, who was buried, according to the Confederates, "with his niggers, where he belongs." Once again black soldiers had demonstrated their ability to fight with courage and determination. In the words of Allan Nevins, all black Americans "stood on higher grounds after Fort Wagner."

Yet in July 1863, at the very time when, in South Carolina, black soldiers were preparing to storm Fort Wagner, a bloody four-day riot broke out in New York City to protest the passage of the Conscription Act of March 1, 1863. In this, the worst riot in American history, several hundred blacks were killed, and thousands more fled the city. There were riots at the same time in other Eastern cities. However, the blacks' performance in battle in 1863 did much to break down resistance to black troops, although, as one newspaper put it, Copperheads would not be convinced that blacks made good soldiers even if they successfully stormed the gates of hell. Nonetheless, the argument was increasingly heard that black soldiers saved white lives. "I have never found the most shaky constituent," said a Pennsylvania Congressman, "who, when drafted, refused to let the blackest Negro in the district go as a substitute for him." Charles Halpine's "Private Miles O'Reilly" expressed the same sentiment—in his "enormously racist song" entitled "Sambo's Right to Be Kilt" which his biographer says helped reconcile the New York Irish to the policy which they most strongly opposed—the involvement of blacks in the war.

> Some tell us 'tis a burnin' shame
>   To make the naygers fight;
> And that the thrade of bein' kilt
>   Belongs but to the white.

> In battle's wild commotion
>   I shouldn't at all object
> If Sambo's body should stop a ball
>   That was coming for me direct

> So hear me, all, boys, darlins!
>   Don't think I'm tippin' you chaff,
> The right to be killed we'll divide wid him,
>   And give him the largest half!

Throughout the rest of the war, blacks made an increasing contribution to the actual fighting. In 1864 the outstanding black engagement of the war took place—the charge of the 3d Brigade of the 18th Division on Confederate fortifications near Richmond. For their role in this engagement thirteen blacks received the Congressional Medal of Honor.

The war witnessed the advent of an era of new educational opportunity for blacks, and the army played a major part in providing education to its black enlistees. Thousands first learned to read and write in army schools conducted by Northern civilians, army officers and enlisted men, chaplains, and the wives of officers. As Professor Bell Wiley has noted, former slaves were "the most numerous and earnest pursuers of learning." Indeed, so great was their desire for education that in a number of instances the black soldiers built their own schoolhouses and pooled their own money to hire teachers. By the war's end army schools had educated about 200,000 black soldiers and freedmen. In the Department of the Gulf alone, 50,000 blacks were said to have learned to read and write during the war. One visitor to the hospital at Benton Barracks in Missouri reported that a "very large proportion of the blacks had books in their hands, or within reach on their beds," and the colored convalescents were organized into a school. After their discharge many of these men and other members of the 62d U.S. Colored Infantry stationed at Benton contributed $5,000 and raised additional funds to help establish Lincoln University in Jefferson City, Missouri. The librarian of that university has written, "Lincoln . . . itself is a living memorial to the members of the 62d and 65th Regiments who, having just emerged from slavery, gave of their meager savings so that a school could be established."

Yet black soldiers in the Union army did not enjoy equal rights with white soldiers. The army maintained a strict color line throughout the conflict, and refused to enlist blacks as regulars. Black soldiers also faced discrimination in such matters as pay, pensions, opportunities for appointment as officers, and provisions and equipment. One newspaper characterized the barracks of the Michigan black volunteers as a "disgrace to the community." "There is not a barn or a pigsty in the whole city of Detroit," it went on, "that is not more fit for habitation of a human than the quarters at Camp Ward." The black soldiers were also assigned a disproportionate share of heavy and dangerous labor in the construction of bridges and fortifications, and digging trenches as well as performing tedious fatigue details. "Many officers," Nevins writes, "were disposed to use Negro units only as labor outfits." When used in combat, black regiments were often sent into battle with less training than white regiments had received and with weapons inferior to those issued to whites. Allegations arose that they were rushed into battle without proper rest or were required to make impossible charges. Some historians, such as Eugene Genovese, have charged that black troops were used as cannon fodder. There is no doubt that proportionately they suffered heavier casualties than whites, their medical facilities were primitive, and their doctors were scarce.

A most serious problem for black troops was the pay issue. At first it had been assumed that the black regiments would serve primarily in noncombat support and labor duties and that the whites would do most of the fighting. Their pay, therefore, was set at the rates paid to laborers and not soldiers. White privates received $13.00 a month plus a clothing allowance of $3.50, while black soldiers were paid $10.00 a month, from which $3.00 was deducted for clothing. All blacks, regardless of rank, received the same amount. This discriminatory pay scale bred deep resentment among black troops. According to General Ullmann, writing to Senator Henry Wilson from Port Hudson, pay discrimination was "the constant subject of conversation among them. . . . They are deeply sensitive to their gross injustice." Rather than accede to this unequal treatment, large numbers of black soldiers refused, as a matter of principle, to accept any compensation at all when army paymasters sought to pay them less than a soldier's salary. In a moving letter to President Lincoln, Corporal James Henry Gooding of the 54th Massachusetts Regiment asked: "Now the main question is, are we soldiers, or are we laborers? We have done a soldier's duty. Why can't we have a soldier's pay?"

In November 1863 the Massachusetts legislature provided a special appropriation of state funds to make up the difference in pay for the black soldiers of that state. But these soldiers refused to accept the equalization offer because it came as a gesture from the state rather than in the form of merited pay from the federal government; they continued to serve without compensation. This refusal to accept any compensation until their pay was equalized by the federal government aroused the country and made the pay differential a national issue. In February 1864 the Reverend J. P. Campbell used the opportunity presented by a meeting in Baltimore to encourage the enlistment of black men "to mobilize pressure upon Congress to achieve passage of a bill equalizing the pay of colored soldiers." His remarks were pointed:

> We ask for equal pay and bounty, not because we set a greater value upon money than we do upon human liberty, compared with which, money is mere trash; but we contend for equal pay and bounty upon the principle, that if we receive equal pay and bounty when we go into the war, we hope to receive equal rights and privileges when we come out of the war. If we go in equal in pay, we hope to come out equal in enfranchisement.
>
> Is that an unreasonable hope, or an unjust claim? It takes as much to clothe and feed the black man's wife as it does the white man's wife. It takes as much to go to market for the black man's little boys and girls as it does for the white man's little boys and girls. We have yet to learn why it is that the black soldier should not receive the same compensation for labor in the service of his country that the white soldier receives.

On June 15, 1864, Congress enacted legislation granting equal pay, retroactive to January 1, 1864, for all black soldiers and retroactive to the time of enlistment for those blacks who were free on April 19, 1861. This measure led to the so-called Quaker oaths: Many blacks said that they were free by God's law if not by man's. In September 1864 men of the 54th Massachusetts received their full back pay from May 1863, at a rate equal to that of the white troops—constituting a sum of $170,000 for their "eighteen months of unsalaried service." Finally, further protests led to the passage of a law on March 3, 1865, granting full retroactive pay to all black soldiers.

Black chaplains also suffered discrimination in pay and demanded equal treatment. Originally they were paid at the same rate as colored troops, while white chaplains received one hundred dollars per month. One chaplain, Samuel Harrison of Massachusetts, appealed to Governor John Andrew, who wrote President Lincoln denouncing the principle by which "a man in holy order in the Christian Church has, by reason of his color . . . been refused the rights, immunities, and privileges pertaining to his office and character." In April 1864 Attorney General Bates ordered Harrison paid at the same rate as white chaplains, and subsequently this was extended to include all black chaplains.

Very few blacks achieved officer status. General Butler commissioned more than seventy-five blacks in the 1862 Louisiana regiment. However, white officers treated them discourteously, and General Banks, who succeeded Butler in 1862, dismissed them from service with Secretary Stanton's approval, replacing them with "poorly qualified whites." Not until early 1865 was this stand reversed. However, fewer than a hundred blacks (excluding chaplains) gained commissions in the Union Army.

The pattern was different in the case of noncommissioned officers. When first formed, black regiments were staffed largely with white noncoms, who were promised promotion into the commissioned ranks as vacancies occurred. When this promised advancement lagged they became bitter, and many were transferred to white regiments and replaced by black noncommissioned officers.

Another urgent problem confronting the black troops was their treatment when captured. The Confederacy announced that it would not treat captured black combatants as conventional prisoners of war but rather as escaped slaves or insurrectionists. The implication was that black prisoners would be sold into slavery or put to death. While the rebel government never officially enforced this policy, some Confederate commanders had little interest in taking black prisoners. "One encounter in Arkansas, according to a Confederate participant," wrote Nevins, "left the battlefield a sickening sight, for, defying all restraint, the Southerners fell on the surviving colored soldiers and butchered them in great heaps."

The most notorious atrocity against black soldiers was the Fort Pillow massacre of 1864, perpetrated by Confederate General Nathan B. Forrest, a former slave-trader, who later played a major role in the organization of the Ku Klux Klan. After capturing Fort Pillow, in Tennessee, he apparently massacred more than a hundred surrendered black troops. For many black soldiers afterward the battle cry rang, "Remember Fort Pillow." In July 1864 Lincoln announced that the United States would give "equal protection to all its soldiers"; for every Union soldier killed, he directed the execution of a rebel soldier, and for every black Union soldier enslaved, a Confederate soldier would be put to hard labor until the end of the war. Some cynics saw Lincoln's action less as an affirmation of the equality of men than as a pretext to end the exchange of prisoners at a time when the Confederates were suffering a severe manpower shortage. In practice, black captives were treated as prisoners of war, but the exchange of prisoners ended in 1863 when the Confederacy refused to free black and white captives alike. No further exchanges occurred till the end of the war.

Finally, black troops suffered mistreatment at the hands of white officers as well as fellow white soldiers. In spite of the behavior of black soldiers in combat, many officers shared the pervasive belief in black inferiority, and others were racists who not only made no effort to submerge their hostility to blacks but reviled and abused them in every conceivable way. On April 14, 1863, the surgeon Robert L. Smith addressed a letter from New Orleans to General Phelps in which he graphically revealed the antipathy of some white officers in command of black regiments to their own troops as well as his confidence in the black as a soldier. He said he had examined more than 4,000 black recruits and found they exceeded his expectations. Their talent and skill in drill and "all the prerequisites of discipline and soldierly conduct" were "truly remarkable."

The Negro Regiments now number five and Gen'l Groves, who has command of two, treats them like brutes. He declared openly to Col. Nelson of the 2nd that his men should have no opportunity to distinguish themselves, in fact they should not fight—"that he would not disgrace his white soldiers, by permitting them to fight by the side of Niggers." That "if the government expected him to command Niggers it was welcome to his commission" (and yet he does command them whenever he can injure and refuses to exercise the command when it will benefit them).

In light of the serious disadvantages under which they served, it is remarkable that few disciplinary problems arose among black troops. As Bruce Catton notes: "With the black troops, some of the problem of army discipline seemed to be nonexistent. Desertion was utterly unknown and there was very little drunkenness." There was a "near-mutiny" in the 55th Massachusetts and a minor mutiny in the South Carolina regiment over the pay issue. The most serious instance was a brief mutiny at Fort Jackson, Louisiana, in December 1863. A recent study of that event concludes that the black troops had been brutally treated by racist and incompetent white officers and were virtually "provoked to rebellion." But this did not dampen the black soldiers' enthusiasm. A popular camp song expressed the typical attitude:

> So, rally, boys, rally, let us never mind the past;
> We had a hard road to travel, but our day is coming fast,
> For God is for the right, and we have no need to fear,
> The Union must be saved by the colored volunteer.

There were sixteen all-black regiments, making a total of 186,000 blacks in the Union armies; countless other blacks assisted these armies by performing work as laborers, cooks, servants, and teamsters. Ultimately the blacks fought in 449 engagements of which 39 were major battles. Sixteen black soldiers earned the Congressional Medal of Honor for bravery in battle. Although black enlisted troops were not commissioned at any time during the war, a number had the opportunity of displaying extraordinary leadership on the battlefield. After all the white officers of the Ohio 5th U.S. Colored Troops had been either wounded or killed during the battle at Chapins Farm, Virginia, on September 29, 1864, four black noncommissioned officers assumed command of companies. On

April 6, 1865, they were awarded the Medal of Honor for gallantry in a battle in which 28 black soldiers lost their lives and 185 more were wounded.

Black women also made significant contributions to the Union forces in the Civil War. Generally assumed to be insignificant domestics, black women infiltrated Confederate ranks to collect intelligence data. Lucy Carter provided valuable military intelligence to the 16th New York Cavalry stationed in Vienna, Virginia. Elizabeth Bowser, a former slave from Richmond, similarly served as a Union spy. She was placed behind Southern lines as a domestic to Jefferson Davis in the Confederate White House at Richmond. Pretending illiteracy, she was able to collect valuable military information, which was relayed to Union generals. Susie King was one of the many black nurses who worked with Clara Barton tending the sick and wounded.

Both Sojourner Truth and Harriet Tubman, famous black abolitionists, served in the Union forces, the former as a spy and nurse and the latter as a nurse and scout. Harriet Tubman has been described as "the head of the intelligence service in the Department of the South" and as "the only American woman to lead troops black and white on the field of battle, as she did in the Department of the South." Of one raid in South Carolina, planned and guided by Harriet Tubman, the Boston *Commonwealth* commented:

> Col. Montgomery and his gallant band of 300 black soldiers, under the guidance of a black woman, dashed into the enemy's country, struck a bold and effective blow, destroying millions of dollars worth of commissary stores and cotton . . . and brought off near 800 slaves and thousands of dollars worth of property, without losing a man or receiving a scratch.

Many slaves also served as spies for the Union Army. Allan Pinkerton, chief of the Secret Service, attested to their importance. Southern blacks, because of their knowledge of climate and terrain, guided Northern prisoners who escaped and provided invading Northern armies with invaluable intelligence on the location of supplies and the disposition of the Confederate armies. "Most invading forces," wrote Dr. W. E. B. DuBois, "wander, blind and helpless, while these armies had free guides who knew every foot of terrain, every path, hill and hollow; every person and family, every movement of man and beast." And Professor Wiley notes that "disorder and unfaithfulness on the part of Negroes were far more common than post-war commentators have usually admitted."

Of particular note was black participation in the Union Navy. Months before the army accepted them, black men were fighting on Union naval vessels. Confronted with an acute manpower shortage, the navy, on September 20, 1861, decided to enlist blacks. Barred from enlisting in the army, blacks flocked to join the naval service. From the war's outset, Secretary of the Navy Gideon Welles ordered that blacks be accepted into the service, but they were not to rank above first-class "boys" and were to receive lower pay than their white counterparts. But in the spring of 1862, as many white seamen on ships in the Gulf of Mexico contracted tropical fevers, Welles opened the rank of seaman to blacks. Of 118,044 enlistments in the navy during the Civil War, almost 30,000 were blacks, representing a much larger proportion of that service than they did of the army. Massachusetts provided more men for the Union fleet than any other state. In general, blacks performed well in naval engagements. The efficiency of blacks in handling naval ordnance was praised by Captain Samuel F. du Pont after his victory at Port Royal in November 1861. Their proficiency with heavy artillery encouraged the later formation of black artillery battalions in the army.

Segregation and discrimination were minimal in the naval service. There were, however, complaints of prejudice on the part of some white officers. Captain Andrew H. Foote, while trying to man his gunboats for the campaigns on the Western waters, cautioned one of his recruiting officers that "as there are objections or difficulties in the Southern country about colored people, we do not want any of that class shipped." D. D. Porter, the self-proclaimed hero of New Orleans, was a prime offender. In July 1863 he ordered segregation instituted on ships under his command, and in 1864 he barred blacks from jobs such as lookout, for which he felt they lacked the necessary intelligence.

Blacks served in all capacities in the navy short of petty officer. Four black seamen received the Congressional Medal of Honor. Probably the most dramatic incident involving a black at sea was that of the South Carolina slave Robert Smalls. Smalls had been impressed by the Confederates to serve on the naval craft the

Planter. Early in the morning of May 13, 1862, while the vessel's officers were asleep ashore, Smalls and a crew of seven slaves, accompanied by their wives and children, piloted the craft out of Charleston harbor and surrendered it to the blockading Union forces. Smalls was rewarded by an appointment in the Union Navy. After the war's end he became the black political leader of the South Carolina Sea Islands, serving in Congress until the 1880's.

Herbert Aptheker notes that the contribution of blacks, both enlisted and civilian, to the operations of the Union fleet, particularly in terms of information concerning the enemy, was invaluable; at times, such activities even led to "the destruction or capture of entire vessels." Aptheker concludes his article on "The Negro in the Union Navy" as follows: "The role of the Federal fleet in determining the outcome of the Civil War long has been recognized as decisive. The role of the Negro members of that fleet was of primary importance."

Lincoln and others commented most favorably on the performance of the nearly 200,000 blacks who served as volunteers during the Civil War and asserted that without their aid the Union could not have won. Many officers and enlisted men who were originally skeptical came to respect and admire black soldiers and to believe with Lincoln that their help was the decisive factor in the Union's ultimate triumph.

Blacks suffered extremely high casualties during the war. Some 38,000 black soldiers lost their lives, a mortality rate that was proportionately 35 per cent greater than among other troops, notwithstanding their late entrance into the armed forces. On December 26, 1865, the New York *Tribune* said: "The Negro gave one in three of his number to the cause of freedom. Did we with our valor do half as well?" And Colonel Higginson recalled: "Till the blacks were armed, there was no guarantee of their freedom. It was their demeanor under arms that shamed the nation into recognizing them as men."

By the end of the war, the Confederacy had grudgingly decided to use black troops rather than accept defeat. About 975 free blacks in New Orleans had been permitted to serve in a militia unit in 1861, but they performed only parade, drill, and guard duty during their period of service. The Confederacy also used blacks as laborers in armories, mines, and munitions factories, on the railroads, and in a variety of other fields. The Mayor of Richmond advised the free blacks that "it was no less their duty than that of the whites to do something for the good of the country; since they could not fight, they could work." Not until defeat seemed imminent did the Confederacy prepare to use blacks in combat.

Patrick Cleburne, a Confederate major general, was one of the first to suggest the use of black slaves in the Confederate Army. In 1863 he recognized the need for more troops and pinpointed blacks as the only potential source of fresh recruits. In December 1863 Cleburne, his concern over manpower unallayed despite Jefferson Davis's efforts to tighten up draft exemptions, increase state quotas, and enroll all men whose work could be done by slaves, demanded more drastic measures. In a proposal addressed to Davis, Major General Cleburne traced the South's desperate situation to the poverty of its manpower resources. Valuing Southern independence far more than the South's "peculiar institution," he advocated the immediate training of a large reserve of slaves and guaranteeing freedom to any slave "who shall remain true to the Confederacy in this war."

Although several of his fellow officers approved of Cleburne's proposal, a council of the Army of Tennessee rejected it, and General Albert Sidney Johnston refused to refer it through channels to President Davis. The views of the plan's opponents were summarized by General Clement H. Stevens:

> I do not want independence if it is to be won by the help of the Negro. . . . I contend that slavery was the irritating cause of the war . . . and the cry of Union and rebellion are only a subterfuge to enlist the masses in a crusade against slavery. . . . The justification of slavery in the South is the inferiority of the Negro. If we make him a soldier we concede the whole question.

General Cleburne died in battle in November 1864. Ironically, in the same month, President Davis stated bluntly that "should the alternative ever be presented of subjugation or of the employment of the slaves as a soldier, there seems no reason to doubt what would be our decision." But the Confederate Congress refused to act until a letter from General Robert E. Lee was released early in 1865, in which the general said:

> I think we must decide whether slavery shall be extinguished by our

enemies, and the slaves used against us, or use them ourselves at the risk of the effects which may be produced upon our social institutions. My own opinion is that we should employ them without delay.

Lee predicted that the slaves' habit of obedience would make them good soldiers. Finally, in March, the Confederate Congress authorized the enlistment of 300,000 slaves. These "slave soldiers" were not to be emancipated without the consent of the owners and of the states in which they resided. Nevertheless, everyone seemed to take it for granted that freedom was to be the reward for service. The step was taken too late. Although some companies were raised, none ever saw action.

The war and the conduct of black Union troops led to modification of Northern racism. For one thing, as George M. Fredrickson has noted, the effect of enrolling blacks in the Union Army was "to dispel rather dramatically any lingering sentiment in favor of government-sponsored colonization." It was difficult to ask a man to fight for a nation without recognizing his right to live in it. Perhaps no one reflected the change in racial attitudes better than Lincoln himself, who had long been a proponent of colonization and had always denied that blacks were entitled to suffrage. In his last public address, in April, 1865, Lincoln indicated his belief that as the Southern states drew up new constitutions for readmission into the Union, the right of suffrage should be conferred on "the very intelligent [blacks] and those who serve our cause as soldiers."

During the war, both abolitionists and black leaders pressed demands for black equality before the law in the North, and they made some progress against racial discrimination. Northerners apparently felt bound to protect certain basic rights for those who had contributed so much to the Union cause. The legislatures of Illinois, Iowa, and Ohio repealed state laws barring black immigration. The Rhode Island lower house passed a school desegregation measure. In New York City, blacks and abolitionists forced the desegregation of transportation. Massachusetts enacted a state public accommodation law, and the Bay State's Senator Charles Sumner persuaded Congress to take several antidiscrimination measures during the war, including repeal of an 1825 law barring blacks from carrying the mails. Black troops were cheered as they paraded through the streets of major Northern cities in 1864 and

1865. One year after the draft riots, a mass reception was held for the 20th U.S. Colored Troops in New York. These events signaled a breach in the system of racism, but the battle was by no means won. The call for enfranchisement issued by blacks in October 1864 fell on deaf ears.

In many respects, the Civil War was a war of self-emancipation for the blacks. Large numbers of blacks demonstrated resourcefulness and courage in escaping from plantations and fighting in the army. Many black Reconstruction leaders were later to emerge from among the men with army experience. For example, three blacks who had been sergeants in Colonel Higginson's regiment were delegates to the South Carolina Constitutional Convention of 1868. Morally, psychologically, and physically, the blacks participated directly in their own liberation.

Perhaps the most significant statement on the meaning of black military service was made by a black corporal, Thomas Long, of the 1st South Carolina Regiment:

> If we hadn't become sojers, all might have gone back as it was before; our freedom might have slipped through de two houses of Congress and President Linkum's four years might have passed by & notin been done for we. But now tings can never go back, because we have showed our energy & our courage & our naturally manhood.
>
> Anoder ting is, suppose you had kept your freedom widout enlisting in dis army; your chilen might have grown up free, & been *well cultivated* so as to be equal to any business; but it would have been always flung in dere faces—"Your fader never fought for he own freedom"—and what could dey answer. *Neber can say that to dis African race any more* (bringing down his hand with the greatest emphasis on the table). Tanks to dis regiment, never can say dat any more, because we first showed dem we could fight by dere side.

4

Blacks in the Post-Civil War Army

Black soldiers did not disappear from the military scene following the surrender at Appomattox. Instead, after the war the radical Republicans insisted that, in order to meet the need for additional troops in the West, the "blacks in blue" should be given a place in the regular army. In March 1866 the Senate began discussing an army bill that provided for an army consisting of sixty-seven regiments—five of artillery, twelve of cavalry, and fifty of infantry, with eight of the latter to be composed of black troops. Ohio's Benjamin F. Wade proposed that two of the cavalry regiments should be composed of black enlisted personnel. His amendment was accepted, and the amended bill passed the Senate by a vote of 27 to 5. One writer of a letter to the *Army and Navy Journal* endorsed the Senate action:

> We have given him his liberty. 'Tis but too nearly liberty to starve. Every branch of business or remunerative labor has been seized upon by the whites. . . . We refuse the negro work. . . . We do not permit him to serve himself, let him have an opportunity to serve the country.

The bill, as it finally passed, provided for the first black contingent in the regular army consisting of six regiments—the 9th and 10th Cavalry and the 38th, 39th, 40th, and 41st Infantry.

In March 1869 Congress, in reorganizing the Army, reduced the number of regular infantry regiments; the four black infantry units were merged into two—the 24th and 25th regiments. Thereafter sections 1104 and 1108 of the Revised Statutes stipulated that the enlisted men of the two regiments of cavalry and two of infantry should be "colored."

Despite numerous problems, many of which reflected prejudice and discrimination both within and outside the army, the experiment launched in 1866 can be counted a success. Regimental pride and morale in the black units were high; alcoholism, "the bane of most frontier regiments," was virtually unknown among the black regulars; their desertion rate was the lowest in the army. Only about 4 per cent of blacks deserted in 1867 and 1 per cent in 1868, while the white rate for those years was 25 per cent. "The Ninth Cavalry," the *Army and Navy Journal* later recalled, "astonished the Army by reporting not a single desertion for twelve months."

Between 1869 and 1890, the period of the Indian Wars, black soldiers won fourteen Congressional Medals of Honor, nine Certificates of Merit, and twenty-nine Orders of Honorable Mention. Four Medals of Honor were won by a remarkable organization known as the "Seminole Negro Indian Scouts," comprising about fifty blacks who had been removed from Florida during and after the Second Seminole War and who subsequently migrated to Mexico. In 1870, Major Zenas R. Bliss, 25th Infantry, brought them to Texas with promises of land and food in return for their service as U.S. Army scouts. For nine years they served under Lieutenant John Bullis, whose Civil War service had been largely with black troops. They participated in twenty-six major expeditions without a single death or serious injury. Major Bliss described them as "excellent hunters and trailers and brave scouts . . . splendid fighters." And in 1898 Colonel Loomis H. Langdon declared that the black soldiers had fully "justified the action of the Government in availing itself of their services."

Black soldiers considered themselves representatives of their race. "They are possessed of the notion that the colored people of the whole country are more or less affected by their conduct in the Army," noted Chaplain George M. Mullins of the 25th Infantry in 1877. And, while white regulars were dismissed with contempt by white civilians, the black community thought very highly of its soldiers. Lithographs of black soldiers in action hung in the homes of blacks as "symbols of hope for a better day." Rayford Logan has said: "We Negroes had little, at the turn of the century, to help sustain our faith in ourselves except the pride that we took in the Ninth and Tenth Cavalry, the Twenty-fourth and Twenty-fifth Infantry."

Black soldiers helped significantly in making the West safe for white settlers. They were used to control Indians, guard the mails, protect railroads, and meet the other needs of the frontiersmen. Scouts and patrols opened new roads, mapped vast areas of uncharted country, and pinpointed water holes. During the Indian War period, the "Buffalo Soldiers," as the Indians called the black troops, participated in "nearly two hundred engagements, major and minor." On several occasions black cavalry troops rescued beleaguered white troops and won a number of Medals of Honor and other citations for heroism. When the Utes almost destroyed Major Thornburg's command in 1879, a troop of the 9th Cavalry, despite the loss of its horses, succeeded in reaching it. Finally, during the Pine Ridge campaign in the winter of 1890, four companies of the 9th, after several forced marches under blizzard conditions, rescued elements of the 7th Cavalry.

The nation's press praised the role played by the troopers of the 9th Cavalry. The *Army and Navy Journal* noted that "the spirit of true comradeship between white and black soldiers" had been strikingly exemplified on the battlefield. And the *Cleveland Gazette*, a black newspaper, declared:

> There is considerable cause for a feeling of pride upon the part of our people over the splendid part the Ninth Cavalry played in the recent trouble with the Indians out West. . . . It is but the part any other company of Afro-American soldiers in the Government's service would play had they the opportunity. . . . [Their] bravery, activity, and endurance literally wrings deserved praise from a people extremely conservative when it comes to treating anything of interest or value to our people.

In the late spring of 1892, black soldiers restored calm in the wake of the Johnson County cattle war in Wyoming. They were employed during a strike in the Coeur d'Alene mining region of Idaho in the summer of 1892, again when armies of jobless men marched on Washington in 1894 to demand relief from Congress, and again during the Pullman strike later that year. The Anaconda *Standard* of Missoula, Montana, complimented the 25th Infantry for its service in that community during the railroad strike, declaring: "It is a splendid regiment and worthy of unstinted praise." It is one of the ironies of American history that the black soldiers had to earn their reputation as proficient troops by assisting in the suppression of another minority people and by acting as strike-breakers.

The post–Civil War army depended for its strength upon voluntary five-year enlistments. Volunteers had to be unmarried, between the ages of eighteen and thirty-five, and physically healthy. The ability to read and write was not required until the 1890's. In the years after the war, blacks constituted about 10 per cent of the effective strength of the army. The typical black recruit was an illiterate laborer or farmer, about twenty-three years old, to whom enlistment in the army meant a steady income; food, clothing, and shelter; the chance for some basic schooling; and "elevation of status." And, because their economic opportunities outside the service were few, substantial numbers of the black regulars re-enlisted. As the *Army and Navy Journal* noted in 1896, there were "seldom any vacancies in the colored regiments," in contrast to the white regiments.

Upon induction the recruit was sent to a depot, where he received clothes, quarters, food, and training until he was assigned to a unit. Black and white recruits were sometimes mixed in recruit companies, but in their regular units they were segregated and remained so throughout their term of service.

In the post–Civil War period, both black and white soldiers received a basic starting pay of $13 a month for the private, with annual increases of one dollar per month after the second year of service and a bonus after each enlistment of five years. As the soldier rose in rank, his pay increased accordingly. Both races suffered alike from the bleak living conditions on the frontier. For example, the housing provided was often no better than mud huts, affording little protection against inclement weather, dust, and insects. A white officer described the housing provided the black soldiers at Fort Quitman as "not fit to stable cattle in." And the regimental commander of the 25th Infantry, reporting in 1875 on the housing for black troops at one post in Texas, wrote:

> I have visited the band quarters several times during the past summer to find everything saturated with rain, the dirt floor full four inches deep of mud, and the men sitting at meals with their feet in more

than an inch of water, while their heads and backs were being defiled with ooze from the dripping dirt roof.

The soldier's regulation uniform was too hot in the summer and not warm enough in the winter, and his diet consisted primarily of bread, salt pork, and some kind of fresh meat. Fresh vegetables, dairy products, and eggs simply did not exist in the legal ration. "If the troops of the Indian-fighting army craved fresh fruits or vegetables," writes the military historian, S. L. A. Marshall, "they had either to grow them or steal them. And they did both." Many enlisted men also spent a portion of their pay to purchase food from the post traders as well as many items of clothing not included in the stipulated uniform.

While all soldiers on the Western frontiers performed a considerable amount of manual labor, black soldiers complained they had more than their fair share of such duties. Nor did the accomplishments of the black troops always bring them the recognition or rewards they deserved, and in some cases had been promised. For example, government agencies failed to recognize the agreement made with the Seminole Negro Scouts and refused to provide the promised land and food. On September 1, 1875, the *New York Times* reported that the scouts "are now living in great destitution, bordering upon starvation." Repeated appeals for relief were unsuccessful, and in 1881 the scouting unit was disbanded.

For all soldiers, too, the hardships of frontier service were aggravated by the monotony and boredom that characterized life at small Western posts. But black soldiers suffered more from these conditions. Because white citizens generally objected to having black soldiers near them, the army, in order to avoid racial friction, sought to station these troops in isolated posts west of the Mississippi River. In 1889 a black newspaper, noting that the black troops had performed frontier service "for the past twenty-five years," asked: "Is it not time to give those faithful soldiers a taste of garrison duty in the East? We think so." Prior to 1898, however, only one company of black soldiers was temporarily stationed east of the Mississippi, garrisons of others being on the frontiers, although occasionally near a Western city. Black soldiers were most often stationed near small frontier communities. The arrival of the armed black troops generally evoked less than enthusiastic comments from among local residents. Newspapers frequently published derogatory statements. And, when outside the fort gates during their leisure hours or on other occasions, black soldiers were often the objects of hostility, prejudice, and harassment. In June 1890 an officer wrote that "a sick colored soldier," returning from the Army General Hospital at Hot Springs, Arkansas, to his post at Fort Bayard, New Mexico, "had to go 48 hours without food because neither on the train or at a station could he buy even a cup of coffee."

A black soldier suspected of some violation would become the target of unrestrained abuse and violence at the hands of the local police. In January 1877 Adam Paine, a black Seminole Scout and a Medal of Honor recipient, was shot from behind and killed by a Texas sheriff. It also seemed to be a general rule that white civilians could murder black soldiers with impunity. A Texan, John Jackson, murdered a black infantryman stationed at Fort McKavett and then shot and killed two other black soldiers while eluding the law. When he was finally captured a jury quickly acquitted him. During one eighteen-month period in the late 1880's, three black soldiers from a post at Fort Robinson, Nebraska, "one a holder of the Congressional Medal of Honor, were murdered in the vicinity." All three crimes went unpunished. Ironically, it was after the 25th was transferred from Texas to the North that it lost two soldiers by lynching. When confrontations between white civilians and black soldiers erupted, the army made no effort to help the soldiers. It also did little to apprehend the killers of these soldiers.

The presence of racial groups even lower than blacks on the frontier social ladder—Mexicans, Chinese, and especially Indians—tended to temper somewhat this hostility and to create a more tolerant attitude among local whites toward the black troops. In effect, such frontier communities already had "niggers" to serve as their principal targets. In addition, certain economic and military factors also helped to neutralize the resentment among townsmen near posts garrisoned by black troops. Many merchants invited the business of black soldiers. Moreover, black troops helped to furnish the military protection frontiersmen needed. One historian concludes:

> Racial conflict frequently marred relations between Negro soldiers and white civilians, but the need for military security and the purchasing power of the blacks convinced many westerners of the folly

of antagonizing the Negro soldiers and contributed to an uneasy racial truce in garrison communities.

Military authorities failed to provide or encourage organized recreation for servicemen. Few posts had even the simplest kinds of gymnastic or athletic equipment. Lacking facilities, soldiers had to rely on their own ingenuity and determination or those of interested officers. Colonel B. H. Grierson, commander of the 19th Cavalry and a former teacher of music, organized a band for his regiment. Upon discovering that no issue of instruments could be obtained, he and his officers contributed to a fund to purchase them, and each enlisted man chipped in 50 cents. The Colonel also taught some of the players.

In 1866 Congress directed that each permanent army post establish a school, and it made regimental chaplains responsible for the education of black soldiers. However, necessary appropriations were never made, instructional buildings and room were rarely available, and regimental chaplains found impossible the tasks of personally conducting classes at several widely scattered frontier posts. The chaplain found it difficult to find assistance; officers in black units were reluctant to act as elementary school teachers, and few enlisted men possessed teaching competence.

In spite of these obstacles the educational program had some gratifying results. The Fort Clark chaplain reported in 1872 that "the colored soldiers, even under all the disadvantages of the present system of education, are known to the present writer to have made great improvement."

In 1875, George M. Mullins, a Kentuckian with a master's degree from the University of Kentucky, was appointed chaplain of the 25th Infantry and for years devoted much energy to his educational assignment. When Mullins assumed his post he was convinced that blacks were inherently different from and inferior to white men. In time he recognized that many of the defects he noted were environmental, and he applied himself vigorously to remedying them. He organized a post school with regularly scheduled classes, trained several assistants, and succeeded in persuading the post commander at Fort Davis to assist in the operation of the school. Orders obliged all noncommissioned officers to attend school and directed subordinate commanders "to arrange their regular duties so as not to interfere with school attendance."

Many black soldiers took advantage of the opportunity to receive a basic education in reading and writing. Attendance during the first four years averaged daily over 100 men. When the post school was closed by severe storm damage, the men kept their books and studied nightly in the barracks. In 1878, Chaplain Mullins reported that in the preceding three years more than 160 of his men had learned to read and write, and twenty-four of them had been given assignments as regimental clerks. He maintained that the men who had learned to read and write soon developed "a sense of self-respect and a pride of soldiership."

The black press frequently reported the donation by black soldiers of time and money to worthwhile causes. For example, in January 1872 the *New National Era* reported that Company E, 24th Infantry, had contributed $200 for victims of the Chicago fire "without regard to race or color." Early in 1886 Sergeant John M. Harper of the 25th Infantry, stationed at Fort Meade, Dakota, read in the New York *Freeman* that Mrs. Prudence Crandall Phileo, then in her old age, was living in poverty. The paper recounted the story "of this truly heroic woman," the privations and suffering she had endured in 1832 and thereafter from the citizenry of Canterbury, Connecticut, because she had persisted in her determination to maintain a free school for black girls. The story moved Sergeant Harper to collect contributions from the men at his post in her behalf, and he sent the *Freeman* $27.40 to help "put this worthy lady above want.' Four years later, Corporal James Hardy of the 24th Infantry read in the Cleveland *Gazette* that John Brown's daughter and her husband were in serious financial difficulties and unable to meet the mortgage payments on their home. He too solicited contributions from his regiment. On May 30, 1890, he sent the *Gazette* $23 to the fund "for the worthy daughter and son-in-law of the great hero, John Brown."

Although both black and white soldiers experienced difficulties with their officers, the black soldiers had special problems. When the black regiments were established in 1865, most white officers, convinced that blacks were inferior mentally and could not make good soldiers, expressed their clear preference for assignment to white regiments, despite the prospect of more rapid promotion in black units. Some officers even requested assignment at a lower rank in a white regiment rather than accept appointment in a black regiment. To a large degree, West Point cadets rejected service in black units. A cadet assigned to a black regiment regarded it as an inferior post and quickly requested transfer to a white unit. Cadet Hugh L. Scott, later Army Chief of Staff, graphically revealed the feelings of many cadets about service with a black regiment. He requested an assignment to the 10th Cavalry despite the prejudice against commanding black soldiers, because the unit had four vacancies at the time "and soon to be another."

> I would like much better to get into a white regiment but my class is crazy for the cavalry and there are few vacancies. As for them being moxies I would have near as much to do with them personally as you would with a black cook. . . . I have taken up all this time to justify myself for such a proceeding for most of the men here will hoot me, but I don't care so long as I see it is to my advantage.

Upon graduation, Scott received a commission in the 9th Cavalry. Within a month of his graduation, Custer's defeat occurred, decimating the 7th Cavalry. Through the influence of his uncle, a general, Scott obtained a transfer to the ill-fated regiment.

For years officers accepted assignment to black units reluctantly. Some preferred to resign rather than accept a vacancy existing in a black regiment. In January 1871 the New York *Tribune* carried the following report from Washington: "The only vacancy now existing in the army is in the Colonelcy of the 25th Colored Regiment. Colonel D. J. Stevenson was assigned to this regiment, but disliking to serve with colored men, resigned at the last moment."

Racial prejudice among the officers did not wholly explain this aversion to service with black troops. An officer viewed assignment to a black unit as a reflection on his competence, hence a blot on his record and an impairment to his standing with his fellow officers. Besides, service in a black unit demanded more from the officers: For a long time black units contained few if any skilled and literate personnel, so most of the clerical and technical work had to be handled by the officers themselves. Still another reason white officers did not like to serve with black units was the conviction that they would be compelled to serve permanently at the more isolated and disagreeable posts where the military authorities, to avoid protests from white citizens, traditionally kept the black soldiers. As late as 1906, one captain wrote that "officers assigned to duty with colored troops simply must give up all hope of ever enjoying the Eastern atmosphere." Officers of black units frequently suffered social ostracism by the white citizens of the surrounding communities since the public generally assumed that an officer assigned to a black unit was fit only to command "inferior" troops. In 1881, Colonel Grierson complained to General O. O. Howard about "the prejudice and unjust discrimination that I have had to meet and for nearly fifteen years contend against." All these problems were aggravated by the near impossibility of transferring out of a black unit, for few officers would willingly exchange places with those seeking to leave such units.

Sentiment against service in black units ran so strong that graduates of West Point showed "a marked preference" for the artillery, which had no black troops, even though the prospects of promotion there were especially dim. A young officer told Colonel Charles J. Crane at Fort Monroe in 1883 that he would "rather be a second lieutenant of artillery than a captain of niggers." The colonel further noted that some graduates of West Point requested assignments as "additional second lieutenant" in a white regiment rather than accept appointment to a vacancy in a black regiment.

Most newly graduated officers assigned to black regiments shared these attitudes. Although many underwent changes after some experience with the troops and even came to feel that such service had its rewards, their basic attitude toward blacks retained significant elements of prejudice or paternalism. Captain T. A. Baldwin of the 9th Cavalry reflected the views of many officers when he wrote that the only thing black soldiers "care for is someone to look after them, they never will think for themselves."

In 1887, the *Army and Navy Journal* published a letter from an officer who, it said, had had "experience with colored troops."

> I am no admirer of the African, believing he will ultimately destroy the white race. . . . Yet I think the world of the men of my company. When I look at them I do not see their black faces, I see only something beyond. For the comfort and pleasant life of the officer on the frontier they are far ahead of white troops, they are more like a lot of devoted servants and retainers, faithful and trustworthy in every respect and brave and gallant.

Some officers seriously questioned the value of the black troops to the service. In testimony before a Congressional committee in the 1870's, General William T. Sherman stated crisply: "If I were compelled to choose 5,000 men to go into a fight with, I would rather take 5,000 white men." General E. O. O. Ord, commander of the Department of Texas, complained that black soldiers required "more care than ordinary white troops," claimed he needed at least twice as many officers because the black noncoms were not the "best men," and asked for the replacement of the black soldiers assigned to him. Major Thomas M. Anderson bluntly suggested the four black regiments be mustered out of the service because "the more efficient armies are homogeneous." Like General Ord, he contended that black troops were more expensive than white:

> I do not believe that under the best administration it is possible to make them otherwise. The colored men have not the habits of thrift, economy, or an adequate idea of responsibility, and they are, with few exceptions, thieves and liars.

Even those officers who accepted the continued presence of the black contingent in the service insisted that they must be under the command of whites, strictly limited to service in infantry and cavalry units, and excluded from the more specialized and technical branches of the service, because they lacked the intelligence to perform those duties. The initial postwar army bill had provided for a black artillery regiment. General Grant had objected to this provision, however, and the final bill eliminated the unit. Recruiting officers thereafter assigned black enlisted men exclusively to the four infantry and cavalry units, closing to them the branches of artillery, engineers, ordnance, and the signal corps. For years they never made the positions of hospital steward or ordnance, commissary, or quartermaster sergeant.

Some critics objected that it was unfair to permit the black citizen to enlist and then inform him that certain branches and positions were closed to him. "It is wrong," George W. Williams, the black historian, wrote in 1882, "and Congress should place these brave black soldiers upon the same footing as the white troops." Secretary of War Redfield Proctor proposed in his annual report of 1889 that black soldiers make up two additional regiments of artillery, since their record in the service had been excellent. In December of that year a proposed bill for seven regiments, authorizing the President to enlist blacks at his discretion, was introduced and failed, as did a similar one in the next Congress. In March 1898 Congress authorized two new regiments of artillery but, despite the plea of a black Congressman, George A. White of North Carolina, made no provision for a black regiment. In May 1898 Captain Henry H. Wright of the 9th Cavalry, when asked why the black soldier was not represented in the artillery, responded: "He lacks the brains. . . . He is brave enough and willing enough; but if we let him enlist in the artillery our shooting would . . . resemble the . . . marksmanship of the Spaniards."

The law establishing the black regiments did not specifically require white officers, nor did it exclude blacks from the commissioned grades of other regiments and corps. As one officer wrote, "There is, in fact, nothing of the law of the land to prevent a full-blooded Zulu from becoming the colonel of any one of our regiments, or the chief of any corps."

In this period there were three methods of obtaining a regular commission: by graduation from the United States Military Academy, by direct appointment from civilian life, and by promotion from the enlisted ranks after passing a qualifying examination. For years enlisted men had complained that it was nearly impossible to achieve a commission. Congress reacted in 1878 with provisions for the promotion of deserving noncommissioned officers, who had served for a minimum of two years, had been recommended by their company officers, and had been approved by a board of officers. The act of 1878 was hailed as a genuine step forward to insure advancement of enlisted men. Every man, it was said, now carried a commission in his knapsack. However, both within and outside the service, many observers questioned whether black regulars would benefit from the 1878 legislation.

An anonymous 9th Cavalry man stationed at Fort Robinson underscored these doubts:

> I would most emphatically say, my colored brother, do not come, you will never get there. . . . Since the organization of the four colored regiments now in the service, not a single colored soldier has been promoted from the ranks to the grade of an officer. . . . It is not that they do not possess the necessary qualifications for the office, but that the sentiment of the army is decidedly against it, and any ambitious aspirant for shoulderstraps in the ranks is promptly and effectually given to understand that "spades are not trumps" here.

Military authorities denied these charges, insisting that regulations did not prohibit the commissioning of black officers and that there was nothing to prevent the promotion of ambitious and qualified black noncommissioned officers to the commissioned ranks.

In June 1892 Congress passed a law modifying significant sections of the act of 1878 governing promotion to a commission. This legislation not only opened the door to commissions to privates but also enabled the soldier himself to initiate the application, rather than having to depend upon the recommendation of his commanding officer. The new law was called the soldier's Magna Carta. Whatever the merits of this characterization, the fact is that not a single black enlisted man rose from the ranks to a commission prior to the Spanish-American War. And no matter how often military authorities insisted that any black soldier able to pass the required examinations could become an officer, the black community and press remained convinced that the army meant to keep the black soldier "in his place."

Between 1870 and 1889 twenty-two black youths were appointed to the United States Military Academy. Until the end of Reconstruction in 1877, these appointments were made by black Southern Congressmen and their white Republican allies; subsequently, most appointments were from the North. Only twelve of the twenty-two passed the West Point entrance examination, and only three managed to overcome four years of social ostracism and a host of other tribulations and discriminatory obstacles to graduate from the Academy. Henry Ossian Flipper in 1877 became the first black graduate of the Academy, and he was followed by John Hanks Alexander in 1887 and Charles Young in 1889. No other black was graduated from West Point until 1936. Flipper was assigned to the 10th Cavalry but was court-martialed and dismissed from the service in 1882 as a result of alleged irregularities in his account as commissary officer of Fort Davis, Texas. Alexander died on duty as a second lieutenant in 1894, leaving Young as the only black line officer and graduate of West Point still on active duty at the outset of the Spanish-American War. Young was a first lieutenant on the rolls of the 7th Cavalry, a white regiment, but serving as a military instructor at the all-black Wilberforce University in Ohio and not in direct command of troops, a fact that black Americans deeply resented.

The attitude of West Point toward black candidates was

summed up in the annual report for 1880 of General J. M. Schofield, a Superintendent of the Military Academy:

> To send to West Point for four years' competition a young man who was born in slavery is to assume that half a generation has been sufficient to raise a colored man to the social, moral, and intellectual level which the average white man has reached in several hundred years. As well might the common farm horse be entered in a four-mile race against the best blood inherited from a long line of English racers.

Similar disparities arose in the appointment of chaplains. Although Congress, in 1866, provided assignment of a chaplain to each of the black regiments, until 1884 only whites were appointed to these positions. In that year the first black, Henry V. Plummer, was appointed captain and chaplain of the 9th Cavalry. One year later Allen Allensworth, a black minister and educator, was made chaplain of the 24th Infantry with the same rank. He was convinced that a soldier needed a basic education to perform efficiently in the service and to adapt himself to civilian life afterward. He too tried to instill within each soldier a favorable attitude toward education. At Fort Supply he instructed the soldiers in the history of the United States and in English. When the regiment moved to Fort Bayard, Allensworth expanded the post school to include four instructors to teach the 118 men enrolled. It became the practice to select noncommissioned officers from among those who had attended these classes. Faced with a paucity of educational funds, Allensworth often contributed much to the financing of these classes himself. In addition, he delivered lectures to the men, using a stereopticon and slides to add interest. He also established technical schools to train printers, bakers, and telegraphers, and he personally conducted a normal school for prospective army teachers. His efforts contributed to the passage of additional legislation in 1889 to promote education in the army.

The army, however, refused to deviate from its policy of maintaining separate black units except for the assignment of white officers. It repeatedly rejected the requests of black regiment chaplains for the assignment of white enlisted men to teach black units at posts billeted by black and white soldiers. Indeed, the army opposed integrated educational facilities so strongly that a provision of the Army Regulations of 1881 read: "If the command consists of white and colored troops, it *necessitates* two schools or two separate rooms." The room for blacks was to be "equally well fitted up and as comfortable as the room used for the white soldiers."

Defenders of segregation argued that it averted serious racial conflict in the service and helped to maintain morale and efficiency. Other proponents of separate units defended them as the only guarantee that blacks would be permitted to remain in the army. These arguments recurred during the debates in 1876 and 1878 on proposals to eliminate the two sections of the Revised Statutes that required four black regiments. Although these bills appeared designed to advance black rights, critics contended that their sponsors lacked "the honesty and courage" to advocate openly the disbandment of the black regiments and that passage of the bills would inevitably eliminate almost all blacks from the service or limit them to nonmilitary menial duties. Representative Edward M. Mackey, a white Republican Congressman from South Carolina, charged during the 1876 debate on one such bill that it sought "under the guise of a worthy motive, to accomplish the unworthy one" of virtually eliminating black men from the army. "The repeal of the law which now provides for these colored regiments," he insisted, "is only an indirect way, therefore, of getting rid of colored soldiers in the army."

Senator James G. Blaine of Maine made the point even more sharply during the debate in 1878 on another bill, which had the strong support of General Sherman. Blaine cautioned his colleagues:

> Do not let us deceive ourselves. Let us vote on this bill with the understanding that, whereas as a recognition of the services of the colored man in the Army of the Union during the war, we gave him a place and a recognition in the Army, we now declare an end to that, and that he shall not hereafter serve in the Army of the United States nor wear the uniform of the United States soldier.

This bill also failed of passage. On the other hand, some genuinely concerned people condemned the existence of all-black units. As early as 1866, the antislavery publication *Independent* said of the proposal for separate black regiments: "The injustice and impolicy of such a measure are so patent that we do not see how anyone who advocates the political equality of all men, without respect of complexion or race, could give his support to such a measure."

Thereafter, critics of the system disputed the legality and necessity of racial segregation in the service. They pointed out that the law requiring such separation was passed in 1866, before ratification of the Fourteenth Amendment, which made the black a citizen and gave him the right to serve in all units. They noted that at posts where white and black companies served together their relations were devoid of friction. They called attention to the fact that only the army practiced separation; the navy made no distinction among personnel on the basis of color. And they emphatically denied that either the black enlisted men or the black population benefited from the separate units in the army.

In 1874 a black enlisted man contended that it was just as important for the prosperity of his race in the United States to have mixed soldiers as it is to have mixed public schools. A number of white officers shared his sentiments. In 1869 a Lieutenant Colonel Hinks of the 25th Infantry advocated desegregation of the army and predicted that, if such a policy were adopted, "great harmony" would prevail in the service. And in 1882 General Samuel B. Holabird called upon Congress to abolish "the language of distinction between white and black troops in our statute books."

Following the Civil War, as the naval forces were reduced, the proportion of blacks in that service declined. The navy continued the policy of enlisting blacks on a fully integrated basis but limited black seamen to service in the ranks. Black sailors who could qualify served as regular seamen, gunners, or gunners' mates. They slept and lived together with whites "in the crowded quarters of American warships of the predreadnaught era." In the post–Civil War era two black sailors won the Congressional Medal of Honor. Yet prejudice permeated the service. An "American seaman," writing in 1885 to the New York *Freeman* from a ship "in European waters," complained that there was "at present too much prejudice" toward black seamen. The officers, he felt, tried to be fair but usually dealt out more severe punishments to blacks who broke the rules. The white sailors, and especially the foreign element in the service, "growl like the dog in the manger" about sharing watches, quarters, and mess with black men. Four years later prejudice surfaced again in the navy, as orders were given for Frederick Douglass to travel by naval vessel to his new post as Minister to Haiti. One commander resigned, another declared his ship unfit for service, and a third requested transfer to a new command rather than share the captain's table with Douglass.

Between 1872 and 1897 five blacks were appointed to the United States Naval Academy at Annapolis, and three—James H. Conyers, Alonzo C. McClennan, and Henry E. Baker—passed the entrance examinations. None of the three graduated. All three midshipmen were forced to endure the same social ostracism and harassment black cadets faced at West Point. Not until 1936 was another black admitted to Annapolis, and it was not until 1949 that the first one graduated from the Academy.

Probably the most controversial example of military service by blacks in the post–Civil War era was their involvement in Southern militias during radical Reconstruction. By the act of March 2, 1867, the word "white" was struck from the recruiting regulations of the federal militia laws, thereby including blacks among those eligible for militia duty. Many Southern Republican governments, unable to fill their militia ranks with loyal whites, turned to blacks, although the units were usually not composed exclusively of blacks. The militia units were used to maintain the Republican governments in the face of continued hostility from unreconstructed Southerners and political conservatives, who often formed paramilitary units like the Ku Klux Klan. The sight of armed blacks, almost all of them recently emancipated slaves, was considered an outrage by most Southern whites, and one of the main aims of the Klan and similar organizations was the disarming of the black militia. In a few cases, Southern governors (all of whom were white) used the militia effectively to put down Klan violence, most notably in Arkansas. But more typically the governors, fearful of precipitating full-scale racial warfare, did not mobilize the militia until it was too late. As a result, in states like Mississippi and South Carolina the black militia were often disarmed by white violence and proved unable to prevent violent overthrow of the Reconstruction governments. After the end of Reconstruction, blacks were almost entirely excluded from militias in the South and from an increasing number of those in Northern states. On the eve of the Spanish-American War, a black newspaper in Philadelphia commented: "If in times of peace the white brother would sink his prejudices and act squarely there would be well-drilled regiments of colored men in every State today."

The period from the end of Reconstruction to the early twentieth century has been called the nadir of black life in America. Those were the years when blacks were systematically deprived of the right to vote in the South, and rigid segregation laws were applied to all other aspects of Southern life. Mob violence and lynching of blacks were widespread, and not confined to the South. Northerners increasingly seemed to accept the precepts of social Darwinism and racial superiority, which made them reluctant to intervene to protect the rights of blacks.

Ironically, during those years the Secretary of War eliminated some of the barriers confronting black men in the army. In April 1884 W. Hallett Greene, a black member of the graduating class of the City College of New York, applied for enlistment in the Signal Corps. General William B. Hazan, chief officer of the signal service, rejected the application, stating that Congress had restricted black soldiers to two regiments of infantry and two of cavalry. Secretary of War Robert Todd Lincoln overruled this interpretation, and on September 26, 1884, Greene was enlisted in the Signal Corps. This action opened the way for the acceptance of a handful of black enlisted men into other technical branches, such as the Hospital Corps, the Ordnance Corps, and the Quartermaster and Commissary departments.

On April 28, 1891, Secretary of War Proctor further breached the "color line." Despite protests from local citizens, he issued an order assigning Troop K of the 9th Cavalry to Fort Myer, Virginia, outside the national capital, as a reward for their service in the recently concluded Indian campaigns at Pine Ridge. One month later, Troop K left Fort Robinson, Nebraska. Not long afterward the *Washington Post* reported that, for the first time in its history, "beautiful Fort Myer" was garrisoned "by colored cavalrymen." The *Southern Argus* published the following dispatch by its Washington correspondent, headed "Race Moves":

> A company of colored soldiers is now guarding the national capital. . . . There has never been a colored soldier stationed here since the war until now; not that colored boys had not made good soldiers and done brave deeds, but on account of a mean, narrow prejudice they have always been kept away.

During the same period, a correspondent writing to the *Army and Navy Journal* urged that the black soldiers receive "the same appreciative recognition" as to stations as that awarded "to their more fortunate white comrades in arms." In 1896 such recognition finally came to the members of the 24th Infantry Regiment, which had been kept for many years in Arizona and New Mexico. Chap-

lain Allensworth explained his own important role in bringing
about the desirable transfer. The opportunity arose when a recently discharged black soldier, Shanks Davis, informed the chaplain that he did not intend to re-enlist because of the poor stations
assigned to the regiment. Allensworth arranged for an article to be
written setting forth the reasons why the soldier would not re-
enlist and sent it to the New York *Age*. After its publication, he
sent a copy of the article to the black Congressman John M. Langston and urged him to do something about the matter. Langston
replied in March 1896, informing Allensworth that he had taken
the article to General Nelson A. Miles, the army commander in
chief, and raised with him the issue of better stations for the black
troops. General Miles had assured him that something would be
done to meet the problem, and Langston was confident that the
black troops would be given such change of stations for the future
as "may tend to please the officers and give to the regiments ample
opportunity for the best display of their individual and collective
good behavior."

On September 18, 1896, Secretary of War Daniel S. Lamont
announced the transfer of the entire 24th Infantry to Fort Douglas, Utah, removing the regiment from the frontier for the first
time in twenty-two years. General Wesley Merritt, the department
commander, characterized the new assignment as "in the nature
of a promotion" for a "splendid regiment." But not everyone in
Salt Lake City shared his enthusiasm. The Salt Lake City *Tribune*,
the leading newspaper of the city, published an editorial entitled
"An Unfortunate Change," which described serious apprehension
among "the best people in the city" that they might be forced into
"direct contact with drunken colored soldiers on the way from the
city to Fort Douglas."

The War Department refused to yield to arguments that it re-
voke the order, and on October 11 Company F left Fort Bayard, as
an advance contingent, for Fort Douglas. Private Thomas A.
Ernest, of Company E, wrote in a letter to the *Tribune*, shortly
afterward:

> The enlisted men of the Twenty-fourth infantry, as probably the
> people of Salt Lake City know, are negroes. . . . They have en-
> listed to uphold the honor and dignity of their country as their
> fathers enlisted to found and preserve it. . . .
> We object to being classed as lawless barbarians. We were men

before we were soldiers, we are men now, and will continue to be men after we are through soldiering. We ask the people of Salt Lake City to treat us as such.

A year later, on the occasion of the first anniversary of the regiment's arrival, the *Tribune* apologized for its misgivings. It observed, "The regiment has lived down the apprehensions awakened when the announcement of their coming was made and they are now appreciated at their worth, as citizens and soldiers above reproach."

On the eve of the Spanish-American War, the New York *Tribune* featured a lengthy tribute to "The Colored Troops," which concluded with an optimistic prediction:

A huge army of colored men would give a splendid account of itself in case of a war with Spain, although in such an event it is probable that the American spirit would soon rise high enough in the Army to obliterate all invidious dividing lines, and there would be but one soldiery, as there is now but one form of American in the navy.

On June 1, 1898, after the outbreak of the war, the Chicago *Tribune*, in an editorial titled "Wipe Out Race Prejudice," went even farther and expressed the wish that the war would reverse the tide of racial oppression in the United States:

If the colored men respond to the call for their services in carrying out this war . . . and prove themselves the brave soldiers they did towards the close of the civil war and have done since, it is to be hoped that it will have the effect to remove the prejudice which has stripped them of their political rights in so many of the States and so often made them the innocent victims of mob violence. If the bravery and patriotism manifested by colored men . . . shall accomplish this result, it . . . will be worth all the war will cost them and the nation at large.

These forecasts failed to materialize. The display of patriotism on the part of black Americans and their outstanding military service in Cuba did not improve their status in American society. Instead, the intensification of racism that underscored American life during and after the war was reflected in the deterioration of the position of blacks both in civilian life and in the armed forces. This new setback for black Americans, as one historian has noted, "also dramatized the frustration and disappointment suffered by Negroes who envisioned participation in a patriotic cause as a means of achieving first-class citizenship."

5

From the Spanish-American War to World War I

From the outset of Cuba's struggle for liberation from Spain, black Americans expressed great sympathy with the rebel cause. Pronouncements supporting the insurrection emphasized the considerable black population in Cuba and the role played by black soldiers in the Cuban revolutionary armies. General Thomas Jordan, formerly of the Cuban Liberating Army, wrote in a letter to a meeting of black citizens in the United States: "Former slaves are fighting fiercely in the ranks of the Cuban army, not in separate organizations as in the United States, but in the same companies side by side with white people, and I have seen white men commanded by blacks."

Yet even after the sinking of the U.S.S. *Maine* in Havana Harbor on February 15, 1898, in which 22 black sailors were among the 250 killed, there was considerable division of opinion among black Americans as to their role should war come. Pro-war spokesmen claimed that participation by blacks would win respect from whites and improve their status at home. They argued that economic opportunities would open up for blacks once the islands came under American influence and that the race prejudice of white Americans would diminish as contacts with predominantly "colored" cultures increased.

Anti-interventionists maintained that it was hypocritical for the American Government to undertake a crusade to free Cuba from Spanish tyranny unless it was prepared to insure the constitutional rights of black citizens at home. And they warned that a Jim Crow war would result in a Jim Crow empire, which would inevitably doom black Americans, as well as the black population of the Spanish colonies, to even greater oppression.

As soon as war had been declared against Spain, however, misgivings about intervention apparently disappeared; blacks rallied to the flag on the wave of the patriotic upsurge, although "many blacks continued to question the wisdom of being for democracy in Cuba when conditions at home left so much to be desired." Booker T. Washington, one of the earliest and most persistent advocates of black participation in the Spanish-American War, stated that "the Negro . . . will be no less patriotic at this time than in former periods of storm and stress." The black man, he continued, "was an American through and through," and the President need not fret about divided allegiance, because there were "no hyphenates among us."

During the war in Cuba black soldiers, called "Smoked Yankees" by the Spaniards, were in the forefront of the fighting. According to correspondent Stephen Bonsal, no four white regiments could be compared to the four black units in terms of service and sacrifice to the nation. After the Spanish war, black regulars and volunteers participated in many of the operations in the Philippines.

Some black soldiers became regular correspondents, sending reports to the black press, which, among other things, revealed the high hopes of black military personnel that their valor and loyalty would earn the appreciation of whites and lead to an easing of the oppression of blacks. But the war led to a reconciliation between North and South, as men from Mississippi marched into Camp Jackson singing:

> Hurrah for the blue! Hurrah for the gray!
> Hurrah for the sons of them all.
> Together we come and united we stand
> To answer humanity's call.

As usual, the blacks were not included in the renewed national unity. Instead, the consequence of this reconciliation, along with the racism inherent in the entire imperialist adventure, was heightened by discrimination and violence against blacks. Paradoxically, the Progressive era coincided with one of the high points of racism in American history. It reached its zenith during the administration of Woodrow Wilson.

This period also witnessed the organization of militant black intellectuals, among them W. E. B. DuBois and Monroe Trotter, protesting the accommodationist policies of Booker T. Washington and the increasing trend toward racial proscription. At this time, too, a significant change occurred among the black soldiers. Aware that they had performed well on the battlefield, they became less obsequious in manner, increasingly imbued with racial pride, less disposed to accept discriminatory treatment and physical violence, and resentful of ostensible praise that was couched in patronizing terms and racist innuendos. In May, 1898, for example, the correspondent of the Boston *Evening Transcript* wrote from Tampa:

> The Negro soldiers who come here from the North and West . . .
> are under the impression that they are as good as white soldiers . . .
> they think that the willingness to die on an equality with white men
> gives them a claim to live on something like an equality with them.

One year later, Sergeant Presley Holliday expressed exasperation with those who contended that "the Negro is not fit to exercise command." "Our motto for the future," he concluded, "must be 'No officers, no soldiers.' "

In 1906, the *New York Times* featured a dispatch from Washington under the headline "Race Feeling Among Negro Soldiers." The correspondent reported that army officers were openly commenting on "the surprising change in bearing that has taken place in the Negro regiments in the last few years." "It is usually described," he went on, "as a strange development of 'cockiness' on the part of the men." Black soldiers showed their feeling about higher liquor prices for blacks by smashing beer glasses. In 1911, they touched off a riot in San Antonio by refusing to ride behind Jim Crow signs on the streetcars. Black soldiers objected to minstrel shows as degrading, and during a six-month period in Hawaii in 1915, on at least three occasions, they halted showings of racist movies and performances of racist plays, "once by pelting the theater with rocks." In July 1917, members of the 24th Infantry contributed nearly $150 to a relief fund for black victims of the East Saint Louis riot. In the same year the regimental chaplain of this unit advised Dr. DuBois that the entire command of his regiment was prepared to assist in every way his "noble fight for manhood rights of our people."

Even before the outbreak of war with Spain in 1898, the Secretary of War, in the mistaken belief that black men were immune to tropical diseases, ordered the four black regiments to proceed from their Western posts to the South to prepare for the expedition to Cuba. On April 21, 1898, the 24th Infantry marched from Fort Douglas to the railroad depot to begin its journey eastward. "The citizens, school children, university students, and the state officials turned out en masse to witness their departure and bid them bon voyage," wrote the *Broad Axe*, the local black newspaper, "and many flowers were showered upon them by the spectators."

The black community took great pride in the decision to give black troops a key role in the crusade to free Cuba. Bishop Abram Grant, at a session of the African Methodist-Episcopal Church, pointed out that, unlike 1861, when not one black was allowed to enlist, now black soldiers were "the very first" called for service. "Let us hope," the Bishop added, "that this nation will be led by the contemplation of this fact to forget the color of all its citizens."

The Bishop's hope proved overoptimistic, for no sooner had the black troops entered the South than their experiences changed markedly. While local blacks gave them a warm reception, white Southerners quickly demonstrated that their hospitality did not extend to black units. "It mattered not if we were soldiers of the United States and going to fight for the honor of our country," a black soldier commented bitterly, "We were 'niggers,' as they called us, and treated us with contempt."

This hostility probably resulted in no small part from the fact that a black soldier in uniform contradicted the stereotype of a subservient inferior, fit only for drawing water and hewing wood. What was especially galling to white Southerners was the prospect of black troops exercising authority over whites. When members of the 24th Infantry escorted a number of Spanish prisoners from Tampa, Florida, to Fort McPherson, Georgia, whites objected noisily. All along the route crowds displayed sympathy for the prisoners while hurling jeers and insults at the black soldiers. At Macon, Georgia, several white ladies went to the train and distributed flowers among the white prisoners. Upon their arrival at

the fort, the members of the guard heard a Catholic priest from
Atlanta declare, "It is an outrage that white men have been subjected to the humiliation of having Negro guards over them."

While stationed at Camp Chickamauga, the members of the
25th Infantry objected to the indignity of being compelled to ride
in Jim Crow cars when they went into town and pledged not to
travel on segregated public transportation again "unless ordered to
by official army command." Instead they hired private convey-
ances or walked.

Once in town, black soldiers were barred from recreational and
amusement facilities. Cafés, saloons, and restaurants refused to
serve them, and stores refused them purchases across the same
counters as whites. On the streets they endured insults and taunts.
They were arrested by the local police on flimsy pretexts, in sharp
contrast to the tolerance shown white troops for even serious offenses. The Memphis *Commercial Appeal* warned the "colored
soldier" not to forget "his place" and presume that "he was
changed" or "benefited [in] his social condition by wearing a blue
coat and carrying a gun." The Denver *Statesman* warned: "No
man can long . . . be made a target for the enemy and also for
the blasphemy of his supposed countrymen."

From Chickamauga Park the black troops moved on to Tampa,
the port of embarkation for Cuba. Dressed in regulation blue flan-
nel and wool, while drilling in the tropical sun they suffered from
the heat. But they suffered even more from prejudiced and hostile
white Floridians. On May 8, Colonel Jacob Kent of the 24th Infantry wrote to his wife from Tampa, "This is not a nice town for
my men. The feeling is strong against their color."

From the moment of their arrival, the black troops gave notice
that they would not accept the discrimination customarily heaped
on local blacks. "The colored infantrymen stationed in Tampa and
vicinity have made themselves very offensive to the people of the
city," reported the Tampa *Morning Tribune*. "The men insist
upon being treated as white men are treated, and the citizen will
not make any distinction between the colored troops and colored
civilians." In these circumstances, racial conflict was inevitable. In
Lakeland, a civilian was killed by a stray bullet when members of
the 10th Cavalry opened fire into the air, after one black trooper
was denied a drink of soda water and a white barber refused another a shave.

The mounting racial tension erupted in a serious clash in Tampa on the night of June 6. The riot was triggered by a group of white volunteers of an Ohio regiment who "decided to have some fun" with a two-year-old black boy and forced the child to serve as target for a marksmanship demonstration. The incident prompted "already angered" black troops to intervene forcibly. The white 2d Georgia Volunteer Infantry was assigned to restore order, and did so with such relish that a dispatch from Tampa claimed that the streets of the city "ran red with Negro blood." Twenty-seven black soldiers and several Georgia volunteers, "all with serious wounds," were transferred to Fort McPherson. While the black press condemned the "slaughter of black troops" by the Georgia regiment as "inhuman and uncalled for," the *Atlanta Constitution* argued that the Tampa affair clearly demonstrated that "army discipline has no effect on the Negro."

Two days after the riot, the black regiments boarded transports together with white troops and prepared to sail for Cuba. Departure was delayed as rumors spread that a Spanish warship lurked in the vicinity. While the transports waited at Tampa, the black regiments remained on board except when taken ashore under escort, although white troops were free to disembark at will. On board the transports, black soldiers were segregated, assigned to the lowest deck, and forbidden to mix with whites. On at least one vessel the color line was drawn with black troops on the starboard side and white troops on the port side.

The expedition finally left for Cuba on June 14, and on June 22 it arrived off the Cuban port of Daiquiri. Once on Cuban soil the black units participated in all the engagements of the short campaign and, according to accounts, performed creditably on the field of battle. The black troopers of the 10th Cavalry won considerable praise for their courage in The Battle of Las Guasimas. They further distinguished themselves at El Caney, where, after a costly battle, the 25th Infantry, along with the 12th Infantry, captured the village. The 24th Infantry played a part in the famous assault on San Juan Hill.

After this engagement, the Rough Rider and future Secretary of the Navy Frank Knox wrote to his parents that "in justice to the colored race, I must say that I never saw braver men anywhere." And the commander of the 24th declared, "Too much cannot be said of their courage, willingness and endurance." The Army awarded five Medals of Honor and twenty-six Certificates of Merit to blacks for their heroism in the Cuban campaign.

In the two-week period preceding the surrender of Santiago, black soldiers, in torrid heat and short of supplies, dug trenches for days on end. As the days passed their situation deteriorated. A letter from a black soldier vividly describes their misery: "Now we are almost naked, no medicine, not much to eat, hot water to drink, sleeping on the bare ground and no papers of any kind."

During the siege of Santiago, observers commented on the black soldiers' cheerfulness under the most adverse conditions. To shorten the hours, they sang or played musical instruments. They readily shared the little food they had with those who had none. One of Colonel Theodore Roosevelt's officers said that he had "never met a braver and a kinder set of men." "When the Negroes were helping white soldiers in the Cuban camps to improve their hard conditions," the New York *Tribune* declared, "nobody heard any complaint that a white man's dignity was lowered by taking a piece of hard-tack or a cup of coffee from a black hand."

On July 15, the day the Spanish surrendered, the 24th Infantry was assigned to duty in the yellow fever camp at Siboney, "after eight regiments had refused this assignment." The chaotic conditions at the camp led the surgeon in charge to ask the commanding officer for volunteers to assist him by working as nurses in the hospital. The members of the 24th offered to perform this task. The first volunteers, about sixty-five in number, soon fell victim to the disease, and another contingent of the regiment promptly replaced them. As the days passed, virtually everyone in the regiment fell ill; only twenty-four of its men escaped malaria or yellow fever. On one particular day the morning report listed 241 of the 456 men in the regiment on sick call. Correspondent Bonsal wrote that the battle they fought in the yellow fever hospital "was more gallant" than their performance in battle, and more costly. On August 22 the regiment received orders to return to the United States. As the weary troops marched to their transport, "they received an ovation from the white soldiers."

While the four black regular army regiments recuperated at Montauk Point, New York, they continued to receive enthusiastic commendation from the press for their "excellent service in the field." Their record was considered especially noteworthy in view of the difficulties they had experienced before leaving for Cuba. The New York *Tribune,* among many other papers, paid its respects to the black soldiers who, despite determined attempts to make life unpleasant for them at Chickamauga and in Florida, went to Santiago and showed "that they knew how to fight for the United States with the best of soldiers, that they could march and suffer and die with white men, even if they couldn't ride in the same car."

Prominent citizens and the general public showered the black soldiers with gifts, special luncheons, and victory parades. Addressing a rally of blacks in his campaign for the governorship of New York, Theodore Roosevelt spoke of the black regulars as "brave men, worthy of respect." "I don't think any rough rider," he added, "will ever forget the tie that binds us to the Ninth and Tenth Cavalry." On October 8, the 10th Cavalry, on its way to Huntsville, Alabama, marched down Pennsylvania Avenue to the cheers of the citizens of Washington, D.C., and a review by President McKinley and his Cabinet. The *Army and Navy Journal* commented, "Never in history has the Negro advanced himself so rapidly in public estimation as in this war."

The black press and community naturally manifested great pride in the performance of the four regular units. In many homes, prints of the charge up San Juan Hill could be found hanging on the wall. It was optimistically asserted that recognition of their achievements in the war foreshadowed an improved status for black soldiers and civilians. Captain John Bigelow of the 10th Cavalry declared that the exploits of the black troops had "enhanced the self-respect and stimulated the aspirations of colored people in general and of the soldier in particular."

These expectations were soon shattered, however, as black civilians and soldiers were confronted by a renewed upsurge of racial hostility in the immediate postwar period. White Southerners increasingly resented the way newspapers and the general public were playing up the role of black soldiers in the war. They said such outpourings of sentiment had given the blacks an exaggerated sense of their own importance, which threatened to upset the Southern system of white supremacy. One Southerner was quoted in a Washington press report as saying, "The trouble is that the press and the public have made such a fuss over the exploits of the Negro troops in

Cuba. . . . This has set up the Southern Negroes, especially, in their own estimation, and its effect upon them has been bad." The situation was aggravated by reports from Florida, where black veterans of the Cuban campaign, en route to Montauk Point, not only had defied Jim Crow restrictions but also had undertaken to defend and protect black civilians. As a result there had been clashes between white civilians and black soldiers. In discussing these developments, Professor Willard B. Gatewood, Jr., writes:

> The attitude of both white civilians and Negro soldiers seemed to have undergone changes that make such clashes inevitable: the determination of whites to keep black troops "in their place" obviously had become more pronounced, while the soldiers displayed more aggressiveness in combatting what they considered racial injustices.

The Southern response to this alleged threat to its "racial patterns" ranged from a new wave of disfranchisement to mob action and a series of brutal lynchings, several of which culminated "in the most barbarous burnings at the stake" and "terrible massacres." In Wilmington, North Carolina, a reign of terror directed against local blacks "in the wake of an impassioned political campaign" succeeded in keeping them from the polls. After the Democrats triumphed in the election, armed bands of whites, including leading citizens of the community, raided the black section. Estimates of the number of blacks killed ranged from 12 to 100, and hundreds fled from their houses in terror in the bloody race riot.

Enthusiasm for the black soldiers cooled noticeably. On October 22, 1898, the Cleveland *Gazette* published a communication from George W. Prioleau, the black chaplain of the 9th Cavalry, describing the arrival of that regiment at Kansas City, Missouri, where the 1st Cavalry had arrived only a few minutes earlier:

> The two regiments, regulars of the U.S.A., were there together. Both were in Cuba. Both were under the same flag; both wore the blue. And yet these black boys were not allowed to stand at the counters of restaurants and eat a sandwich and drink a cup of coffee, while the white soldiers were welcomed and invited to sit down at the tables and eat free of cost.

Late in November, Little Rock, Arkansas, learned that the War Department had ordered a contingent of the 25th Infantry to nearby Fort Logan H. Roots. Local whites besieged Washington officials with requests that the order be revoked. The *Arkansas Democrat* called it "a serious mistake" to station black soldiers in communities where they were likely to have a disruptive effect on race relations. It pressed for their transfer to a Western or Northern post, where their presence could not incite other members of their race "to acts of hostility toward the whites." The governor of Arkansas joined with the press and local citizens in protesting the War Department's order. On November 29, the War Department announced that, owing to the "earnest and emphatic remonstrances" of residents, it was canceling the original order and was dispatching a detachment of the white 12th Infantry to the post.

The accomplishments of the black regulars were now "sedulously minimized" and the quality of their soldiery disparaged. For example, Theodore Roosevelt, who had earlier extolled the bravery of the black troops in a widely publicized magazine article, now declared that they were "peculiarly dependent upon their white officers," and that black noncommissioned officers generally lacked the ability to command and handle the men "like the best class of whites." He described an incident during a critical period of the fighting at San Juan Hill, when the Spaniards were laying down an intense barrage of fire. Under the strain, "none of the white regulars or Rough Riders showed the slightest sign of weakening," but he had to draw his revolver to stop a group of black infantrymen from fleeing to the rear. Faced with the threat of being shot if they did not return to the front, the black soldiers "flashed their white teeth at one another, as they broke into broad grins, and I had no more trouble with them."

Roosevelt's attributions of cowardice to black soldiers on San Juan Hill aroused indignation in the black press and the black community in general, and among black soldiers in particular. Writing to the New York *Age*, Sergeant Presley Holliday of the 10th Cavalry charged that Roosevelt's maligning of the black troops was "uncalled for, uncharitable, and ungrateful," and had done them "an immeasurable lot of harm." According to Holliday, the black soldiers were following a white lieutenant's order to move to the rear and bring up more ammunition and entrenching tools, and were on their way there when Roosevelt stopped them. Roosevelt had been so informed by this officer and had come to the line of the black troops on the following day, where he told the men that he recognized his error and "found them to be far different men from what he had supposed."

At the end of December 1898 the *Washington Post* published a special dispatch from Richmond, Virginia, under the headline "No Praise for Negro." The correspondent related how a "packed audience" at the Academy of Music in that city had reacted with anger when Mason Mitchell, an actor who had served with the Rough Riders in Cuba, in the course of a dramatic presentation on the late war, paid tribute "to the gallantry and bravery of the Tenth Cavalry":

> From all parts of the building came cries of "put him out" and "stop him," and hisses drowned the voice of the speaker. Mr. Mitchell rebuked his audience, but to no purpose. . . . The hisses were continued until Mitchell had to ring down the curtain and retire from the stage.

But the 10th Cavalry had to contend with more than hisses. Toward the end of January 1899 it left Huntsville for San Antonio, Texas. Outside of Meridian, Mississippi, and again on the outskirts of Houston, Southern whites fired upon the train carrying the regiment. The officer in charge requested aid so that his troops "could pass an area which they were supposed to protect 'without danger from hidden assassins.'"

There were also a growing number of troublesome incidents along the Texas border arising primarily from racial animosity between the black troops and white civilians living near army posts. One white officer said that, while several companies of the 25th Infantry were stationed at Fort Sam Houston from November 1899 to July 1900 their soldiers were "subjected to continual persecution by the citizens and police of San Antonio on account of their color." Another officer wrote that, when several companies of the 25th Infantry were stationed at Fort Bliss in 1900, there was "a relentless persecution of the men by the police and others of El Paso on account of their color."

In November 1899 tension between the civilians of Rio Grande City, Texas, and the black troopers of the 9th Cavalry stationed at the nearby garrison of Fort Ringold, culminated in an armed attack on the post by several hundred citizens. Three months later, on February 16, 1900, a member of the 25th Infantry was arrested and imprisoned in El Paso on charges of drunkenness and disorderly conduct. That evening several members of the regiment invaded the local jail to force the release of their comrade. A policeman and a black corporal were killed. While not condoning the assault on the jail, both Lieutenant Colonel C. C. Roberts of the 13th Infantry, who was assigned to investigate the incident, and Colonel Chambers McKibbin, the department commander to whom the report was sent, placed a good measure of the responsibility on the bitter resentment in the South against "colored men in uniform" and on the failure of local police to enforce impartially the law.

A black soldier would be arrested for offenses that, when committed by a white, would be overlooked, and the black would also be subjected to abuse though behaving "with perfect propriety." As long as this attitude and treatment prevailed, there would continue to be "troubles of one kind or another." Colonel McKibbin pointed out: "There is unquestionably a very strong prejudice throughout all of the old slave states against colored troops. . . . It is not because the colored soldier is disorderly—for as a rule, they behave better than white soldiers . . . but because they are soldiers."

Two thousand blacks served in the navy during the Spanish-American War. One of them, John Jordan, chief gunner's mate on Admiral George Dewey's flagship, the *Olympia*, was the man who fired the first shot at Manila Bay. Another black sailor, Robert Penn, won the Congressional Medal of Honor for saving a shipmate's life while the fleet lay off the Cuban coast.

After the war there were approximately 500 black men in the enlisted force of the navy, serving on the same ships as white men and eating in the same messes. The *Army and Navy Journal* called them "excellent sailors." But black seamen complained that, although in the recent war they had once again demonstrated their loyalty and ability, their chances of advancement in the service were very poor as compared with those of white sailors, even whites with less education and skill. One black sailor described the lot of his fellows:

His promotion to higher rates depends entirely upon the recommendation of officers through whose veins, in most cases, runs the poisonous blood of Negrophobia, with a baleful effect unimaginable. Sea and shore are alike in this particular for the representatives of our race. Filled with true patriotism for the country and the flag, he is a hero in time of war, and in peace suffers a caste prejudice more deadly than the poisonous fangs of the *fer-de-lance*.

In addition to the four black regular regiments that served during the Spanish-American War, some 8,000 to 10,000 blacks eventually entered the volunteer army. On April 23, 1898, President McKinley issued a call for 125,000 volunteers. Blacks seeking to enlist immediately encountered obstacles, since, under War Department instructions, the governors filled their quotas by mustering their national guard regiments into the federal service. Few states had black militia units, and those that did showed little inclination to muster them into federal service. In the end, only the governors of Alabama, Ohio, and Massachusetts accepted black units as part of their state's quotas on the first call.

On May 26 the President called on the states for 75,000 more volunteers. Under this second call Alabama's black battalion was raised to regimental strength and designated the 3d Alabama Infantry. In addition, the governors of a number of states, failing to meet their federal quotas with whites and at the same time feeling the pressure of black politicians, decided to accept black units. The Populist governor of North Carolina, Daniel L. Russell, whose election in 1896 owed much to the black vote, had authorized the formation of a black volunteer battalion under the first call. The Battalion was now increased to regimental strength and mustered into the federal service as the 3d North Carolina Infantry. In Kansas, Governor John W. Leedy, another Populist elected in 1896 with black support, had similarly authorized the creation of two black battalions, and they were now mustered into federal service as the 23rd Kansas Infantry. In Illinois, the Republican governor, John R. Tanner, increased the all-black 9th Battalion of the Illinois National Guard, organized in 1891, to regimental strength, and the new 8th Illinois Regiment was recruited, equipped, and mustered into federal service under the second call of President McKinley. The Democratic governor of Virginia, J. Hoge Tyler, after considerable hesitation, finally decided to accept a black volunteer regiment—known as the 6th Virginia Volunteers—to meet that state's quota. The governor of Indiana mustered in two black companies of infantry, which occupied the status of "separate colored companies." A few so-called mixed units, usually containing no more than two or three black volunteers, were also set up.

Meanwhile, Congress was debating the formation of several units of volunteers who were supposedly immune to yellow fever and malaria. As finally passed, the bill called for the recruitment of ten regiments "possessing immunity from diseases incident to tropical climates" to be known as the United States Volunteer Infantry (USVI). The War Department decided that only four of these regiments, the 7th, 8th, 9th, and 10th USVI, would be made up of black enlisted men. The President received the power to appoint the officers of the "immune" regiments.

But blacks were not content with being allowed to join the volunteer army. From the outset, black citizens had waged a vigorous campaign to have black officers placed in command of the black volunteers. The black press further urged black men to volunteer only if they were commanded by men of their own race. Foremost among these agitators was John Mitchell, Jr., of the Richmond *Planet*, who coined the phrase: "No officers, no fight!"

In response to the clamor for black officers, John R. Lynch, a prominent black Republican from Mississippi, received a temporary appointment as paymaster of volunteers with the rank of major. Another black paymaster was Major R. R. Wright of Georgia.

Subsequently, ninety-nine blacks received temporary commissions as first or second lieutenants in the line companies of these new regiments; approximately thirty of them were soldiers in the regular army. Several were commissioned in recognition of "their particularly gallant and meritorious service" at Santiago.

The black press and the black community expressed satisfaction that the authorities had finally recognized that a black soldier could serve no less effectively as an officer than he could as a private. On the other hand, the fact that, with but two exceptions, blacks would be permitted to serve only as lieutenants, and the failure of the War Department to recommend blacks for commissions in the regular army were strongly protested. It was pointed out that, once the volunteer units were mustered out, the newly commissioned officers on temporary duty from the regular army would have to either resign or return to their units as enlisted men. Chaplain Prioleau complained, "Promotions have been made, but they are not what we want. . . . Give us promotions as regulars for regulars and not as regulars for volunteers."

Black officers served with the black units recruited by the states, except in Alabama where, save for a black chaplain, Governor

Johnson replaced the officers of his all-black units with whites. Robert L. Bullard, a native of Alabama and a captain in the regular army, was placed in command of the 3d Alabama. Virginia's Governor Tyler appointed blacks as battalion and company officers and selected Richard C. Croxton, a white Virginian and a lieutenant in the regular army, as regimental commander. In September, Croxton called upon the black officers of the 2d Battalion to stand examination before a review board. Convinced that the order was merely "a maneuver to discredit them," nine officers of the unit resigned and were replaced by whites.

Three of the all-black volunteer regiments mustered into the federal service had complete rosters of black officers. Governor Leedy of Kansas issued commissions to twenty-nine blacks and appointed James Beck, a black long active in the Populist Party, as commander of the 23d Kansas Volunteer Infantry with the rank of lieutenant colonel. Governor Russell of North Carolina also appointed a full roster of black officers for the 3d North Carolina Infantry, headed by James H. Young, who was commissioned a colonel in the volunteer service. The 8th Illinois Regiment was the third unit "whose every man from bugler to colonel was an Afro-American." Its commanding officer was Colonel John R. Marshall.

The 9th Ohio Battalion had nineteen black officers. Lieutenant Charles Young was appointed its commander and commissioned as a major in the volunteer service. Two Indiana companies had six black officers with two black captains. Company L of the 6th Massachusetts Regiment had a full complement of black officers. "The officers of Company L," said the Cleveland *Gazette*, "are college graduates and professional men and are among Massachusetts' best citizens of color."

Of the more than 200,000 volunteers called up during the Spanish-American War, no more than 35,000 left the country or were even assigned to expeditions before the armistice in August. The only black volunteer unit sent into combat was Company L of the 6th Massachusetts, which took part in the invasion of Puerto Rico. Late in August, after the armistice, three black volunteer regiments —the 9th USVI and two state units, the 8th Illinois and the 23d Kansas—were selected by the War Department to perform garrison duty in Cuba. The three regiments established camp at the town of San Luis, where they performed a variety of jobs creditably, including construction of roads and bridges. Cordial relations developed between the Cubans and the black soldiers, and several men of the Kansas regiment married "Cuban senoritas."

The rest of the volunteers sat out the war in camp, growing increasingly restive and unhappy over their failure to see action. As expectations of glory faded, boredom with routine garrison duty strained tempers. Although there is no evidence to indicate that black volunteers were any less disciplined than their white counterparts, the white press singled them out for special denunciation. Every incident involving blacks was made into a grave breach of discipline, while similar violations by whites were either overlooked or "treated with tolerance and levity." "No disturbance occurred," wrote one black soldier, "but what the puppet so-called journalism chronicled it, with that effete style of 'darkey' . . . and those terms which all true men of this new age hope have died with slavery." The Washington *Bee* accused the *Post* of that city of featuring "every minor incident" involving black soldiers while overlooking serious breaches of discipline by white volunteers. It added:

> If the *Post* had taken the same pains to ascertain and publish the numerous crimes and misdemeanors committed in the various white camps that it has those alleged to have been committed by colored troops, it would be found that the white soldier far outstrips his dusky comrade in all that tends to cast a blot on the name of American citizenship and valor.

The problems faced by the black volunteers in the Southern training camps were as severe as those confronting the black regulars. They often suffered racial insults, abuse, and violence from white soldiers, local white citizens, and the police. When members of the 3d Alabama Infantry were assaulted in Anniston by white soldiers and civilians, the black soldiers formed a column of fours, ignored their attackers and marched back to camp. Their regimental commander wrote: "It was a wonderful display of discipline and control the like of which I never before saw and will probably never see again." On November 24, 1898, the Alabama black volunteers retaliated against "their tormentors." The "battle of Anniston" left in its wake one black soldier dead, one white soldier seriously wounded, and several soldiers and civilians slightly wounded.

Black volunteers stationed at Camp Haskell, near Macon, Georgia, ran into trouble as a result of their disinclination "to abide by Jim Crow customs or to tolerate insults." At least four members of the 3d North Carolina Infantry were killed by white civilians, who easily won acquittal from all-white local juries. By the end of their stay, at least three black volunteers had been killed by street-car conductors in fights resulting from the blacks' refusal to ride in the Jim Crow trailers hitched to the trolleys. The trials of the conductors also resulted in acquittals. A soldier of the 6th Virginia, who signed himself "Ham," wrote to the Richmond *Planet*: "Hasn't a week passed since we have been in this pest hole of the South that some of Uncle Sam's black boys in blue, haven't been 'justifiably homicided,' at least this is the only word that seems to strike the minds of all juries who try cases for 'killing nigger soldiers.' "

Beginning early in 1899, the troops were mustered out of the volunteer service. When the black volunteer regiments were disbanded, the black officers lost their commissions and returned to their units as enlisted men. Chaplain T. G. Steward said their commissions "were too short-lived, and too circumscribed, to be much more than a lively tantalization, to be remembered with disgust by those who had worn them."

The other black volunteers, after being officially discharged, returned to their homes by troop train. As discharged soldiers they were subject to local police rather than to the provost guard. When the train carrying the 3d North Carolina from Macon reached Atlanta, members of the police force climbed on board and engaged in "much clubbing," with the result that "the train that pulled out of Atlanta for Raleigh contained 'many bloody heads.' " Another assault upon black troops occurred in Tennessee. When the train carrying the 8th USVI reached Nashville, the black soldiers were asleep in their coaches. About 75 policemen and 200 citizens entered the cars armed with pistols and clubs and proceeded to beat the men "over the heads and bodies." A sheriff who participated in this affair stated gleefully:

> "It was the best piece of work I ever witnessed. . . . The way they went for the Negroes was inspiring. . . . And if a darky even looked mad, it was enough for some policeman to bend his club double over his head."

Even as the Spanish-American War army was being demobilized, other black regulars and volunteers were being sent to do battle with Filipinos rather than Spaniards. The American forces that had landed on the islands turned out, to the dismay of the Filipinos, whose aim was immediate independence, to be "an army of occupation, not of liberation." On February 6, 1899, the Senate gave its consent, with one vote to spare, to a treaty to annex the Philippines. Two days before, however, the shooting of a Filipino soldier by an American soldier "had set off the spark for the mass insurrection of the Filipino people against American rule." On March 2, 1899, Congress authorized the President to enlist 35,000 volunteers to serve until July 1, 1901.

From the outbreak of hostilities on February 4, 1899, to March 10, 1901, when the United States forces broke the back of the insurrection with the capture of insurgent leader Emilio Aguinaldo, the Filipinos fought against American annexation by conventional and guerrilla methods. "Every tree seemed to shoot at us," wrote Lieutenant Michael J. Lenihan. The two years of relentless warfare claimed the lives of at least 4,000 Americans and no fewer than 250,000 Filipinos. On July 4, 1902, the insurrection was declared officially over by President Roosevelt, who had taken office upon the assassination of McKinley.

There was much discussion among American blacks as to whether it was right for them to fight against the Filipinos seeking their independence. On the one hand, certain spokesmen called upon blacks to rally to the flag now that a state of war existed between the Filipinos and the United States. The *Freeman* of Indianapolis came out strongly for upholding the nation's honor at all costs, insisting that "the enemy of the country is a common enemy." Blacks were assured that service in the Philippines would go far toward combating racial prejudice and securing first-class citizenship. But a highly vocal element in the black community, including a large segment of its press, "had by now become disenchanted with the imperialist ventures of the United States" and took a strong stand against American intervention in the Philippines. This attitude was prompted by sympathy for the aspirations of "another people of color," by the brutality of the suppression of the insurrection, by reports of the establishment of a system of racial discrimination in Cuba, by the intensification of discrimination and repression of blacks in the South, which the McKinley Administration did nothing to halt, and by the unjust treatment of black veterans of the Spanish-American War. Referring to the black veterans, the Cleveland *Gazette* asked: "What has been his reward? Has honor, promotion, assured citizenship, or protection crowned his career at El Caney or San Juan Heights? Ingratitude, discrimination, humiliation are the only trophies which, so far, he can thank his country's star for."

Black opposition to American intervention in the Philippines became so vocal and widespread that the War Department for a time questioned whether black volunteers should be sent to the Philippines. Black regulars, however, were considered reliable, and in the late spring of 1899 the first black troops—companies of the 24th and 25th Infantry—were dispatched to the islands. "We are on trains bound for Ft. Presidio [the Presidio of San Francisco], Cal.," wrote a member of the 25th Infantry to the Cleveland *Gazette* early in June 1899, "where we will embark on the U.S. transport *Pennsylvania* for the Philippines." On June 19, while the 24th was awaiting orders to sail, the San Francisco *Chronicle* published a letter from a correspondent who signed himself "Lieutenant." He charged, on the basis of statements being made openly by members of the black regiment to visitors at the Presidio, that it would be dangerous to send black troops to the islands, since they would not fight against the dark-skinned Filipinos as they had against the Spaniards in Cuba. "They say," he went on, "that the white men are trying to coerce the natives of the Philippines as they have coerced the Negro in this country. Instead of fighting the Filipinos, they will aid them."

The next day the *Chronicle* sent a reporter to the Presidio to elicit the reaction of the black troops to these charges. He found them furious over what they termed "a libel on the regiment." A veteran of the Cuban campaign who was said to speak for the others declared: "We are American citizens and we have at heart the interests of our native land in the same manner as do all Americans." The correspondent concluded that "no taint of disloyalty" existed in the regiment. On July 2, while the 24th was en route to the Philippines, the *Chronicle* published a lengthy tribute to the black soldier, which concluded with an appeal to the nation to remember "that this is a man and a brother, no longer the bond slave but a citizen who of his own free will gives of heart and brain and brawn to the cause of the republic."

The first black troops arrived in Manila in mid-July 1899. These companies of the 24th and 25th Infantry were joined during the next two years by other units of these regiments as well as by those of the 9th and 10th Cavalry. In August 1899 the army undertook to organize two black volunteer regiments for service in the Philippines and to staff these new units with black officers below the grade of major, to be chosen from among black regulars who had distinguished themselves in the Cuban campaign and those with superior records in the state volunteer units. While blacks were pleased that they could now become captains in units set up by the army, it did not escape their notice that, just as in the Spanish War, their assignments were to the temporary volunteer regiments and not the four black regular units. "In the regular army," the Richmond *Planet* noted, "no colored man can hope for promotion beyond that of non-commissioned officer."

The two regiments of black volunteers, known as the 48th and 49th Infantry USV, had an aggregate of seventy-five officers, most of whom had been officers in the volunteers during the Spanish-American War. Fifteen enlisted men of the regular army who had distinguished themselves in the Cuban campaign were among those appointed as company-grade officers. The two black volunteer regiments began arriving in the Philippines early in 1900 and remained there until their commissions ended eighteen months later.

During the skirmishes and campaigns against the Filipino insurgents, black regulars and volunteers saw action all over the islands and were also used for scouting, garrison, and reconnoitering activities. Black units participated in the operations at Las Piñas, the capture of O'Donnell, the attack on Mount Arayat, the expedition under Captain Joseph B. Batchelor in which one battalion of the 24th Infantry made a successful march through 200 miles of difficult and unknown country, and countless other engagements.

During their stay in the Philippines, the black soldiers associated "on terms of equality" with the local population. When peace was restored, more than a thousand blacks remained, married indigenous women, and made the Spanish-speaking islands their permanent address. "In sharp contrast," white soldiers "almost without exception and also many officers" continually disparaged the Filipino people as "niggers" and otherwise behaved toward them in an offensive manner. John W. Calloway, a battalion sergeant in the

24th Infantry, reported to the Richmond *Planet* that the local population could not help but appreciate the differences in their treatment by black and white soldiers. According to a white volunteer from Idaho, A. L. Mumper, such prejudiced behavior on the part of enlisted men was encouraged by the racial views of superior officers. Mumper wrote: "It kept leaking down from sources above that the Filipinos were 'niggers,' no better than Indians, and were to be treated as such." White soldiers also delighted in taunting black soldiers by addressing them as "coons" and "niggers" and "by singing 'All coons look alike to me' and 'I don't like a nigger nohow.'" The *Army and Navy Journal* became so agitated by the constant use of the term "nigger" that it suggested the word be banished from "the vocabulary of the Army."

A version of the American color line was introduced to the Philippines. Local facilities that catered to Americans adopted Jim Crow standards. Black soldiers were barred from "whites only" restaurants and barbershops, which proliferated after the color line was established. Black officers also had a rough time of it. White enlisted men showed a reluctance, if not outright refusal, to salute black officers or otherwise give them the respect due their rank. Many white officers were guilty of personal discourtesy to them. One observer noted that black officers were ignored socially and were treated officially almost like enlisted men. The Topeka *Citizen* complained that the black officers' treatment was "not only insulting, but cruel and brutal."

The Filipino insurgents made special appeals to the black troops, urging them to return home where their fighting talents could be put to better use against lynch mobs, or to come over to the Filipino side, where they would be treated as equals. One historian notes that these pleas were largely ignored; only about five blacks "took up the cause of the Filipinos and fought for them," but another speaks of the "relatively high rate of desertion among Negro regiments." Nevertheless, he notes that "most Negro soldiers" regarded their tour of duty in the Philippines as a job that had to be done. "We are now arrayed to meet a common foe," wrote M. W. Saddler, a member of the 25th Infantry, in September 1899, "men of our own hue and color. Whether it is right to reduce these people to submission is not a question for a soldier to decide. Our oaths of allegiance know neither race, color, nor nation."

With the official end of the war in the Philippines on June 30, 1901, the War Department began to send most of the regular army and all of the volunteers home. Any black volunteers who wished to join one of the two black regular infantry regiments was given an opportunity to do so. But the black volunteer officers were not treated as generously. The act of February 2, 1901, increased and reorganized the regular army and created 1,135 officer vacancies. Every colonel of the volunteers was permitted to designate those officers of his regiment whom he considered best qualified for appointment to the regular army. Oswald Garrison Villard, editor of *The Nation*, pointed out that "hundreds of white officers were selected in this way, but not a single colored officer." "What does this mean?" the *Colored American* inquired angrily. "Does it mean that the brave black soldiers who volunteered to stand by the flag are to be ignored in the reorganized army? . . . It would seem so."

Three blacks were more fortunate than these volunteer officers. On February 8, 1901, John R. Lynch, a paymaster and major of the volunteers, was appointed a captain in the Paymaster Department of the regular army to become the first and only black paymaster of that service. And on March 21, 1901, the New York *Tribune* reported that among the twelve enlisted men who had passed the examination for commissions in the regular army was Benjamin O. Davis, who had served during the Spanish-American War as a first lieutenant in the volunteers. Upon his discharge he enlisted in the 9th Cavalry, with the aim of qualifying for a commission and went with that unit to the Philippines. "Sergeant Davis," the report continued, "will be the first Negro to rise from the ranks to a commission in the regular army." On the following day the *Tribune* featured a lengthy interview with "an officer of the regular army" who expressed disapproval of "the appointment of Negroes as officers of the regular army." He insisted that black enlisted men would resent the fact that a black ranked above them and on this account would become "insubordinate and hard to control." He added: "The Negro is the best of soldiers, but so far as he has gone his forte is in the ranks, and not among the officers. If he improves by the next generation, it may be the part of wisdom to give him the shoulder straps, but for the present I do not believe it to be so." Nevertheless, Davis was appointed to the rank of second lieutenant in the regular army on May 19, 1901. Lieutenant Davis was assigned to the 10th Cavalry and remained with that organization when it returned from the Philippines. Chaplain Prioleau hailed the promotion as proof that the army was not hostile to the idea of black officers. "The door is open. Who will be the next to enter?" he asked.

In July 1901 the army announced that Corporal John E. Green of the 24th Infantry, having successfully passed the required examination, had been appointed to the rank of second lieutenant in the 25th Infantry. Villard was confident that many more blacks would rise from the ranks, "if the same admirable spirit of fair play continues to rule in the army and is not altered by outside prejudice."

As the years passed, however, there were no additional promotions of black soldiers from the ranks. The military authorities continued to insist that any black candidate of talent and ambition could receive a commission by passing the required series of examinations. This drew the response that, so long as white officers believed that black soldiers must be led by whites, there was no likelihood that more blacks would rise to the commissioned ranks. The recognition extended to Davis and Green was called a token gesture to silence criticism. On July 10, 1904, Blanche K. Bruce, black former senator from Mississippi, wrote to Emmett J. Scott, Booker T. Washington's confidential secretary, that the military leaders "are determined to prevent Colored men from being officers in the army."

The black community was further concerned by the lack of support for their efforts to eliminate discriminatory features in other areas of the service. It is true that, despite the heightened racism that gripped the nation and the army after 1898, black soldiers continued to be treated as the equals of white soldiers in such aspects of military life as pay and educational and recreational opportunities. But the repeated appeals of blacks for additional regiments, branches, and positions were "constantly disappointed and frustrated," with the exception of a much publicized victory achieved by Booker T. Washington and his associates in 1908 when President Theodore Roosevelt ordered the replacement of the white regimental chief musicians of the four black regiments by blacks. On the other hand, despite a determined campaign by blacks, no new black units were added in the postwar reorganization and increase of the army. As the years passed, the percentage of blacks in the service steadily decreased. Writing to Scott on February 24,

1907, Sergeant Holliday of the 10th Cavalry complained that "the four known regiments by which we are represented in the army give a ratio to our population not at all equal to that of the white regiments to the white population."

The War Department also resisted efforts to open the artillery branch to blacks, because many officers continued to believe that, as an Army War College report stated in 1906, they were "inferior to the white race in intelligence and mental ability." There was also the complaint that the military authorities still failed to assist the black soldiers when they came into conflict with local white citizens in the South or when their civil rights were jeopardized. But there was more than the failure to eliminate the prewar restrictions against blacks; there was also an actual deterioration in the status of the black soldier. Professor Marvin E. Fletcher stated it most aptly when he wrote:

> As for the Army's treatment of the Negro enlisted man himself, the decline in the quality of officers assigned to the regiments, the deletion of the bi-racial picture in the recruiting booklet, the segregation of recruits in the recruit depots, and the attempt to enforce a color line are all symptomatic of the Army's increased awareness of the color of the soldier's skin.

This "increased awareness" was brought home most sharply in November 1906, when it was revealed that, in violation of the legal principle of the presumption of innocence, the army deprived a whole battalion of blacks of a basic right of an American soldier—fair trial by court-martial. In the spring of 1906 the 1st Battalion of the 25th Infantry—Companies B, C and D—was ordered to move from Fort Niobrara, Nebraska, to Fort Brown, a military reservation just outside of Brownsville, Texas, a small town across the Rio Grande from Mexico. When the residents of the town learned that a black battalion would be coming to replace the 26th Infantry, a white regiment, they were outraged. There was an outpouring of protests to the War Department and appeals for a revocation of the transfer orders. Secretary of War William Howard Taft refused to comply. Responding to a protest from the U.S. Commissioner in Brownsville, the Secretary wrote:

> The fact is that a certain amount of race prejudice between white and black seems to have become almost universal throughout the country, and no matter where colored troops are sent there are always

some who make objections to their coming. It is a fact, however, as shown by our records, that colored troops are quite as well disciplined and behaved as the average of other troops, and it does not seem logical to anticipate any greater trouble from them than from the rest.

The War Department, however, did modify its original order and directed that, before occupying Fort Brown, the 1st Battalion, together with the rest of the 25th Infantry, participate in the maneuvers of the regular army and Texas National Guard to be held near Austin on July 21. As soon as it completed this assignment, the battalion was to go to its new station. The reaction of the white officers and the black regimental chaplain, T. G. Steward, to the new directive was one of dismay. Recalling how black troops were continually subjected to "unprovoked assaults and abuse" by white soldiers of a Texas National Guard regiment during joint maneuvers in 1903 at Fort Riley, Kansas, and fearful of a repetition of such incidents, if not worse, they wrote to the regimental adjutant expressing their misgivings. "I protest against the 25th Infantry being sent to Austin," wrote Captain Samuel P. Lyon, "and subjected to the insult and abuse which will be the lot of the entire personnel of the regiment." Chaplain Steward seconded this appeal: "Texas, I fear, means a quasi-battleground for the Twenty-fifth Infantry." The regimental commander, responding to these appeals, requested that the black troops not be sent to Austin, and the War Department revoked the new directive. Late in July the black battalion left Nebraska and, proceeding directly to Fort Brown, arrived in Brownsville on July 28.

From the time of their arrival, relations between local citizens and the soldiers were strained, and they grew steadily worse with each passing day. The soldiers resented the Jim Crow arrangements and other discriminatory features that prevailed in most of the town, as well as the abuse they received. Some of the saloons had segregated bars; other excluded blacks entirely. Two soldiers set up their own bars near the post to accommodate the black troops. "There was just a mean bunch of people in Brownsville," one black infantryman reminisced years later. "They didn't want Negro soldiers there. They had a sign at the park. It said, 'No Niggers and no dogs allowed.' " On at least two occasions, black soldiers were either pushed or knocked down for allegedly jostling or speaking disrespectfully to whites. On August 13, the town buzzed with the rumor that a black soldier had attempted to rape a white woman, only to be driven off by her screams. That night some sixteen to twenty armed men moved through the streets of Brownsville shooting at random into buildings, killing a bartender and wounding a policeman. The garrison was aroused and the roll was called. All the soldiers were found to be present and accounted for. Shortly thereafter several cartridge cases fitting the new army rifle were picked up along the garrison road by the mayor of Brownsville. On inspection the next morning, the battalion rifles were found to be clean and the ammunition was accurately accounted for. On the same day a Brownsville Citizens' Committee, which had already concluded that the shots were fired by soldiers protesting segregated bars, quickly found them guilty of the assault upon the town. The predetermination of guilt on the part of the committee is reflected in the following question addressed to a witness:

Q. We are inquiring into the matter of last night with a view to ascertaining who the guilty parties are. We know they are Negro soldiers.

The same presumption of guilt was made by the several government investigators sent by President Roosevelt to ferret out the parties responsible for the shooting. At no point did they attempt to see if there might be any other explanation for the incident or to seek out other evidence. After two days of inquiry, the first of the investigators, Major Augustus P. Blocksom, Division Assistant to the Inspector General, Southwestern Division, reported that the shots were fired by a number of soldiers protesting racial slurs and Jim Crow arrangements, and recommended the removal of the black battalion. The troops were transferred to Fort Reno, Oklahoma Territory, where Blocksom continued his investigation.

Meanwhile, twelve soldiers had been confined in the post stockade on warrants issued by the State of Texas, charging them with murder and conspiracy to murder. Before leaving Brownsville, troop officers were instructed to transfer the suspects to Fort Sam Houston near San Antonio to await action by a grand jury. After taking evidence for three weeks, the grand jury was unable to indict any members of the battalion. The prisoners, however, were not released but continued to be held in confinement at Fort Sam

Houston. On August 29 Major Blocksom submitted his final report, in which he repeated that soldiers stationed at Fort Brown had been guilty of raiding the town. Since every soldier disclaimed any connection with or knowledge of the shooting, Blocksom concluded that a "conspiracy of silence" existed in the battalion. He recommended that, unless the guilty ones confessed or unless those who knew the guilty parties came forward and identified them, all the enlisted men of the battalion should be discharged without honor and barred from re-enlistment. He concluded by asserting that the black soldier was "much more aggressive" than he used to be "on the social equality question."

President Roosevelt next sent Brigadier General Ernest A. Garlington, Inspector General of the Army and a South Carolinian, to identify the members of the 1st Battalion who had participated in the raid. He was authorized to warn the soldiers that they would all be ousted unless the guilty confessed or others came forward and revealed who had committed the shooting. The ultimatum proved unavailing. Finding that every soldier continued to deny knowledge of the shooting incident, Garlington agreed with Blocksom's conclusion that some black soldiers were guilty and the others were shielding them in a "conspiracy of silence." He too recommended that all enlisted men of the three companies be discharged without honor and barred from future service in the armed forces and from government employment. Asked later whether he thought "colored people, generally, are truthful," when testifying about a crime, Garlington responded: "No, sir; I do not."

Roosevelt accepted Garlington's findings and recommendations and, on November 5, instructed Secretary Taft to carry out the dismissal of the enlisted man. However, "for fear of its effect on the colored vote," the decision was not made public until the day after the 1906 Congressional elections, held on November 9. From November 16 to 26, 167 black soldiers, one of whom had served twenty-seven years and twenty-five of whom had served more than ten, were discharged from the service without honor, denied all back pay, allowances, and benefits; and were declared ineligible for pension, as well as barred from re-enlisting and excluded from civil service employment. Six of the blacks dismissed were Medal of Honor winners, and thirteen had citations for bravery in the Spanish-American War.

The punishment understandably attracted wide attention; sides were taken, and the President's action was hotly debated. Most whites felt the President had acted correctly and supported the administration. The South applauded the discharge order as a "courageous application of justice." "Whatever may be the value of Negro troops in time of war," the New Orleans *Picayune* commented in a typical Southern editorial "the fact remains they are a curse to the country in time of peace." Leading journals such as *The Outlook, The Review of Reviews,* and *The Nation* also sided unequivocally with Roosevelt. And the *New York Times* reported that "the almost unanimous opinion" at the War Department upheld the legality and justice of the President's action and argued that the soldiers had only themselves to blame. But the *Army and Navy Journal* disagreed, repeatedly characterizing the summary discharge of three companies without trial by court-martial as a "drastic and arbitrary exercise of authority." On November 17, the *Journal* said that the President's order, based on the recommendation of an officer who was a native of South Carolina, "savors too much of oriental methods." A week later it declared: "The finding against the Negro soldiers is based upon the testimony of white men given under circumstances that deprive it of all value as legal evidence." Three months later it insisted that the great mistake was "in treating the men of the 25th Infantry as a lot of 'plantation niggers' instead of as soldiers wearing the uniform of the Army."

Most of the black community and press had no doubts on this point. "The race," Booker T. Washington wrote to Taft, "feels . . . hurt and disappointed." A black columnist said that the outrage felt by blacks was unequaled "since the overthrow of the Sumner Civil Rights law" by the Supreme Court twenty years earlier. This resentment stemmed in no small part from disillusionment with the Republican Party, to which blacks had a traditional allegiance, and with a President with whom Booker T. Washington had a special relationship and whom he had ardently defended in the past. The New York *Age* urged the remaining blacks not to reenlist when their terms expired, since they could not expect to be treated fairly while in the service. In Thomasville, Georgia, the Reverend William Decker Johnson reminded the nation of the contributions of black soldiers and went on to express the mood of the black community: "The Spanish-American was not the last war this country is going to be involved in, there will yet dawn a day when this country will be glad, yea, will court and beg the services of the Negro in time of warfare."

The Constitution League of the United States, an interracial civil rights organization, conducted an independent investigation and on December 10, 1906, submitted to Congress a report that accused all the investigating agencies of having presumed the guilt of the soldiers and of having failed to give them a fair hearing. It noted the absence of such legal safeguards as trial by court-martial and the opportunity to cross examine accusers and challenge the veracity of witnesses. Finally the report called for a Congressional investigation by a committee empowered to summon and examine witnesses and report remedial legislation.

The report was instrumental in persuading Senator Joseph B. Foraker, an Ohio Republican, to champion the cause of the blacks, although his critics insisted that he was motivated more by ambition for the Presidency than by a desire to correct an injustice. Foraker introduced a bill calling for an investigation by the Senate Committee on Military Affairs, which passed in an amended form. During February and March 1907, as the committee was beginning its hearings, both Major Charles W. Penrose, commanding officer of the black battalion, and Captain E. A. Macklin, officer of the day on August 13, were court-martialed at Fort Sam Houston for neglect of duty. The court concluded that the shooting had been done by the soldiers but found the two officers not guilty.

The Senate committee conducted hearings intermittently between February 4, 1907, and March 10, 1908, and one day later submitted majority and minority reports. The majority found that the shooting had been done by soldiers but was not able to identify any specific individuals. The minority said that neither a motive for the raid nor any convincing evidence to indicate soldiers had done the shooting had been presented. Two members of the Committee, Senators Foraker and Bulkeley, went even further, and in a separate section attempted to prove the soldiers' innocence. Foraker then proposed a bill enabling the soldiers to re-enlist on formal application supported by an affidavit of innocence of all charges. Concluding a stirring plea for the readmission of the blacks on April 14, 1908, Foraker said: "They ask no favors because they are Negroes, but only for justice because they are men."

Consideration of Foraker's bill was postponed until December 1908 because of the forthcoming Presidential election. Secretary of War Taft was the nominee of the Republican Party. Because of bitterness over Brownsville and the refusal of Booker T. Washington to criticize Roosevelt's action or do anything in behalf of the soldiers, some blacks, led by W. E. B. DuBois and Bishop Alexander Walters, supported William Jennings Bryan, the Democratic candidate. But most blacks, responding to Booker Washington's appeals and reluctant to support the Democrats, "remained loyal to the Republican Party and voted for Taft in spite of Brownsville." Nevertheless, the Brownsville affair placed Washington in a difficult position and in the end strengthened the hand of his opponents in the black community.

In the Congressional session following the election, a revised version of Foraker's proposal, with the Ohio Senator's reluctant approval, was passed by Congress and signed by President Roosevelt on March 3, 1909, on his and Foraker's last day in office. The measure gave the Secretary of War the power to appoint a five-man court of inquiry made up of retired army officers. The court was empowered to hear testimony and, within one year, to report on which soldiers were eligible for re-enlistment. Under the rules set up by the War Department a soldier who desired reinstatement could apply to the court and submit evidence of his innocence, although how he was supposed to find evidence remained a mystery.

The five retired officers chosen for the court of inquiry began their hearings early in May 1909. Under the original instructions drawn up by the War Department, the court had been directed to "determine whether there was such guilt" as to warrant the action taken by the former President. Because of objections from the new Secretary of War, Jacob M. Dickinson, these lines were deleted, and the court was confined to the question of the readmission of soldiers. Not only was Roosevelt's action not questioned, but the court refused to search for any evidence that might clear the soldiers. Moreover, only eighty-two soldiers were allowed to appear before the court. More than seventy others who had asked to be called were waiting to appear when the court announced that it would not hear any more witnesses. On November 15 the court concluded its investigation and, after a week of deliberating, announced its decision. The court concurred with the earlier findings that some soldiers were guilty of shooting up the town, but it ruled that fourteen of the 167 blacks were eligible for re-enlistment and entitled to the rights and status they had at the time of the discharge. No reason was given as to why the others were not readmitted. "The court of inquiry," said the New York *World*, "has done all that could possibly be asked of it to make this Brownsville burlesque upon justice a triumph of absurdity." Within a year eleven of the fourteen eligibles had re-enlisted and received pay for the time they had been discharged. The Brownsville Affair—or what an Army spokesman years later called the only documented case of mass punishment in its history—was seemingly brought to a close.

But for the black community and its friends the case was not closed. In November 1910 the first issue of *The Crisis*, official organ of the National Association for the Advancement of Colored People (NAACP), published an article by Moorfield Storey, a white liberal who served as chairman of the NAACP board of directors, in which he contrasted the Brownsville decision with the treatment accorded a group of white soldiers in 1904. Storey noted that in that year between fifty and seventy-five white soldiers tried to break open a jail in Athens, Ohio, in order to release a comrade. During the attempt the soldiers killed one militiaman and wounded at least two others. Contending that, no matter how guilty a man was, "he was entitled to be defended by counsel," Secretary of War Taft assigned a representative of the War Department to defend the accused and arranged for an attorney from the Department of Justice to assist in the defense. The Secretary explained his active intervention in behalf of the soldiers: "An enlisted man is more or less a ward of the government, and if the government steps in merely to see that he is tried according to law, it seems to me that it is an exercise of a discretion which the Government has."

Only two years later, Storey pointed out, an entire battalion of black troops was discharged without honor, without being offered a trial or any assistance. Why, he asked, were the soldiers of the 25th Infantry not considered "wards of the government" as well as those at Athens? "The soldiers of Brownsville," he concluded, "were colored."

On September 28, 1972, the army finally cleared the records of the 167 black soldiers discharged for the shooting incident in

Brownsville. Declaring the original action a gross injustice, the army ordered the discharges changed to honorable but also ruled out back pay for survivors or allowances for their descendants. An army spokesman added that it had simply acted to right a wrong. Others, however, believed the action resulted from a speech in which California's Representative Augustus Hawkins, a black, had argued their innocence. Subsequently, Hawkins identified a Minneapolis man, Dorsey Willis, eighty-six, as the sole survivor. On December 27, the New York *Times* reported that Willis, "old, arthritic and resentful," after his discharge had been reduced to working as a porter and shoeshine man. "That dishonorable discharge kept me from improving my station," Willis told the reporter. "Only God knows what it did to the others." He added bitterly, "None of us said anything, 'cause we didn't have anything to say. It was a frame-up straight through." Late in 1973, Congress passed a bill granting Willis $25,000 as compensation and providing him with medical care at veterans' hospitals.

Black sailors, too, suffered a deterioration in their status. Gradually the navy began to restrict blacks in the service to the messmen's branch, established on April 1, 1893. In time black men were no longer eligible for other ratings; they were permitted to enlist only as messmen and could rise only to the position of officer's cook or steward. This restriction regarding blacks was put into effect "apparently by verbal instructions to the recruiting service rather than by written orders."

In August 1903 the story was widely circulated in the press that the Navy Department had decided no more blacks were to be enlisted, and those then in the service would be gradually mustered out until the enlisted force was composed exclusively of whites. In the opinion of many naval officials and officers, discipline and efficiency would be greatly improved by the elimination of black sailors. Not only were blacks inferior sailors, they contended, but the white enlisted men were discontented because they were placed in close contact with blacks aboard ship, compelled to associate with them, and treated as their equals. The promotion of blacks caused additional difficulty. White sailors deeply resented finding themselves under the authority of blacks. A white petty officer of twenty years' service wrote to the New York *Herald* endorsing this position: "It is indeed high time the department took some action in this matter. Among the many causes of discontent and desertion in the navy the presence of the Negro is one of the most potent."

Soon thereafter the *Herald* published a reply from a correspondent who contended that, in view of the contributions blacks had made to "some of the greatest naval victories in our history," it would be a "backward step" for the nation now to say, "No room for you in the navy." The Cleveland *Gazette* was more blunt: "Any disposition . . . to exclude Afro-Americans from the navy would be as criminal as it is unjust." Naval authorities emphatically denied their intention of eliminating blacks from the service. The *Army and Navy Journal* agreed that such a step would be a "plain violation of the Federal Constitution." It concurred with a number of naval officers that the solution to the vexing problem of "race antipathy" was not "the absolute exclusion of Negroes" but their consolidation into black crews under white officers, as had been done in the army, where the organization of black soldiers into separate units had successfully resolved "the racial question." The *Journal* and these officers held that blacks made good sailors, they would be more useful and efficient if organized into separate crews, and such a setup would give them opportunities for advancement that were then largely denied to them. Lieutenant Commander J. P. Magruder declared:

> The Negro himself would doubtless prefer this plan to the present system, since it would give him a better chance for promotion; he would have more company of his kind and be freed from the prejudice of a few of another color who may not be his superior physically or in the qualifications for the ratings they hold.

The plan ultimately adopted was not to establish separate black crews but increasingly to limit the presence of blacks on board ship in ratings other than those of the messman's branch. The first step came during 1907–8, as the Great White Fleet assembled at Hampton Roads, Virginia, in preparation for its round-the-world cruise. Tension had been mounting between the United States and Japan over discrimination against Japanese on the Pacific Coast, and there was fear that the Japanese stewards in the navy might act as spies and saboteurs. As a consequence, the Japanese stewards were discharged and replaced by blacks in the mess branch. A recent study of the Great White Fleet has asserted: "Negro volunteers, who had joined the Navy in good faith, were chosen to fill the gap. They resented their assignments as waiters and busboys, and, as the months went by, would sometimes become so 'impudent' that they would have to be beaten."

In February 1909 the fleet returned, and black petty officers were transferred to shore duty. Charles F. Parnell, one of those transferred, subsequently wrote: "Every one of us was transferred. We knew that the end of a colored man being anything in the Navy except a flunkey had arrived." In November 1909 a black sailor with two years' service accused the Navy Department of instructing recruiting officers to enlist black applicants only in the mess branch. As a consequence it was becoming virtually impossible "to come across a Negro seaman."

This situation was dramatically brought home to black civilians when the navy joined in a number of exposition and centennial celebrations during those years. In the fall of 1909, naval crews paraded in New York City during the Hudson-Fulton centennial. The black press was struck by the absence of black seamen and charged that they had been forbidden to participate. Soon thereafter an article appeared in the New York *Age* in which officials of the Navy Department denied that there was "any studied attempt to discriminate" against blacks. The explanation offered for their absence was that the deck crews—landsmen, sailors, gunners, and so forth—were the only ones permitted to parade and there were few blacks in these ratings. It was further stated that the navy was eager to enlist blacks, even "giving them preference over white men . . . as messmen, stewards, cooks and firemen."

The altered status of black seamen was again highlighted on October 12, 1912, when not a single black was to be seen among the 6,000 sailors who paraded in the National Naval Review in New York City.

On April 12, 1913, a number of black leaders of New York wrote to Secretary of the Navy Josephus Daniels, directing his attention to the charges of discrimination against blacks in the navy. The Secretary responded that careful consideration would be given to "the alleged discrimination against colored men in the naval service." The communication was turned over to Rear Admiral Charles J. Badger, in command of the Atlantic Fleet. On May 26 the *New York Times* reported: "Secretary of the Navy Daniels and

Rear Admiral Charles J. Badger have completed an investigation of the charge of discrimination in the navy against colored enlisted men and find that the charge is unwarranted as there is no evidence of discrimination." The admiral conceded that the only blacks in the navy were in the messman branch but pointed out there were also some white men in that branch and that neither black nor white messmen were permitted to parade. The only sailors authorized to parade were those composing the deck and gun crews. Secretary Daniels dispatched the report to his New York correspondents along with a letter that read: "The department believes with Admiral Badger that you are misinformed as to the conditions of colored men in the navy." On the eve of World War I, two men passed the navy test to become wireless operators. One, a white man, was accepted for this specialty but the other, a black, was informed that he was "eligible for the mess service only."

Meanwhile, on December 24, 1912, the *Washington Post* published a report that further aroused deep concern in the black community. It read: "The proposal to eliminate the Negro as an American soldier is a topic slated for consideration when the conference of the ranking officers of the army is held here January 8." The Washington correspondent of the *New York Evening Post* characterized this scheme as an attempt to drive the blacks out of the army as they had been eased out of the navy, save as "servant, messboy, or any other post of a comparatively menial nature." Many groups appealed to the Secretary of War to retain the black units, pointing to "their splendid record in time of war in Cuba and the Philippines." The Chicago *Defender* declared: "First in war, first in peace, but usually last in the hearts of their countrymen, the record of the colored soldier stands." Secretary of War Henry L. Stimson responded with the statement that the black regiments had performed "creditable and even distinguished service," and that only Congress could eliminate them.

Late in January a bill was introduced in the House calling for repeal of the statutes authorizing the formation of four black regiments. The measure never came to a vote. The same happened to a bill introduced in July 1914, which prohibited blacks from serving as commissioned or noncommissioned officers in the army or navy. On March 9, 1916, General Pancho Villa crossed from Chihuahua, Mexico, into New Mexico and attacked the town of Columbus. The following day the War Department instructed Brigadier General John J. Pershing to lead a punitive expedition across the Mexican border in pursuit of Villa. The 10th Cavalry formed part of one of the two invading columns against the *Villistas*. On June 21, 1916, Troops C and K of the 10th Cavalry had "a fateful fight" at Carrizal in which ten black soldiers were killed and a number of others were captured.

In June 1916, while black troops were engaged in the Mexican expedition, Congress passed the National Defense Act, increasing the size of the regular army. In spite of appeals from the NAACP, the measure made no provision for additional black units or for the inclusion of blacks in the artillery. At the same time, Southern Congressmen sponsored a bill to eliminate black soldiers and sailors from the armed forces by preventing the enlistment or re-enlistment of "any person of the Negro or colored race" in the military service of the United States. The new Secretary of War, Newton D. Baker, spoke out strongly against the proposal, noting that black soldiers had performed "brave and often conspicuously gallant service" as part of the American forces since the time of the Revolution and adding: "In the most recent instance, at Carrizal in Mexico, these colored troops conducted themselves with the greatest intrepidity and reflected nothing but honor upon the uniform they wore."

The Secretary's strong words proved effective, and the measure was defeated. When war broke out with Germany on April 6, 1917, the black component of the regular army still consisted of four regiments of enlisted men and three black line officers—Colonel Charles Young, First Lieutenant Benjamin O. Davis, and First Lieutenant John E. Green.

In addition to the regular regiments, there were a number of black National Guard units, constituting about 5,500 men and 175 officers. These included the 8th Illinois and the 15th New York regiments and single companies from the District of Columbia, Maryland, Ohio, Tennessee, and Massachusetts. The 8th Illinois alone had a complete roster of black officers. The 15th New York had a famous regimental band, led by Lieutenant James Europe and with Sergeant Noble Sissle as its drum major.

At the beginning of World War I, approximately 20,000 of the 750,000 men in the regular army and National Guard were black.

The war would see an intensification of the armed forces' racist orientation and a further deterioration in the status of the black soldier and sailor. Military leaders now came to believe that the ability to serve in combat was largely a matter of race and that blacks were not suited to such a role. If used at all, their service should be limited to that of labor troops in the army and menials in the navy. As Don Lacy says in his work, *The White Use of Blacks in America*: "The general white policy was to make use of blacks to help fight the war, but to do so in ways that reinforced rather than denied the conception of them as different, inferior, and not fit to serve as equal men."

6

World War I and Black Servicemen

In April 1917, when President Wilson asked for a declaration of war against Germany, he told Congress, "The world must be made safe for democracy. Its peace must be planted upon the tested foundations of political liberty. . . . We are but one of the champions of the right of mankind." With very few exceptions, black spokesmen, convinced by this democratic rhetoric as well as by official promises of significant improvement in racial affairs, urged blacks to aid the country's war effort, raising the cry that the "race is on trial." A faculty and student group at Howard University commented: "If we fail, our enemies will dub us COWARDS for all time; and we can never win our rightful place. But if we succeed—then eternal success."

In an editorial headed "The Black Soldier" in the June 1918 issue of *The Crisis*, W. E. B. DuBois declared that out of victory for the armies of the Allies would rise "an American Negro with the right to vote and the right to work and the right to live without insult." One month later he called upon blacks to put aside their "special grievances" for the duration of the war, insisting that the objective of winning the war must take precedence over the fight for black rights. "We make no ordinary sacrifice," he added, "but we make it gladly and willingly with our eyes lifted to the hills."

A small group of black radicals led by Asa Philip Randolph, a young activist and labor leader, and Chandler Owen, a law student at Columbia University, dissented from this consensus. Both Randolph and Owen were active Socialists and edited the *Messenger*, a radical black journal of opinion, which conducted a vigorous campaign against black participation in the war. The *Messenger* noted the bitter irony implicit in blacks' being called upon to risk their lives in defense of freedoms that were denied them at home. It rejected the contention that by their service in the war blacks would succeed in eliminating race prejudice and would bring to an end discrimination, disfranchisement, and lynching. In the January 1918 issue of the *Messenger* Owen wrote:

> Since when has the subject race come out of a war with its rights and privileges accorded for such participation? . . . Did not the Negro fight in the Revolutionary War, with Crispus Attucks dying first . . . and come out to be a miserable chattel slave in this country for nearly one hundred years after? . . . Did not the Negro take part in the Spanish-American War? . . . And have not prejudice and race hate grown in this country since 1898?

However, sentiment among blacks was overwhelmingly in favor of serving, and they responded enthusiastically to the draft calls. Indeed, their major concern was that they might be excluded from the military and that their hope for achieving greater democracy at home might be frustrated. But enthusiastic participation by blacks failed to produce the anticipated changes. Instead, once again, both during and immediately after the war blacks found themselves the victims of violence at the hands of white citizens determined to keep them in their prewar status. "The promise of equality brought by the war," the Saint Louis *Argus* bitterly complained, "was succeeded by the lynch mobs of 1919." This time, however, blacks refused to be "passive victims of the white man's violence" but fought back vigorously in the many "abrasive and bloody encounters" that took place during what has become known as the Red Summer of 1919.

With the entry of the United States into the European war, the War Department implemented the addition to the regular army authorized by the National Defense Act of June 1916. All the regiments were brought up to maximum strength by voluntary enlistments. Black volunteers brought the four regular units to full strength within a week. Since it was army policy to allow black enlistments only to fill vacancies in these regiments, the War Department suspended further enlistments by blacks. Whites faced no such restrictions on the number of units in which they might enlist. As a consequence, while 650,000 white volunteers were accepted, only 4,000 blacks were allowed to enlist.

However, United States involvement in World War I required the rapid recruitment of a massive army. To accomplish this Congress passed and the President signed the Selective Service Act, which required all able-bodied American male citizens between the ages of twenty-one and thirty-one to register with their local draft boards. The applicants were then examined and classified according to their availability and usefulness, with deferments granted because of dependents, occupations, illiteracy, and medical disabilities. The armed forces, essentially the army, determined the monthly draft calls and set the physical and mental standards for induction.

The draft legislation contained no specific racial provisions. The same local boards registered and classified blacks and whites. Blacks found eligible for service were inducted separately, in line with the army's policy of strict segregation. "There is no intention on the part of the War Department," said Secretary of War Baker, "to undertake at this time to settle the so-called race question." But Baker assured the NAACP that the army would be free of racial discrimination and that black soldiers would be "justly treated."

In spite of Baker's assurance, blacks confronted gross prejudice and discrimination at every stage. The local draft boards, which exercised wide discretion in deciding who would be drafted and who deferred, were composed almost exclusively of whites. Across the nation, local boards required registrants "of African descent" to tear off one corner of their registration questionnaires so that they could be more easily identified. The boards eventually accepted a greater proportion of black registrants than whites for military service. Approximately 2,291,000 black men registered for the draft, and by the time the war ended 367,710 had been inducted into the armed forces, representing a 34.1 per cent rate of acceptance as opposed to 24.04 per cent for whites. Although black Americans were but 9 per cent of all those registering for the draft, they furnished 13 per cent of all persons drafted for service in World War I. Because of their advantaged economic position, more whites qualified for occupational deferment. Many single whites with practically no dependents were granted exemptions, while black men with large families dependent on them for support were inducted.

A larger percentage of blacks was also found physically qualified for general military service—74.6 per cent blacks as against 69.71 per cent whites. Draft boards regularly inducted blacks who were physically unfit while excluding whites with similar disabilities. No wonder Randolph complained: "The Negro is tubercular, syphilitic, physically inferior for purposes of degrading him; but physically fit and physically superior when it comes to sending him to the front to save white men's hides."

Blacks entitled to deferment were railroaded into the army, while whites with "no legitimate excuse for exemption were allowed to escape the requirements of the draft system." In parts of the South, black sharecroppers were not drafted if the planters whose land they worked filed requests for their exemption, whereas independent black farmers with large families were arbitrarily drafted. Out of 815 white registrants in Fulton County, Georgia, the local draft board exempted 526, while only six out of 212 blacks were excused from service. In this case and two others Secretary Baker suspended the boards for violations and appointed new members. "All told," wrote one observer, "it appears that many Negroes who had sufficient claim for exemption were drafted and sent away to camp."

With few exceptions, blacks accepted the call to service willingly, despite the discriminatory actions of the local boards. Indeed, there are no reported incidents of blacks' refusing to be drafted except in Oklahoma in August 1917, when resentment against the draft led blacks to join whites in a protest action, initiated by white Socialists, called the Green Corn Rebellion. A Kansas editor observed: "It is generally acknowledged that on the whole the Negroes of the United States have responded more universally and cheerfully to the call of the Government than the white man. When called under the selective service draft they have rarely asked for exemption."

The War Department decided to construct a separate cantonment for each of the army divisions and decreed that white troops must constitute a majority in each cantonment. Each of the white divisions had a black regiment attached to it for training purposes. The Provost Marshal's office arranged to have white and black draftees travel to the camps separately, and upon arrival they were assigned to separate areas. There were persistent rumors that the black draftees would be assigned exclusively to service units. In response to protests Baker insisted that this was not War Department policy.

In May 1917 the black community received the disturbing news that Colonel Charles Young, the only black West Point graduate on active duty and then holding the highest rank ever attained by a black officer in the U.S. armed forces, had been retired for medical reasons. Young was sixth in line for brigadier general, and accelerated wartime promotion would have given him this rank. His examining board had already recommended him for promotion, but when he came before the medical board for physical examination he was pronounced unfit because of high blood pressure and ordered retired. To prove his fitness for active duty, Young rode horseback the several hundred miles from his home in Ohio to Washington, D.C., but to no avail. On July 30, 1917, he was retired from active service with the rank of colonel.

To the black community, the medical reasons advanced for Young's retirement appeared to cloak the determination of military officials to remove Young rather than accept a black general. The Chicago *Defender* accused the military of " 'railroading' this man from the army" simply because of color. The New York *Age* wondered what chance there could be for "others not quite so well equipped" if a man like Young, with his splendid record, could be forced into retirement. Young was called back to active duty five days before the Armistice was signed, and was ordered to take charge of trainees at Camp Grant in Illinois. After the war he was sent to Liberia to help organize that country's army. While on furlough in Nigeria, he contracted a fever and died in 1922. He was buried with full military honors at Arlington National Cemetery. But DuBois, in his tribute to Colonel Charles Young, reminded the readers of *The Crisis* how the late officer "had been denied the stars of a general": "They could not stand a black American general."

In the late summer of 1917 serious fighting flared up between black regulars and white policemen and civilians in Houston, Texas. The War Department had ordered the 3d Battalion of the 24th Infantry, an all-black unit, to perform guard duty at Camp Logan, a military training base for National Guardsmen then under construction on the outskirts of Houston. From the time the black troops arrived at the camp, the white community of Houston made no effort to hide its resentment of their presence. Racial insults and abusive epithets were repeatedly hurled at them, and they were denied access to recreational facilities that had been opened to white troops. For their part, the blacks grew increasingly resentful of the segregation and the abuse that was inflicted upon black civilians and themselves. Refusing to accept these humiliations passively, they defied the local Jim Crow restrictions on street cars and in theaters and even tore down offensive discriminatory signs. A Houston motorman testified: "They said, 'We're from New York and we'll sit where we please. We're as good as any white man in town.'"

Members of the regiment's provost guard were allowed to carry only clubs within the city limits. White policemen brutally assaulted and arrested members of the battalion, including the provost guard, for refusing to observe Jim Crow signs. Early in August city detectives severely beat two black soldiers on a street car.

On August 23 a black soldier, Private Edwards, saw two policemen in the act of cursing and beating a black woman and remonstrated with the officers to release her. The policemen turned upon the soldier and beat him to the ground with the butts of their revolvers. They continued to beat and kick him while he was on the ground and then arrested him. Later that day, Corporal Charles Baltimore, a member of the provost guard, approached the officers and asked about the arrest, stating that it was his duty to report the matter to his superior officers. The officers responded by striking Baltimore over the head with their pistols. When the corporal tried to flee, the officers pursued him, beat him and arrested him.

When word of the assaults reached the camp, together with rumors that Baltimore, one of the most respected noncommissioned officers in camp, had been killed and that a mob of white men was planning to attack the camp, angry members of one company seized rifles and ammunition and marched on the city of Houston during that same evening to seek revenge on the police force, particularly those policemen stationed around the black district. After an exchange of fire with policemen and a civilian posse, the blacks gradually returned to camp. In the short but bloody confrontation sixteen whites, including four policemen, and four black soldiers died, one by suicide.

The next day the entire battalion was disarmed and transferred to New Mexico. An officer of the War Department who investigated the violent incident said: "Certain men of the 24th Infantry apparently resolved to assert what they believed to be their rights as American citizens and United States soldiers. . . . It is my belief that the tension had reached that point where any unusual occurrence would have brought on trouble."

Between mid-October and late November 1917 sixty-four black soldiers were court-martialed at Fort Sam Houston for murder and mutiny. After the most perfunctory trial, thirteen of them were sentenced to death, forty-two received life sentences, four were given long prison terms, and five were acquitted. Details of the court-martial as well as the verdict were not made public until after dawn on the morning of December 11, when the thirteen men sentenced to death were summarily and secretly hanged without a review of the sentences by either the President or the War Department "since military law specified that the area commander had final authority in time of war." However, the attorney of the NAACP insisted that this provision applied only to troops in action.

The Northern press joined Southern papers in justifying the execution of the thirteen blacks, but black Americans were furious. The Cleveland *Advocate* reported that the "wholesale execution struck the people dumb." In a speech delivered in Brooklyn's Saint Augustine's Episcopal Church (Colored), the Reverend Dr. George F. Miller condemned the speedy executions as "a military lynching," to placate the South.

In two additional trials, sixteen more men were condemned to death and twelve received life terms. Black organizations, especially the NAACP, worked to mitigate the harsh sentences imposed by the military. In February 1918 the NAACP presented a petition with 12,000 names to President Wilson, asking clemency for the condemned men. In response, the President agreed to review the trial record, and as a result ten of the death sentences were commuted to life imprisonment. The other six men were hanged. All told, the War Department indicted 118 men and convicted all but eight of them who testified against the others in return for promises of immunity. Nineteen were hanged and sixty-three received life sentences. In 1921, President Harding, after receiving a petition containing the signatures of 50,000 persons, reduced the sentences of those still imprisoned. By 1924 a majority of the men had been released from prison, but not until 1938 was the last soldier freed. As a result of this case, Congress passed an article that provided for appellate review at the department level before certain sentences, including the death sentence, could be executed.

In the meantime, to calm the black community and win its cooperation, Secretary Baker appointed Emmett J. Scott, an associate and onetime personal secretary of Booker T. Washington, as special adviser to the Secretary of War on matters concerning blacks. Scott was "to be responsible for all cases of real or alleged discrimination against Negroes in the Army."

At the same time, in response to demands that blacks be permitted to serve as combat troops, two all-black Infantry Divisions, the 92d and 93d, were formed and sent to France. The 92d Division, made up largely of black draftees, took form late in November 1917. It consisted of two infantry brigades and some supporting units. In addition, there were divisional troops and a Field Artillery Brigade.

From the outset, the division confronted serious handicaps. Instead of training in a single cantonment, its various units were split up among seven different camps "hundreds and thousands of miles apart," and were never brought together while in the United States. Only after it reached France was the division formed into a single organization. Major General Charles C. Ballou, in command of the division, had served in the 24th Infantry prior to the war and like the other white officers was chosen "because of previous experience with black troops." DuBois said of Ballou's leadership that, "whenever any occasion arose where trouble had occurred between white and colored soldiers, the burden of proof always rested on the colored man." For example, Ballou issued a command directing officers and men to refrain from going where "they were not wanted" regardless of their legal rights. This directive, known as Bulletin No. 35 resulted from an incident in Manhattan, Kansas. A black sergeant stationed at nearby Camp Funston was barred from entering a local theater by the manager, even though his exclusion violated a Kansas law prohibiting discrimination. Admitting that the theater manager was legally wrong in denying the sergeant admission, the bulletin claimed that nevertheless the sergeant was "guilty of the greater wrong in doing anything no matter how legally correct, that will provoke racial animosity." It concluded with the warning: "White men made the Division, and they can break it just as easily if it becomes a troublemaker."

In January 1918 the second all-black division, the 93d Division, built around black National Guard units, was formed. It had originally been the objective of the War Department to attach the black National Guard units to five under-strength white National Guard divisions. However, the division commanders did not want black soldiers and officers as part of their commands. Not knowing quite what to do with these unwanted black National Guardsmen, the War Department finally organized four regiments drawn from three black National Guard units and another from black Southern draftees officered by whites to form the 93d Division. No supporting units were attached to the infantry regiments. Command of the division was given to Brigadier General Roy Hoffman.

None of the four black regular army regiments saw combat as a unit in France during World War I. Instead, the regiments remained at stations in the continental United States and its island territories, while a large percentage of their soldiers were used to provide noncommissioned personnel for the 92d and 93d Divisions and officer candidates. In line with its traditional policy of having white officers lead black troops, the army at first refused to admit blacks to officer training schools. Before the war blacks had been excluded from the camps set up at Plattsburg, New York, to prepare men as officer candidates. After the war started, fourteen camps were established to train prospective white officers, but none for blacks. Black college students and certain officials of the NAACP, notably J. E. Spingarn, then chairman of its board of directors, as well as other groups, launched a campaign for the establishment of a separate officers' training camp for blacks. DuBois supported this project in the *Crisis*. But other elements of the black press and the more militant members of the black community vehemently protested the proposal, charging that a separate training camp for black officers would constitute tacit approval of racial segregation. Advocates of the proposal, however, insisted that the choice was either a segregated camp or no black officers at all. "We demand Negro officers for Negro regiments," DuBois wrote in the *Crisis*. "We cannot get them by admission to the regular training camps because the law of the land, or its official interpretation, wickedly prevents. Therefore, give us a separate training camp for Negro officers."

In May 1917 Secretary Baker agreed to the establishment of a black officers' training camp, to open on June 15 at Des Moines, Iowa. Of the 1,250 candidates who were trained at the camp, one-third came from civilian life; the remaining two-thirds had been noncommissioned officers in the four regular army regiments. In October 1917 the first group of 639 captains and lieutenants was graduated and commissioned as infantry officers. All told, 1,200 blacks received commissions, "representing about seven-tenths of 1 per cent of the officer strength of the army although 13 per cent of the enlisted troops were blacks." An effective ceiling was placed upon the advance of black officers beyond the company grades "regardless of their ability." As a consequence, except for a few National Guard officers, blacks did not serve in the field grades of major or higher. Moreover, relatively few became company commanders. The great majority remained first or second lieutenants. Colonel Frank A. Denison of the 370th Infantry was the highest-ranking black officer in the war. Next in rank were Lieutenant Colonel Otis B. Duncan of the same unit, and Lieutenant Colonel Ollie B. Davis of the 9th Cavalry.

Civilians launched a systematic effort to humiliate and harass the black officers. Throughout the war, the army made little effort to protect their civil rights or to curb hostile incidents. In a much-publicized case, Lieutenant Charles A. Tribbett, while traveling on a train under government orders, was removed from a Pullman car in a town in Oklahoma and arrested, fined, and jailed for violating the Jim Crow regulations of the state. In response to strong protests from the NAACP, the War Department declared that "the state law prevailed." In November 1918 the New York *Age* reported that a black officer who had returned to his home in Mississippi for a short visit with his family was compelled "to flee the town in disguise" when white citizens threatened that "they would allow 'no nigger' to wear a uniform that a white man was bound to honor."

Within army ranks less overt humiliation occurred. Many white officers made no effort to hide their dislike of black officers, barring them from the officers' clubs, refusing them permission to stay in officers' quarters, and generally viewing them with contempt. Many enlisted men refused to salute them. One black officer wrote, years after the war: "Practically every Negro officer commissioned in World War I can recount personal experiences of mistreatment at the hands of fellow officers, as well as disrespect by white enlisted men, silently condoned by higher authority."

White officers seized every opportunity to discredit black officers by bringing them before white-dominated efficiency boards and having them transferred to labor battalions and replaced by white officers. In asking permission to replace the black officers of the 372d Infantry Regiment with white officers, Colonel Herschel Tupes argued:

> The racial distinctions which are recognized in civilian life naturally continue to be recognized in military life and present a formidable barrier to the existence of that feeling of comradeship which is essential to mutual confidence and esprit de corps.

The request was granted. Indeed, before the war was over, many of the black officers were removed from both the 92d and the 93d divisions.

The blacks assigned to combat duty represented only a small fraction of the black troops in the army—about 42,000 out of 380,000. In spite of assurances to black leaders that a considerable number of black draftees would be permitted to serve with combat units, the overwhelming majority, regardless of their qualifications, were assigned to noncombat service in labor and stevedore battalions. As a rule, no attempt was made to provide service troops with military training. Further, these troops were housed in inferior quarters, without either recreational facilities or proper medical attention. They lived in tents without floors and stoves, and in some cases they were given discarded uniforms, which arrived in crates specifically marked "for the colored draft." At one camp, black soldiers were issued Civil War uniforms. "When one of the organizations thus clad marched through the camp," one historian wrote, "it became the laughingstock of the rest of the soldiers, and the men were humiliated."

In the bitter winter of 1917–18, the death rate among the black draftees was abnormally high. A report to the Secretary of War states that in Camp Alexander, Virginia, "during the winter of 1917–18 men died like sheep in their tents, it being a common occurrence to go around in the morning and drag men out frozen to death."

The War Department received numerous complaints from black

soldiers about mistreatment by white officers and noncoms. By early 1918 complaints from black troops all over the country were pouring into Washington charging that white officers called them "nigger," "darky," and "coon"; physically assaulted them; drove them relentlessly; kept them more closely confined to camp than white troops; denied them passes; meted out severe punishments to them for minor offenses or no offenses at all; permitted racist MPs to abuse them in the most brutal manner; and, when selecting black soldiers for promotion to noncommissioned officer ranks, "showed a tendency to prefer illiterate 'funny fellows' to men of greater ability." As a result of this discrimination and mistreatment, by the end of the war racial clashes and near-riots increasingly plagued the military.

Life for the black soldiers outside the camps was also characterized by mistreatment and insults from white civilians and local police, especially in the South. The blacks were refused rooms in hotels, denied entrance to restaurants and theaters, and openly jeered at in the streets. In October 1917 the 15th New York arrived at Camp Wadsworth in Spartanburg, South Carolina, for three months of training. The regiment received a hostile reception from the local whites. In an attempt to win the goodwill of the community, the regimental officers arranged for the band to give public concerts, but their efforts went for naught. The storekeepers refused to serve the black members of the regiment. A black officer— a Harvard graduate and an attorney—was cursed and forcibly removed from a streetcar.

On October 22, while Noble Sissle, the popular regimental drum major, was buying a newspaper in a local hotel, he was knocked down and kicked because he failed to remove his field cap promptly when ordered to do so by the white hotel manager. Upon learning of this assault, black soldiers rushed to the hotel, determined to wreck it. Only the intervention of Lieutenant Europe prevented a large-scale riot. Nevertheless, the atmosphere remained tense. Emmett Scott was sent to Spartanburg, where he succeeded in persuading the black troops that violence would harm the black people of the nation. In the meantime, the War Department arranged to send the regiment overseas. Two weeks after their arrival, on October 22, the 15th New York set out for France.

Discrimination against black soldiers and officers continued on the transports taking them to France. They were placed in the least desirable locations aboard ship. On the *George Washington*, which carried the 368th Infantry, the white officers were assigned first-class passage on Deck A while the black officers were given second-class passage. Black soldiers were assigned to the poorly ventilated bottom holds. Without mess facilities, they had to eat on deck.

Of the 200,000 blacks sent to France, 160,000 served as military laborers in the Service of Supplies, where they worked night and day, twelve to sixteen hours at a stretch, performing many difficult and necessary tasks. They made up stevedore battalions, engineer service battalions, labor battalions, and pioneer infantry battalions. The black stevedores unloaded the transports, prepared the vehicles to convey the supplies to the battlefields, and built storage depots. The labor battalions built and repaired roads, railroads, and warehouses and performed general fatigue duty. Black laborers salvaged war material, detonated explosives, and buried the dead.

Black combat units were also required to work as laborers. During their first two and a half months in France, the men of the 369th Regiment worked at Saint-Nazaire in the supply service, where "the regiment toiled for weeks building docks, erecting hospitals, laying railroad tracks, and constructing a great dam. The men never saw their rifles except by candlelight."

Just as in the camps in the United States, the black soldiers overseas received inadequate housing, clothing, and food. While white soldiers often spent their off-duty time in nearby towns, black troops were forbidden to leave their bases. They were barred from cafés and other public places. Military police enforced these regulations ruthlessly. One black officer reported that "the spirit of Saint-Nazaire is the spirit of the South."

Black officers eloquently testified to the discrimination and abuse they suffered in the AEF. Rayford Logan, who became an outstanding scholar, said he was never "more humiliated or infuriated" than when he served as an officer in World War I. He recalled with indignation an occasion when the white commander of his black regiment attempted to convert the unit into a singing group to entertain Allied audiences in France with spirituals.

In contrast to the unabated discrimination, prejudice, and violence they suffered at the hands of other Americans, black soldiers and officers were simultaneously enjoying friendly relations with the French military and civilians alike and experiencing a complete freedom from racial discrimination such as they had never known. "I have never before experienced what it meant to be really free," wrote a black officer from France in August 1918, "to taste real liberty—in a phrase, 'to be a man.'" And Moorfield Storey of the NAACP predicted: "The Negroes will come back feeling like men, and not disposed to accept the treatment to which they have been subjected." So freely did black soldiers associate with French soldiers and civilians that the American military authorities issued orders prohibiting them from conversing or associating with French women, attending social functions, or visiting French homes. Black soldiers were arrested when they appeared at functions, even if they had been invited by the local French officials.

The military authorities also distributed to French military and civilian officials a document entitled "Secret Information Concerning Black American Troops." Written by Colonel Linard, the French liaison officer at the American GHQ, it warned the French that Americans resented their attitudes of "indulgence" and "familiarity" with blacks and that they might create serious complications for the United States Government. He advised the French that it was important for them to understand fully the inferior status of blacks in the United States and that "American opinion on the color question was unanimous and did not admit of any discussion." The vices of the Negro, he said, were "a constant menace to the Americans who had to repress them sternly." The French Army was further warned against accepting black American officers as equals or treating them in a familiar manner. "We must not eat with them," the document continued, "must not shake hands with them or seek to talk or meet with them outside the requirements of military service." Such intimacy, it went on, would not only alienate the white officers but might result in unrest in the United States after the war. Finally, French officers were urged to see to it that the native population did not "spoil" the black troops, and especially to prevent any expression of intimacy between white women and black soldiers, which would deeply affront white Americans.

Civilian agencies serving the army similarly discriminated against black troops in numerous ways. Nearly all the YMCA facilities, both in the United States and abroad, were segregated. At Camp

Greene, North Carolina, all the YMCA canteens were reserved for white personnel. Even the five buildings located in the black troops' section of the camp were for whites only.

The four regiments of the 93d Division were integrated into the French Army. Equipped as French units, carrying French rifles, and eating French rations, they knew an equality denied them by their own military. They operated in the area of Meuse Argonne near Saint-Mihiel Champagne, and in the Oise-Aisne offensive from the early summer of 1918 to the end of the war.

The total casualties for the 93d Division amounted to more than 3,000, with 584 killed—a casualty rate of about 35 per cent. The 369th alone lost 851 men in five days, and according to its commander that unit spent 191 days at the front, longer than any other regiment in the AEF. In that period, the regiment reportedly never surrendered a foot of ground or had a prisoner taken. By the war's end, about 540 officers and men of the 93d Division had been decorated by either the French or the American Government. Casualties for the 92d Division amounted to more than 2,100, with 176 killed in action.

The only instance of alleged misbehavior in combat involving American black soldiers occurred when the 368th Infantry was assigned as a liaison unit in the Argonne. During a battle, two companies of the 2d Battalion became confused and disorganized. After five days, the regiment was withdrawn from the line. Unquestionably the 368th Infantry lacked training for such an assignment. The regiment was without clear orders or proper equipment. It had no grenades, maps, signal flares, or wire cutters. Nor did it receive artillery support. Nevertheless, the white regimental commander and battalion commanders held the black officers responsible, and Major General Ballou relieved thirty black officers as unfit to command troops. Eventually the Secretary of War exonerated the unfortunate officers. Shortly after the signing of the Armistice, the 92d Division was ordered "to make preparation to be immediately returned to the United States." However, Marshal Foch, the Allied commander, intervened and stated that no groups should leave the war zone until a treaty of peace had been signed. General Robert L. Bullard, Commandant of the Second Army, to which the 92d Division was assigned, reported his reaction: "I told the American Headquarters to say to Marshal Foch that no man could be responsible for the acts of these Negroes toward French women, and that he had better send this division home at once." Apparently Bullard, like many other army officers, was "obsessed with the idea that Negroes must be kept from raping French women." Nevertheless, during its entire stay in France, only one member of the 92d Division—comprising more than 25,000 troops—was convicted of rape. And the Judge Advocate General of the Service of Supply reported: "Since February, 1919, there had been only one assault with intent to commit rape in section 4, 6, 7, and 9, where there were more than 75,000 Negro soldiers. The rape stories seem not to be substantiated."

During the entire period of World War I, the Marine Corps accepted no blacks, and the navy accepted them only as messmen and servants. An exception was made for a group of about thirty black women who were enlisted as yeomanettes and employed in a segregated office in the Navy Department. On June 30, 1918, there were but 5,328 blacks in a navy totaling 435,398 men. The rank and file of these men were either messmen or attached to the fireroom forces as coal passers, although they often performed duties as yeomen on detail. A very limited number of black seamen were in the petty officer grades, with assignments as water tender, electrician, and gunner's mate. An article in *Our Navy*, a magazine devoted to the enlisted men of the naval service, noted:

> True, we have black petty officers here and there in the Navy, and in some cases black chief petty officers. It stands to reason that they must have been mighty good men to advance. They surely must know their business—every inch of it—to advance to these ratings, yet they are not wanted in these ratings because they involve the black man having charge of white men under him. Outside of the messman branch you will find comparatively few Negroes in the Navy today.

On Bastille Day, July 14, 1919, Paris celebrated with a huge victory parade. Both the French and the British had black troops as part of their contingents. Only the United States, of all the Allies, failed to include any black soldiers in its line of march.

Even as black soldiers in France suffered overt discrimination, President Wilson sent Dr. Robert R. Moton, principal of Tuskegee Institute, to remind them about the behavior expected of them when they returned to the States. Moton told the troops: "I hope no one will do anything in peace to spoil the magnificent record you have made in war."

The President's emissary might better have addressed his remarks to whites, for discrimination intensified as black soldiers and officers returned home for demobilization and discharge. Some members of the 92d Division were assigned to sail on the USS *Virginia*. Once aboard, they were ordered removed by the vessel's captain and replaced by white soldiers, with the explanation that "no colored troops had ever traveled on this ship and none ever would."

Walter D. Binger, a white officer in World War I, told of the experience of a black captain, one of a complement of 400 casual officers who had been detached from their organizations and sent home on the *Siboney*. The dining room of the ship could seat only 200. As a result, three sittings were arranged for each meal—200, 199, and a third sitting for the black officer. Binger recalled:

> Each night before retiring it was my habit to take a number of turns around the deck and the Negro captain did the same, walking in the opposite direction. The first time we passed, I always said "Good evening, Captain," and he would reply "Good evening, Lieutenant." To the best of my belief these were the only words spoken to him during the nearly 10 days we were at sea.

Unlike white servicemen, black Americans returning from military service received little consideration and few accolades from white civilians. Instead, they generally faced hostility, contempt, and mistreatment.

In the South, black servicemen attracted special abuse, since there was widespread concern over the acceptance and recognition given the black troops by the French and an equally widespread determination to keep blacks in the subordinate position they had occupied in prewar society. In order to eradicate any notions of equality they may have picked up in France, returning black soldiers were insulted, stripped of their uniforms, and beaten by white ruffians and police.

The revitalization of the Ku Klux Klan and an increase in the number of lynchings further dashed any hopes of the returning black soldiers that their loyalty and patriotism would be rewarded by an end to their second-class citizenship. The *Nation* said:

When the Negro went so willingly to war for the United States, he, of course, had faith that a new attitude of justice toward him might result. The Negro fighting in Europe was not simply fighting Germans, he was fighting indirectly for his privileges at home. With what result? . . . There were sixty-two lynchings in 1918—twenty-four more than in 1917.

But the experience of black servicemen during the war had spawned a new spirit—a determination "not to accept passively the assaults and indignities that had been their lot in the past," but to fight for their rights. In the words of DuBois: "We return. We return from fighting. We return fighting."

The new militancy of the black soldiers resulted in intensified violence. In 1919, seventy-seven blacks were lynched. Ten of the victims were war veterans, several of them still in uniform. "Negro soldiers, clamoring for equality and justice," wrote Carter G. Woodson, "were beaten, shot down, and lynched, to terrorize the whole black population." During the bloody months from June to December, 1919—a period known as the Red Summer of 1919—twenty-six incidents of serious racial violence erupted in American towns and cities in which police authorities gave little or no protection to black citizens. The most serious riots occurred in Washington; Longview, Texas; Chicago; Knoxville; Omaha; and Elaine, Arkansas. In many of these riots, black veterans armed themselves and fought back against white mobs. To the charge that black unrest was largely due to the propaganda of the International Workers of the World (IWW) and the Bolsheviks, the *Independent* editorialized:

> Who is foolish enough to assume that with 239,000 colored men in uniform from the southern states alone, as against 370,000 white men, the blacks whose manhood and patriotism were thus recognized and tested are forever to be flogged, lynched, burned at the stake or chased into concealment whenever Caucasian desperados are moved to engage in these infamous pastimes?

In the years after the war, black veterans experienced great difficulty in finding employment. The American Legion restricted and segregated black members. In 1924, when a federal bureau dedicated a plaque inscribed with the names of servicemen killed during the war, it was discovered that the names of the black dead were on a separate tablet. And when, in 1930, the mothers and widows of soldiers buried abroad were invited by the United States Army to visit the graves of their dead, it was revealed that the War Department had arranged for the black Gold Star Mothers to make the trip on separate vessels. This plan for a "segregated pilgrimage" was bitterly denounced as an insult to the black community, but the War Department was unyielding. Three years later Emmett J. Scott secretary of Howard University and special assistant to the Secretary of War during World War I, expressed the profound disillusionment felt by blacks. In an address to the black veterans of the 92d and 93d divisions in October 1933, Dr. Scott contrasted the service rendered by black soldiers with the recognition accorded them by their country in the postwar period. Decrying the ingratitude shown by the nation, he went on to say: "As one who recalls the assurances of 1917 and 1918, I confess personally a deep sense of disappointment, of poignant pain, that a great country in time of need should promise so much and afterward perform so little."

As the discharge of the huge temporary army raised during World War I proceeded, plans were made for the organization of the permanent peacetime army. Many black officers, eager to remain in the service, submitted applications for regular army commissions. The Adjutant General's office assured them that they would be given the same opportunity to qualify as white officers. Many black enlisted men also volunteered for the regular service.

Peace had barely been established when a campaign was launched to discredit the role played by black officers and enlisted men in the war. Commanders of the two combat divisions submitted reports to the War Department and the Army War College on the performance of black troops. What emerged was a racist stereotype that was destined to influence army practices for many years thereafter. Military commanders after World War I insisted that blacks were inferiors, both biologically and intellectually; that they could not adapt to modern combat conditions "because of certain racial characteristics." Black officers were said to have failed because of their lack of character and the inherent distrust on the part of blacks for their leadership. The commanding officer of the 367th Infantry noted: "As fighting troops the Negro must be rated as second-class material; this is due primarily to his inferior intelligence and lack of mental and moral qualifications." General Bullard, in his published memoirs, held that as combat troops blacks were "hopelessly inferior," that he "could not make them fight," and that they "wasted time and dawdled when they did attack." "If you need combat soldiers," he added, "and especially if you need them in a hurry, don't put your time on Negroes." The general conclusions resulting from these views were that the voluntary black officers should be eliminated from the army; that the army should use black troops only in segregated units; that as few black organizations as possible should be established, and that these should be noncombatant, confined to labor and service duties. Indeed, many officers preferred the total elimination of black soldiers from the postwar army.

Under the terms of the National Defense Act of June 1920, which authorized a peacetime army with a maximum strength of approximately 30,000 officers and men, the four regular army black units were retained in the service, largely because "it was generally considered within the Army and by the Negro public that the Negro regiments were required by law" and could not be disturbed without Congressional action. But in spite of the assurances they had received of equal and fair treatment, black officers commissioned during the war were excluded from the postwar army. The application of one black officer who wanted to remain in the service after the war was rejected by a board of army officers on the ground that he was unqualified "by reason of the qualities inherent in the Negro race."

But American military commanders were keenly aware that if losses in future combat were confined solely to white troops, "there would be resentment from families of white enlisted men." A study prepared for the Army Chief of Staff in November 1922 concluded that blacks must be used in combat as well as service units, for

> to follow the policy of exemption of the Negro population of this country from combat means that the white population, upon which the future of the country depends, would suffer the brunt of loss, the Negro population none; the rising white generation 34 per cent, and the rising Negro population nothing.

Although this study emphasized that the successful performance of black troops was dependent upon "proper leadership" by "white officers in command of principal units," it went on to warn that black officers must also be used since "it is not reasonable to expect that the Negro will be willing to serve in the ranks with no hope of a commission." However, the report emphasized that no black officer should be put in a position where he could command white troops.

The study resulted in little change in the status of blacks in the army. There was no increase in the number of black regular units. Black soldiers were confined to infantry and cavalry units, and they were barred from all the specialized branches of the military service. The air corps totally rejected blacks. There were no new black line officers; the total number remained at two.

The exclusion of blacks from the Marine Corps remained complete. Not only were they unacceptable in uniform, but the Marine Corps headquarters in Washington refused to employ blacks even as messengers. Black Americans were enlisted in the Coast Guard only as menials, and from 1919 to 1932 the navy virtually closed its doors to black enlistments. Blacks already in the service were permitted to remain but were limited to labor and housekeeping branches. Black seamen with general ratings were allowed to retain them, but as these men gradually retired they were not replaced by blacks.

After 1933, blacks found additional cause for resentment in the army's refusal to appoint black reserve officers to supervisory positions in the Civilian Conservation Corps (CCC) camps. Although the law creating the CCC included the provision that "no person shall be excluded on account of color or creed," the War Department appointed white reserve officers as camp directors, chaplains, and physicians, while denying to black reserve officers any such positions even within the approximately 200 black camps. Pressure from blacks to alter this discriminatory practice was unavailing. Thus, when Reginald Johnson of the National Urban League urged the appointment of black reserve line officers, he was advised by the War Department that "community pressure made the appointment of blacks as officers impossible." The War Department proved equally unresponsive to demands from black leaders that it use black reserve medical corps officers, explaining that the appointment of blacks would create embarrassment and future difficulties for the army and the CCC.

In late July 1935, as the Presidential election approached, President Franklin D. Roosevelt succeeded in forcing the War Department to summon a few black reserve medical corps officers and chaplains to duty. Only four black chaplains and ten black doctors were serving in the black camps a year after the order was issued. In response to "continuing pressure" from the White House, the War Department authorized the establishment of two black CCC camps officered entirely by blacks—the first in August 1936, an election year, and another in 1937. The next few years witnessed very little progress. As late as November 1940, in the approximately 150 black camps, only nine black doctors and four black chaplains were on duty.

Except for "token appointments" to supervisory positions in the CCC made in response to pressure, the New Deal did little to disturb racist attitudes and practices in the military. After a visit to the posts where the black units were stationed in the summer of 1934, Charles H. Houston, attorney for the NAACP and a former AEF officer, wrote to General Douglas MacArthur, Army Chief of Staff, complaining that black officers had been eliminated from duty with troops and that three of the four black regiments had been reduced "to the practical status of service battalions." He advised MacArthur that the black community resented "the present policy of the War Department" and warned that in future military conflicts black citizens would not be content "with the treatment their fathers received."

In June 1936 Benjamin O. Davis, Jr., whose father was a regular army colonel, became the first black cadet to graduate from West Point since 1889. And on June 15, 1936, for the first time in 61 years, a black, James Lee Johnson, Jr., of Illinois, was admitted to the Naval Academy. Johnson resigned from the Academy in 1937 because of academic deficiency, and blacks explained his resignation by claiming that "it was the cold atmosphere of ostracism that floored the youth" rather than "alleged academic failures." George J. Rivers was appointed to the Naval Academy on June 16, 1937, and resigned on July 7, 1937. Eight years were to elapse before another black would be admitted to the academy at Annapolis.

In 1938, the army adopted a policy requiring that black military manpower be maintained at a ratio approximating the proportion of blacks in the national population—that is, from 9 to 10 per cent. But at no time until late in World War II did the percentage of blacks in the service reach that quota. Indeed, the strength of the four black units was reduced, so that by 1939 the number of black enlisted men had declined to less than 4,000, "far fewer than the total of American Negroes in uniform in 1900." The four units were used to perform overhead duties at various service schools; military training was relegated to a secondary role. In October 1939 a recently discharged soldier with ten years of service in the 9th Cavalry charged in an open letter to the Secretary of War that members of the 10th Cavalry worked seven days a week as orderlies for West Point cadets and officers, and that 9th Cavalry soldiers received so little training that veterans of many years' service were unable to drill in simple military formations. "What drills they get," he went on, "are after hours when they have worked all day as servants, grooms, and stableboys." An inquiry about the 24th Infantry at Fort Benning, Georgia, brought the reply that it was "not a combat unit" at all. Its members, according to this report, were employed as truck drivers, cooks, or grooms.

The total number of black regular army officers in 1939 was five, of whom three were chaplains and only two were line officers—Colonel Benjamin O. Davis and his son, Lieutenant Benjamin O. Davis, Jr. The former had been promoted to full colonel in 1930 and in 1939 received his first major command, a national guard unit in Harlem. Lieutenant Davis commanded the ROTC at Tuskegee Institute. In addition, there were 353 black officers in the Army Reserve. Seven states and the District of Columbia had black National Guard units, all but two staffed by white reserve officers. In Illinois and New York, the organizations were completely officered by blacks.

A shortage of Filipinos resulted in the reopening of enlistments for the messman's branch of the naval service to blacks in December 1932, a decision which one black described as "waiters and bellhops going to sea." The 2,807 black enlisted men in the navy on June 30, 1939, had no opportunities to learn the many trades provided in the naval training program or to become combat seamen. A black youth who enlisted was rated a mess attendant third class at $21 a month and was required to remain in that classification for a year. A white young man enlisting at the same time was eligible for a promotion in rating every three months and at the end of one year could become a petty officer at a salary of $54 a month.

There were 19,477 naval commissioned and warrant officers, not one of them black.

As World War II loomed, the American armed forces faithfully reflected the worst racist excesses of American society. It was a mirror reflection that contained ominous portents. Writing in *The Crisis* on "Jim Crow in Uniform" in March 1939, one perceptive observer warned:

> Judging from prevailing Jim Crow practices in the armed forces of the United States today, the next war . . . will see the same gross maltreatment of the Negro soldiers seen in the World War. For today Negroes are barred from the newer arms of service, including aviation and other branches; Negroes may serve in the U.S. Navy only as menials; . . . Negro regular army soldiers are kept out of active service. . . . These are but a few of the many discriminations.
>
> Now, such a policy is contrary, not only to decency, but to the security and well-being of the American government.

7

World War II and Black Servicemen

During World War II, in a struggle presumably being waged against the twin scourges of fascism and racism, black men were asked to risk and sacrifice their lives, even as they were subjected to flagrant discrimination and segregation. In September 1945 Harry Loren Binsee noted in *Commonweal* magazine:

> Perhaps the sorriest chapter in the story of the war which has just come to an end is the treatment accorded Negroes in the American armed forces. In a war ostensibly fought against a racist ideology we ourselves have practiced precisely the same ideology. Yet thanks to various pressures brought to bear in this connection and thanks to the need for efficient utilization of all our available manpower, there has been considerable improvement in the status of the Negro both in the Army and Navy.

Binsea was accurate on two counts—there had been improvement, and it came about as a result of necessity and unremitting pressure, protests, and demonstrations. The changes, however were not "considerable."

At first the navy accepted a few blacks only as mess attendants, while the army sharply restricted the number of black enlistees recruited and selectees inducted and assigned most of them to noncombat menial jobs. The other branches of the armed forces excluded blacks altogether.

Gradually and reluctantly, the Roosevelt Administration and the armed services found themselves compelled, by both mounting pressure from the black community and the urgent need for military manpower, to take steps to reduce discrimination and remedy some of the indignities suffered by black military personnel. The black press and such organizations as the NAACP, the National Urban League, the newly established March on Washington Movement, and the Congress of Racial Equality (CORE, founded in 1942) played an important role in mobilizing the support of large sections of the black community.

More than a million black men and women, half of whom served overseas, ultimately entered the armed forces during World War II. Furthermore, black men and women participated in more branches and services and in higher capacities than previously. For the first time they were admitted into the Air Force, flew as pilots, and served as commissioned officers in the navy. The army integrated its officer-training schools; the Marine Corps inducted blacks again after a long lapse. Many blacks also found encouragement in the successful integration of a merchant ship crew during the war and in an integrated canteen for the entertainment of GIs in New York City.

Yet the fact remains that only limited concessions were granted to black military personnel and that these were prompted more by the desire to silence the clamor against discrimination and to forestall black political reprisals than out of a genuine commitment to integration. Small wonder that John H. Burma wrote in *Opportunity*, the official organ of the Urban League:

> The Negro was in all branches of the armed forces, but it was a token representation only. Ninety per cent of Negro soldiers were engaged in some sort of labor; 10 per cent were in combat units; less than half of them actually were in combat. There were Negro officers: one general, a few colonels, a handful of majors and captains, and half a million enlisted men. A USO entertaining both Negroes and whites was enough of a rarity to make the headlines. Negro blood plasma, contrary to unanimous scientific opinion, was segregated from white. Infractions of military law by white officers or MPs against Negro soldiers were four times as great as against whites. Negro officers were subjected by force to racial etiquette in the South. Since the place of the Negro in the war effort was not determined solely by his numbers, his ability, and his willingness, he is a second-class citizen.

Clearly, policy toward blacks of the army and other military branches had changed only marginally by the end of the war. Nevertheless, the war did provide a fascinating social laboratory in which to observe a nation's schizophrenic behavior when its professed ideals conflicted with its treatment of one-tenth of its citizenry.

After the Nazis successfully blitzed the Low Countries and France in the spring of 1940, the United States hastily expanded both its defense industries and its armed forces. Blacks seeking to participate in the national defense effort met with repeated rebuffs. They were prevented by discriminatory hiring practices from working in defense plants, while those who tried to volunteer for military service found the armed forces virtually closed to them.

In July 1940 the navy issued a call for 4,700 volunteers, including 200 blacks needed to work as mess attendants, cooks, and stewards. When several blacks sought to enter naval service in other capacities, Rear Admiral Chester W. Nimitz, acting for the Secretary of the Navy, succinctly stated the official position: "After many years of experience, the policy of not enlisting men of the colored race for any branch of the naval service except the Messmen's branch was adopted to meet the best interests of general ship efficiency."

The navy's announcement that it would continue to accept blacks only as mess attendants prompted an angry editorial response in *The Crisis*:

> We hope American Negro citizens appreciate fully what this policy means to them. . . . Our taxes help keep up the Naval Academy at Annapolis where our boys may not attend. They help to maintain the numerous naval bases, Navy Yards, and naval air bases from which we are excluded. . . . The training in numerous trades and skills which thousands of whites receive and use later in civilian life is not for us! The health care . . . the travel and education—all at the expense of the taxpayers—are for whites only! This is the price we pay for being classified, as a race, as mess attendants only! At the same time we are supposed to be able to appreciate what our white fellow citizens declare to be the "vast difference" between American Democracy and Hitlerism.

Blacks were permitted to enlist in the army only to fill the limited number of vacancies in the two infantry and two cavalry regiments provided by law and in an authorized quartermaster unit.

Once these were filled, recruiting stations turned away the many black volunteers seeking enlistment. In addition, black volunteers faced insults, humiliation, and physical violence. In many communities they were bluntly told that "Negroes aren't wanted." A black high school teacher in Charlotte, North Carolina, accompanied four of his students to the army recruiting office but was informed that the recruiting station was for "whites only." When the teacher asked for an explanation, men in uniform broke his jaw as they threw him out of the office. "Negroes cannot help but feel that their country does not want them to defend it," the New York newspaper *PM* observed. Meanwhile, recruiting officers were "beating the bushes for white soldiers." Michigan Senator Arthur Vandenberg angrily exclaimed: "Negro patriots do not have equality of approach to military service. It is unfair. It should be corrected."

In the summer of 1940 Congress was considering a peacetime conscription measure that contained the recommendations of the army and navy for a year's compulsory service. The black community was fearful that, if the armed forces had their way, blacks would again be forced into labor battalions and compelled to endure other discriminatory restrictions. As a result of these fears, the Committee on Participation of Negroes in the National Defense Program, founded in Washington in May 1938, largely at the instigation of the Pittsburgh *Courier*, other black organizations, and the black press launched a vigorous campaign to end the exclusionary practices of the armed services and to open every branch of the armed forces to blacks. Judge William H. Hastie, Dean of the Howard University Law School and the first black to be appointed a federal judge, leveled a sharp attack at the practice of relegating black servicemen to supply units. He vowed: "We will be American soldiers. We will be American aviators. We will be American laborers. We will be anything that any other American should be in this whole program of national defense. But we won't be black auxiliaries."

This campaign succeeded in securing the inclusion of antidiscrimination language in the draft bill. On September 14, 1940, Congress passed the Burke-Wadsworth bill, providing for the first peacetime draft in American history. Two days later, the President signed it into law as the Selective Service and Training Act, which called for the registration of all men between the ages of twenty-one and thirty-five and the induction of 800,000 draftees. Section 4(a) of the law stated that "there shall be no discrimination against any person on account of race or color" in the selection and training of men inducted under the act. However, there was no express provision against segregation. Moreover, Section 3(a) limited induction to those who were acceptable to the land and naval services for training and service, and a corollary provision vested "unlimited discretion" in the military and naval authorities. Still another provision stated that no man should be inducted until sanitary and other facilities were available.

Black leaders immediately identified these provisions as seriously undermining the safeguard against discrimination. Their concern was intensified when, two days after the bill was signed, the War Department announced that black aviation units would be established as soon as the necessary personnel could be trained. It was clear that the basic pattern of segregation was to be continued. Black leaders attacked the administration and demanded that there be no discrimination or segregation in the fighting forces whose responsibility was to defend American democracy. Under growing pressure from the black community as the election approached, and at the urging of Eleanor Roosevelt, the President agreed to meet with Walter White of the NAACP, A. Philip Randolph of the Brotherhood of Sleeping Car Porters, T. Arnold Hill, adviser on Negro affairs for the National Youth Administration, and representatives of the army and navy to discuss the participation of blacks in the armed services.

The meeting took place at the White House on September 27, with Secretary of the Navy Frank Knox and Assistant Secretary of War Robert R. Patterson representing the services. The three black leaders submitted a seven-point program designed to eliminate segregation and discrimination in the armed forces. The main point in the statement was that black officers and enlisted men should be used throughout the services, subject only to the limits of their ability. Another major demand was that existing units of the army and subsequently formed units be staffed with officers and enlisted men without regard to race. The newly reappointed Secretary of War, Henry L. Stimson, who had held that post in the Taft Administration, commenting on the meeting in his diary, made it clear that he did not favor the proposals of "the Negro politicians" for "colored officers and various other things." He then added:

> I saw the same thing happen twenty-three years ago when Woodrow Wilson yielded to the same sort of demand and appointed colored officers to several of the Divisions that went over to France, and the poor fellows made perfect fools of themselves and one at least of the Divisions behaved very badly. The others were turned into labor battalions.

President Roosevelt had promised to get in touch with the black leaders, but nothing happened until October 9, when White House Press Secretary Steve Early released a statement prepared by the War Department and initiated by the President himself, defining the Army's policy "in respect to Negro participation" in national defense. The statement specified that the number of blacks in the army should correspond to the proportion of blacks in the total population. Black combat and noncombat units were to be established in all branches of the service. Blacks were to be eligible for admission to the proposed officer candidate schools, but, except for the three established black National Guard units, black units would be officered by whites. It was further announced that black pilots were being trained and that, when their numbers were sufficient, black aviation units would be formed. Finally, the statement reaffirmed the policy of "not integrating colored and white enlisted personnel in the same regimental organizations." The separation of the races, it said, had proved satisfactory "over a long period of years, and changes would produce situations destructive to morale and detrimental to the preparations for national defense." For similar reasons, the existing regular black units, which were officered by whites, would receive no black reserve officers other than medical officers and chaplains. The statement concluded: "These regular units are going concerns, accustomed through many years to the present system. Their morale is splendid . . . and their field training is well advanced."

The clear implication was that the statement released by the White House had the approval of White, Randolph, and Hill. Indeed, newspapers, in reporting the press release, stated that "the segregation policy was approved after Mr. Roosevelt had conferred" with the three black leaders. They immediately and vehemently denied endorsing the White House statement, noting that they had specifically repudiated the army's policy of segregation in their memorandum to the President. And they firmly challenged the army's contention that morale in the existing black units was high, adding that enlisted men in these units had repeatedly protested against being compelled to serve "as hostlers and servants to white Army officers." They concluded that the army's Jim Crow policy "has never been satisfactory nor is it now to Negro Americans. Such segregation has been destructive of morale and has permitted prejudiced superiors to exercise their bigotry on defenseless Negro regiments."

The NAACP charged that under this army plan only the most limited use would be made of black officers; black regulars and draftees would have white officers exclusively. "The highest Army officials," it went on, "are solidly behind the policy of 'no Negro officers.'" The organization called on its 600 branches, youth councils, and college chapters to protest the War Department's plan and to do so before the 1940 Election Day "to make the protests of Negro Americans most effective." Others joined in the protest. *The Nation* said that experience had proved that separate units meant "discrimination of the most flagrant kind." The Catholic publication *America* declared in an editorial headed "Our Jim Crow Army" that "what the country needs today is not separation, but unity."

These protests, coming as they did in the weeks immediately preceding the 1940 Presidential election, caused considerable concern in Democratic ranks about the black vote. President Roosevelt was reaching for an unprecedented third term. The administration feared that unless steps were taken to placate the blacks, their support might be lost. Early wrote to White expressing regret over the embarrassment caused to the black leaders. Roosevelt did the same and assured White that blacks would be put in all branches of the service and be given training in aviation, that black reserve officers would be called to active service and "given appropriate commands," and that they would be given "the same opportunity to qualify for officers' commissions as will be given to others."

On October 15 the War Department publicly reaffirmed its intention to establish black aviation units and soon thereafter announced the formation of new black combat units. In the week before the election, three more steps were taken. Judge Hastie was appointed as a civilian aide to Secretary Stimson to coordinate policy on black troops; Major Campbell C. Johnson, another black, was made adviser to the Director of Selective Service on all matters relating to racial minorities; and Colonel Benjamin Davis, the senior black officer in the army, was made a brigadier general, the first black to attain that rank in the U.S. Army. The promotion of Davis was widely covered in the press, but not all the reaction was favorable. It failed to impress many black Americans, who viewed it as merely a political device to allay black pressure. The Baltimore *Afro-American* complained: "We asked Mr. Roosevelt to change the rules of the game and he countered by giving us some new uniforms. That is what it amounts to and we have called it appeasement." And Milton R. Konvitz wrote in the *Guild Lawyer*: "The promotion of Davis . . . is another instance of our traditional practice, to single out an individual for honors, at the same time to keep the mass of Negroes in inferior status or suppressed."

But black support for the President was overwhelming. The large Northern urban black electorate voted heavily for Roosevelt. Where Roosevelt had previously captured four of the nineteen black wards in nine Northern cities in 1932, and nine in 1936, he succeeded in winning fourteen of them in 1940. But whether or not the steps taken on the eve of the election mollified blacks, they left unaltered the military's basic policy of segregation.

The Red Cross, in response to pressure from the army and navy, refused to accept blood plasma from blacks for blood banks "on the score that white men in the service would refuse blood plasma if they knew it came from Negro veins." The irony of the situation was that Dr. Charles R. Drew, the pioneer researcher in blood preservation and Medical Director of the Red Cross blood program, was a black. Drew resigned from the Red Cross upon learning that the armed services refused to accept blacks' blood.

The United States Maritime Service adopted a policy of gradually excluding black seamen from jobs as firemen and coal passers on government transport ships. In November, eighteen blacks on the SS *Philadelphia* complained in a letter to the Pittsburgh *Courier* that their work was limited to "waiting on tables and making beds for the officers" and that within the past six months nine blacks had been placed in solitary confinement on bread and water. "We sincerely hope," they continued, "to discourage any other colored boys who had planned on joining the Navy and making the same mistake that we did and become seagoing bellhops, chambermaids, dishwashers, in other words mess attendants, the one and only rating any Negro can enlist under."

Three of the signers were imprisoned and the others received "undesirable discharges for unfitness." On December 13 the NAACP protested to the Chief of the Bureau of Navigation, calling the action of the navy "a denial of the very rights which our country professes to uphold."

In the December issue of *The Crisis* a black enlisted man reported that he found the army to be, "for the Negro, a place impregnated with suppression and racial prejudice." The Army Air Corps still refused applications from black youths, and the NAACP instituted a suit in behalf of Yancey Williams, a student at Howard University, and on behalf of all blacks "similarly situated," for an injunction to require War Department officials to consider his application for enlistment in the Army Air Corps as a flying cadet.

In January 1941 A. Philip Randolph issued a call for a March on Washington to be held on July 1. It was projected that 50,000 to 100,000 black Americans would march to protest the exclusion of blacks "from defense industries and their humiliation in the armed services." The March on Washington Movement (MOWM), whose membership was restricted to blacks, received an enthusiastic response from the masses of the black community. Worried government officials worked to have the march called off. Only when President Roosevelt issued an Executive Order banning racial discrimination in defense industries and the government was the scheduled demonstration canceled.

While this militant black challenge was ultimately successful in helping to place many blacks in war industry jobs, the armed forces remained unchanged. On December 1, 1941, six days before the Japanese attack on Pearl Harbor brought the United States into the war, General George C. Marshall responded to Judge Hastie's proposal to employ soldiers without racial separation by declaring that "the settlement of vexing racial problems cannot be permitted to complicate the tremendous task of the War Department." Even after the attack on Pearl Harbor, the walls of prejudice stood firm in many areas of American life, particularly in the armed forces. Shortly after Pearl Harbor a black journalist commented: "In the last war, in spite of the acknowledged bravery of the Negro troops, they suffered all forms of Jim Crow, humiliation, discrimination, and indeed slander—a pattern being followed today." Not long afterward, a black college student angrily declared: "The Army jim-crows us. The Navy lets us serve only as messmen. The Red Cross refuses our blood. Employers and labor unions shut us out. Lynchings continue. We are disfranchised, jim-crowed, spat upon. What more could Hitler do than that?"

Typical of the prevalent discrimination was the manner in which the Selective Service Act was administered. Under it 1,765,917 blacks registered for service—almost 11 per cent of the total registration. In the whole population, the 1940 census reported 9.8 as the black percentage. Blacks were grossly underrepresented in the selection apparatus. A few blacks were appointed to administrative posts at high levels. Local board members, however, were nominated by governors of the states, and in 1942 only 250 blacks served as members of local draft boards in seventeen states—a little over 1 per cent of the total. Most Southern governors refused to provide any black representation on the local level. Indeed, of the Southern states only Virginia with ten, North Carolina with four, and Kentucky with three had blacks serving as members of local boards. They had no authority over white draftees. Several governors were canvassed to discover why more blacks were not nominated. It was found that the attitudes of the governors "were based entirely upon the probability of racial friction should Negroes be placed in positions where they might hold the balance in determining what might be life or death decisions regarding white registrants." They expressed no concern over granting whites life and death decisions over blacks.

Blacks did not receive a proportionate share of the occupational, dependency, and similar types of deferment. By 1945, blacks held only 4.4 per cent of the deferments for defense employment, 5.4 per cent for occupations essential to national health or safety, 11.8 per cent of the deferments in agriculture, and 7 per cent of the ministerial exemptions. There were practically no blacks among the public officials deferred by law. In contrast to World War I, when blacks were overrepresented in the draft, the rejection rate of blacks in World War II was substantially higher than that of whites. No fewer than 33 per cent of the black registrants were rejected in contrast to only 16 per cent of the whites, with "mental deficiency" being cited most often as the cause of black rejections.

At the outset, no specific educational requirements were set by the armed forces. In the first year of mobilization, more than 13 per cent of those classified 1-A (available for immediate induction) were blacks. Nevertheless, throughout 1941 blacks were largely excluded from the draft. Local draft boards called up only a small number of black selectees. Until 1943 the navy met its manpower needs without the draft. Although the army drew the bulk of its manpower from Selective Service, throughout 1941 it refused to accept a proportionate number of draft-eligible blacks, citing unavailability of units and facilities needed for the separate housing and training of black soldiers. But one historian suggests that "adequate units and housing were not furnished because Army planners and commanders viewed Negroes as undesirable soldier material, and they wanted to induct as few as possible."

The War Department would call on Selective Service from time to time for so many white inductees and so many black inductees. Selective Service complied with these requests by establishing and maintaining separate draft quotas for the induction of blacks and whites instead of calling up men as their names appeared on the local selective service rolls. Selective Service carefully specified the racial components when they sent quota requisitions to local boards. Instead of asking a local draft board for the first 124 men available for induction, for example, Selective Service asked for the first 120 eligible white men and the first four eligible blacks. This practice resulted in the induction of white fathers and married men even though large numbers of eligible single blacks were available.

By early 1943, approximately 300,000 blacks had been passed over. In addition, the army adopted a literacy standard that further reduced the proportion of blacks inducted. Beginning in May 1941 the ability to read, write, and compute on the fourth-grade level became the standard for induction. The army maintained that the new standard was adopted because military commanders had complained that too many illiterates were being inducted and that these men impaired the quality of their units. But a historian asserts that here too the motive was "primarily to reduce the number of black soldiers it [the army] would have to accept." In any event, the new standard served to reduce substantially the number of blacks eligible for the draft. In the first four months after the new standard was instituted, 12 per cent of the blacks examined were rejected for illiteracy, as compared with 1 per cent of the whites.

The Georgia director of Selective Service probably expressed the sentiments of the other state directors when he complained: "The rejection rate is exceedingly high, and it is very difficult for Georgia to fill calls for Negroes—they simply do not want them." Louisiana Representative Charles E. McKenzie also noted that "a deliberate attempt is being made to keep Negroes, single Negroes, out of the service while white fathers are being drafted. . . . Has it actually come to pass in America," he asked plaintively, "that the color of a man's skin is the basis for his being deferred?" The ludicrousness of this situation was not lost on the Pittsburgh *Courier*. In an editorial entitled "Wail from the South," it pointed out: "The irony is that the cause of this maladministration of the Selective Service Act is the government's eagerness to comply with the wishes of the white South, which demands that there must be segregation of the so-called races in every endeavor, including the defense of the country."

In time, protests from blacks and influential whites, combined with the rising need for additional military manpower, led to increasing acceptance of blacks in the services. In March 1942 the Air Corps began to accept applications from some black youths. A month later the navy, yielding to pressure from President Roosevelt, announced that a limited number of blacks would be accepted for general service. The Coast Guard began accepting blacks for various jobs in May 1942. Breaking a tradition of 167 years, the Marine Corps began the enlistment of blacks on June 1, 1942, and formed them into separate units. In October 1942 ratings were opened to black seamen in the navy's SeaBees (construction battalions).

Meanwhile, the war emergency led to an acceleration in the rate of call of black registrants. By the end of 1942 the army's black enlisted strength had risen to 467,883. In December President Roosevelt issued an Executive Order making it impossible to volunteer for any of the armed forces. All the services now had to recruit their men through the draft and accept blacks on an equal basis. A deepening shortage of manpower during 1943 and complaints from whites who had been drafted while eligible blacks remained at home brought about further reversals of previous policies. The army finally reversed its policy of limiting the number of all-black units. Beginning in June 1943 inductees who had previously been rejected as illiterate were sent to Special Training Units established within the army, generally connected to reception centers, for eight to twelve weeks of remedial instruction in elementary reading and writing. When they reached a fourth-grade level of literacy they were sent on to regular basic training. Men who were unable to meet this minimal standard in twelve weeks were discharged. Of the 136,000 black soldiers assigned to the Special Training Units, 85.1 per cent completed the course successfully. This compared with the 81.7 per cent of the 160,000 white soldiers assigned to the remedial course.

During the last years of the war, the number of black inductees steadily increased. By August 1, 1945, a total of 1,030,255 blacks had been inducted—approximately 9 per cent of all draftees. This number was still below the announced goal of 10.6 per cent of total military strength, the percentage of blacks in the general population.

In World War II, but not in World War I, a number of blacks refused to serve in the armed forces for a variety of reasons. As a protest against separate calls and segregated units in the army, several black registrants declined to appear when called up for induction, or accepted jail sentences rather than serve in a Jim Crow army. The case of Winfred W. Lynn attracted national attention in September 1942, when he refused to report for induction on the ground that, though willing to fight for his country, he would do so only in a unit which was not segregated by race. Court action was instituted in his behalf in New York to test the legality of racial quotas and separate calls. When the court ruled that in order to have a case, Lynn must have submitted himself for induction, Lynn agreed to do so, at the same time as he continued to seek legal redress. When the case was scheduled for a hearing by the Supreme Court, Lynn was overseas as a member of the armed forces, and the petition for a writ of certiorari was denied on the technical ground that he was not in the jurisdiction of the commander named in the petition. A petition for rehearing was also denied.

A number of blacks resisted the draft on religious grounds. During World War II members of religious groups, recognized by Selective Service as legitimate claimants for conscientious objector status—such predominantly white religious groups as Quakers, Mennonites, and so on—were assigned to Civilian Public Service Camps. Others who refused to serve on religious grounds were imprisoned. By the end of 1943, 219 blacks were classified as conscientious objectors. But draft officials denied deferment to the disciples of the Nation of Islam—the Black Muslims. Elijah Muhammad, the Muslim leader, was sentenced to five years in prison, and fifty of his followers were sentenced to three years for refusing to register for the draft. On February 3, 1943, the General Messenger of a group of Black Hebrews in New Orleans was sentenced to fifteen years for persuading members of his group to avoid military service on religious grounds. This was probably the most severe sentence given to a draft law violator during World War II. Indeed, the heaviest and most numerous sentences for Selective Service law violations were given to black religious objectors. As one academic sums up the treatment blacks received in the draft: "Although the record of Selective Service during World War II was not as blatantly racist as was the World War I draft system, the virtual exclusion of blacks from Southern boards, the discriminatory deferment criteria, the separate induction calls, and the treatment of black nationalists prove that racism had not been eliminated."

Once inducted, the black recruit's life conformed to the army's policy of rigid segregation. At the reception center, he was assigned to a "special company," tested, interviewed, and classified separately. Along with other black recruits, he was shipped out for basic training in his assigned branch of the service. Despite War Department pronouncements to the contrary, black soldiers were concentrated in the Service Forces branches and small service detachments on the racist assumption that was succinctly stated in an army staff memorandum, which read: "There is a consensus that colored units are inferior to the performance of white troops, except for service duties."

The tendency to concentrate black soldiers disproportionately in the service branches intensified during the war, increasing from 48 per cent in 1942 to 75 per cent by mid-1945. The primary functions of these branches were associated with such unskilled jobs as road-building, stevedoring, laundry, and fumigating.

The army justified its assignments by pointing to the low test scores registered by black enlisted men in the Army General Classification Test (AGCT). This test was given to inductees at the reception center for the purpose of determining their ability to absorb training and to separate the fast learners from the slow. What the AGCT scores really reflected, however, was the extent and quality of a man's schooling. Nevertheless, the army viewed the scores as reliable indicators of a recruit's native intelligence and employed the AGCT as a screening device. Four-fifths of the black soldiers scored in the two lowest grades—grades IV and V—from which the army planned to draw its semiskilled soldiers and laborers. By far the largest number of low-scoring black and white soldiers came from the South, the region that spent the least money on education, and especially on the schooling of blacks.

In 1942, the army activated three combat units composed of black enlisted men and white and black officers—the 92d and 93d Infantry divisions and the 2d Cavalry Division. In the same year, black troops, mostly engineer and quartermaster units, were among the first to be sent overseas. But as the number of black inductees increased, the War Department, ignoring their qualifications, assigned them to noncombat units, in which they performed housekeeping chores or general service duties.

A black biochemist was originally sent after induction to Camp A for training and then assigned to a position in the biological laboratory. Before he could start work, he was shipped to Camp B and enrolled for technical training as an armorer. He passed this course with high honors and was promptly shipped to Camp C, where he was graded as a corporal and assigned to the Army Air Corps. A week later, he found himself at Camp D, assigned to a labor detail and demoted to private. At the conclusion of this ordeal, he wrote to his wife: "It is a mockery, let no one tell you differently, this sudden opening of the so-called exclusive branches of the services to Negroes. We are trained, become skilled—and then the oblivion of common labor."

Upon arrival at the assigned training camp, located most probably in the South or Southwest, the black recruit inhabited a separate area in the most remote and inaccessible section of the post, with living and recreation facilities generally inferior to those provided for his white comrade-in-arms. Racial separation on army posts encompassed theaters, post exchanges, service and enlisted men's clubs, buses, and even chapels. The sign at one post listing the schedules of religious services read: "Catholics, Jews, Protestants, and Negroes." Another black at an air base stated: "It is not like being in a soldier camp. It is more like being in a prison." And a white private wrote from Camp Upton, New York, that white soldiers there were directed by their commanding officers not to "drink with niggers" or "shake hands." He went on: "Of course the Negro draftees are segregated from the minute they come into the camp. . . . The whole picture is a very raw and ugly one. It looks, smells, and tastes like Fascism."

In some localities, the army actually introduced Jim Crow practices where they had not previously existed. "In Cheyenne, Wyoming, where I was stationed," wrote Ulysses S. Keyes, a black soldier from Chicago, "the few Negroes of the town were free to go about as they pleased. But when the Army moved in, signs appeared all over town barring Negroes from certain bars, hotels and movies." Practically all the volunteer groups associated with the armed forces fell into line with the segregation policy. In most places, blacks utilized separate USO and Red Cross buildings and facilities. After much protest, the Red Cross revised its policy and accepted plasma from blacks for blood banks but still kept the blood of blacks segregated.

From time to time throughout the war, black leaders pressed the War Department for an integrated volunteer division. Although widely endorsed by blacks and whites, the proposal was repeatedly rejected. Army spokesmen insisted that segregation was an established American custom and that the military had no responsibility to tamper with the social customs of the country or to conduct experiments within the army for the solution of social problems. Its only task, they maintained, was to create an efficient fighting machine in the shortest possible time.

The segregation policy intensified friction between black and white soldiers. Whites who entered the army without bias against blacks frequently acquired a prejudiced attitude during their military life. "The sight of masses of Negro soldiers constantly blocked off into separate groups and assigned to menial jobs," wrote a white officer, "generates in the mind of the average soldier a powerful feeling of superiority and of being 'different.'"

The army clung to the old and discredited belief that only white officers, particularly Southern officers, knew how to command black troops, and that the black soldiers actually preferred such men for commanders. As a consequence, most of the officers assigned to black units were white, not infrequently men whom the army commanders regarded as "incompetent or deserving of mild punishment." Many of them held to the prevailing stereotype of black inferiority and made no effort to hide their prejudice from their men. A black enlisted man wrote of one officer that "his obvious dislike for Negroes seemed to be a prime qualification for his assignment with Negro troops." Not surprisingly, a survey of black troops in February 1945 found an overwhelming preference for black officers over white officers and for Northern white officers over Southern whites, contrary to the army's prevailing conception.

The black national press actively publicized the discrimination and abuse suffered by black soldiers. As a result, many commanding officers blamed these newspapers for inciting dissatisfaction among their troops. They banned the reading of black newspapers or excluded particular issues from post libraries or from sale in post exchanges. In some instances the papers were taken from newsboys or soldiers and burned.

Prejudiced white officers were accused of "throwing the book" at black soldiers for acts they would ignore or punish lightly if done by whites. One journalist has noted: "When whites contracted venereal disease they received medical treatment. Blacks received courts-martial." Many black soldiers were unjustly convicted by courts-martial, either because their officers assumed their guilt regardless of the evidence or because they wanted to "set an example" for other black soldiers. Walter White of the NAACP, who visited every major war theater as a correspondent, found court-martial procedures used repeatedly to intimidate blacks, particularly those who knew their rights and insisted on exercising them. These men, he wrote, "were considered 'bad Negroes' who were to be assigned the most unpleasant and humiliating tasks to break their spirit and to be court-martialed if other methods failed." A black officer who wrote directly to General Dwight D. Eisenhower to protest certain court-martial sentences imposed on blacks was himself sentenced to six months in the stockade for correspondence out of channels.

During World War II, the army abandoned segregation at all officer candidate schools except those training Air Force pilots. At the peak, there were about twenty camps where white and black officer candidates slept, ate, and trained together with a minimum of friction. Earl Brown, a black newspaperman, in 1942 described these camps as "little islands of free men in an army where the color of a man's skin sets him apart as a different human being." However, there was a problem in getting commanding officers at the various camps to recommend qualified black candidates for officer training. In the first six months of the program, fewer than thirty blacks were selected for officer candidate schools. Subsequently after many protests from black leaders, Secretary Stimson ordered a redoubled effort to secure black candidates for officer training. Commanders were also required to account for their failure to send black soldiers to these schools, an order that produced speedy results. By the war's end, 7,768 black officers had been commissioned. Nevertheless, the opportunities for blacks to become commissioned officers in the army remained quite limited. By March 1945, 11 per cent of white servicemen were commissioned, as compared to less than 1 per cent among blacks. "Negroes, even those of equal education and AGCT level," one analysis stated, "had much less chance than whites to become commissioned officers."

Upon graduation from the officer candidate schools, blacks faced severe limits on their opportunities for assignment and subsequent promotion. At the beginning of the war, army policy restricted black officers to certain designated units and grades and specified that no white officer could be outranked by a black officer in his unit. This meant that, whenever a white officer received assignment to a unit with black officers, a wholesale shifting of officers followed to prevent him from being commanded by a black officer. It effectively prevented all but the few blacks in all-black officered units from gaining command functions or from advancing above the rank of lieutenant. As a result, there were only seven blacks among 5,220 colonels, and Benjamin O. Davis remained the only black among the 776 generals throughout the war. One critic wrote: "The Negro officer always sees before him a cleverly created wall of white seniority which he is not expected to scale. In far the larger number of cases, he is kept a junior officer while whites, no better fitted, are promoted. . . . This practice does not build morale."

Black officers were regularly criticized, abused, and humiliated in the presence of their men by their unit commanders. One black officer recalled briefing sessions in which "white commanders . . . would act as if the Negro officers were not present, punctuating their briefings with off-color, humiliating racial jokes." When a black colonel was unable to find a place to eat on the post at Fort Bragg, an entire barracks was opened for his sole occupancy.

Black officers were required to sit in the back row of an army theater where front seats were reserved for white officers and Italian prisoners. Black officers were assessed dues to support white officers' clubs from which they were barred. Black officers on the battle line in Italy with the 92d Division "were humiliated by being barred from a 'white' officers *club set up by men in their own outfit!*"

When Judge Hastie inquired about the army's position on the use of facilities by black officers, he received the following reply: "The Army has always regarded the officers' quarters and the officers' mess as the home and private dining room of the officers who reside and eat there. . . . For a variety of reasons, the problems in the officers' home cannot be solved by fiat." This strict segregation policy was deeply resented by black officers, and they demonstrated their resentment by frequent acts of defiance.

When, in March 1945, some of the black officers of the 477th Bomber Group, an all-black outfit except for white command, tried to use the facilities of the white officers' club at Freeman Field, Indiana, instead of the former noncommissioned officers' club reserved for blacks, they were refused service and threatened with arrest if they persisted in entering the club house. In addition, the commanding officer issued a regulation requiring black officers to sign a statement in effect agreeing to their own segregation. One hundred one black officers declined to endorse the regulation. Thereupon the commanding officer created a board of six officers, and the officers who had failed to sign the regulation were summoned before the board. When they still refused to sign they were placed under arrest. Roy Wilkins, writing in *The Crisis*, observed: "The 101 young Negro officers arrested at Freeman Field . . . are determined to be treated as officers, not as Negroes. If there is a club for officers, then they intend to use it. If attempting to use it means arrest, then they choose arrest."

The NAACP wrote to Secretary of War Stimson requesting an investigation, release of the arrested officers, and dismissal of charges against them. On April 26 the War Department dismissed the charges and the 101 black flying officers, after being held for almost a month, were released.

In these circumstances, numerous black officers broke down. Many sought transfers and even discharges. One young officer, requesting permission to resign his commission wrote:

> I am unable to adjust myself to the handicap of being a Negro Officer in the United States Army. . . . Prolonged observation reveals that inconsistencies over and above a reasonable amount are rampant. Sins of omission, sins of commission, humiliations, insults—injustices, all—are mounted one upon another until one's zest is chilled and spirit broken.

For the black enlisted men, army life was even more frustrating. Both their letters and the reports of correspondents reported countless instances of discrimination and endless troubles with Jim Crow practices, especially the overt inconveniences, discomforts, and friction associated with segregation on public transportation facilities. At Fort Bragg black soldiers could not board regular buses, although black civilians were permitted to do so. The soldiers had to wait for infrequent buses marked simply "colored troops," with no destination indicated. White civilian drivers operating buses with segregated seating arrangements between army camps and nearby towns frequently refused to transport black soldiers to and from their bases even when they had plenty of room. As a result, black soldiers were delayed for hours in reporting back to camp. When homeward bound on furlough, they were forced to wait as long as twelve hours in railroad stations before ticket agents would sell them tickets. And when the train pulled into the station, they often found the segregated coach reserved for them too crowded to board. "Last Christmas," a reporter wrote, "hundreds of Negro soldiers spent their entire furlough waiting, waiting in vain. They never got home."

Innumerable accounts report the difficulties experienced by black military personnel with segregation on the Jim Crow railroad system, even when they were traveling under government orders. Station restaurants often refused them service, leaving them hungry for hours. Most galling was the denial of the facilities and hospitality that were extended to German prisoners of war. In March 1945 *The Crisis* declared: "Nothing so lowers Negro morale as the frequent preferential treatment of Axis prisoners of war in contrast with deprecatory Army policy toward American troops who happen to be Negro."

On one occasion, a group of German prisoners of war traveling under guard to the West Coast ate with the white passengers in the main section of the dining car, but the black soldiers assigned to guard them were fed behind a curtain at the far end of the car. The poet Wittner Bynner recorded the incident in the following rhyme:

> On a train in Texas German prisoners eat
>   With white American soldiers, seat by seat,
> While black American soldiers sit apart—
>   The white men eating meat, the black men heart.

This situation prevailed throughout the country. In Salina, Kansas, just outside the Air Force base Camp Phillips, "For whites only" signs were on display all over the town. Even the five and ten cent store had a sign in the window reading, "We do not solicit colored patrons." Here too restaurants routinely served German prisoners of war while refusing service to black airmen. "The people of Salina," recalled the black author Lloyd L. Brown, who was an airman in World War II, "would serve these enemy soldiers and turn away black American GIs."

Especially outrageous were the numerous incidents of humiliating treatment, harassment, and violence on the part of white MPs. "Backed by the city police," a black reporter wrote after touring several camps, the MPs "do not hesitate to beat up and kill Negroes in the streets and in the jails." A black officer complained bitterly of the "arrogance and bodily assault" regularly imposed on himself and his colleagues by the military police.

Typical was a situation that developed in and near Gurdon, Arkansas. One evening some 200 to 300 black soldiers of the 94th Engineer Battalion, recently transferred from Fort Custer, Michigan, visited the town in search of recreation. Their reception by the local whites was extremely hostile. Racial epithets and other defamatory comments were frequent. As the atmosphere worsened the soldiers armed themselves with clubs, marched in a group through the town, and returned to their bivouac area. There was no violence. The next day the commanding officer declared the town off-limits and directed the battalion to move to a new bivouac area several miles away. As elements of the battalion were moving along a highway to their new area, state police and armed civilians approached the unarmed soldiers and ordered them off the road and into the ditches and woods. When the unit's white officers protested, they were threatened and insulted, and one of them was struck by a state policeman. Because of these incidents, more than forty soldiers left the battalion and made their way back to Fort Custer, where they turned themselves in. One soldier wrote: "Some of our men began to talk about returning to Camp Custer for protection. That night they left by bus, train, and walking. Three of us hopped freight trains after walking forty-two miles to avoid white people, who we felt would attack us because of our uniforms." Six soldiers were tried by court-martial, and some black officers were relieved of their command for this incident.

At a conference of black editors with War Department officials in December 1941, a colonel in the adjutant general's office responded to protests against the mistreatment of black soldiers by stating: "The Army cannot change civilian ideas on the Negro. . . . The responsibility is upon the complainants in racial friction and clashes."

Early in 1943, the black press carried almost weekly accounts of insults, violence, and homicide directed at black soldiers in the towns surrounding Southern army camps. A black sergeant was killed in March by a city policeman in the streets of Little Rock, Arkansas. On Memorial Day, the town sheriff in Centerville, Mississippi, intervened in a fracas between a white MP and a black soldier. When the MP began getting the worst of it, he yelled, "Shoot the nigger!" The sheriff fired point blank at the soldier's chest and then asked the MP, "Any more niggers you want killed?"

In June 1943 the National Lawyers Guild submitted a report on violence against black soldiers to the War and Justice departments. The report stated in part:

Civilian violence against the Negro in uniform is a recurrent phenomenon. It continues unabated. It may well be the greatest factor now operating to make 13 million Negroes bitter and resentful and to undermine the fighting spirit of three-quarters of a million Negroes in arms. Yet no effective steps are being taken . . . by state or federal authorities to stamp out this evil.

The black soldiers reacted with cynical disillusionment to the discrimination, harassment, and terror. A black sergeant wrote from the China-Burma-India Theater of Operations:

> I have a very clear idea of what we are *not* fighting for. We certainly are not fighting for the four freedoms. . . . The list of insults and discriminations to which we have been subjected because of race since donning the khaki is too long for detailed discussion here, but it is pertinent to state that it has been long and disgusting enough to make the writer indifferent and apathetic with regard to this war and to tempt him on more than one occasion to request imprisonment rather than continue to accept the indignities to which the Army insists on subjecting him.

Other black soldiers responded by fighting back. During the summer of 1943, racial tension in the army erupted into serious disturbances as black soldiers fought white soldiers and police at many bases in the country and in Australia, the South Pacific, and England. Walter White gave the following report of a visit with black soldiers stationed in England:

> As we talked, I was puzzled at the frequency, despondency, and bitterness of the use of the phrase "the enemy." I soon learned that Negro soldiers referred not to the Nazis across the Channel but to their white fellow-Americans. One of them, his face clouded with disillusion and anger, asked me, "What are we fighting for over here? Are we sent to the ETO to fight the Nazis—or our white soldiers?" Having then listened for four hours or more to recitals of transplanted American race prejudice, I had no answer to give him.

Racial conflict within the military was paralleled by similar unrest in the civilian communities. As jobs increasingly opened for them, the influx of blacks into industries and localities where they had not previously been welcome aggravated tensions and led to disputes and outbursts of violence. During the same summer of 1943 serious disturbances occurred in Los Angeles, Detroit, New

York, and Beaumont, Texas. Detroit seethed with racism and ha-
tred—"a keg of powder with short fuse." On June 20 it exploded
into a two-day riot that resulted in thirty-four dead, more than
seven hundred injured, more than $2 million in property losses,
and 100 million man-hours lost in war production.

The Harlem riots that same summer were triggered by a rumor
that a black soldier had been killed by a white policeman. Even
though it was untrue—the soldier was slightly wounded—the rumor
set off an explosion. In a letter to Secretary Stimson, Walter White
described it as "fury born of repeated unrebuked, unpunished . . .
shooting, maiming of Negro troops, particularly in the southern
states, which started the disorders." The *New Republic* commented:

> A growing number of Negro soldiers have been beaten or murdered
> in the vicinity of Southern training camps. . . . It is inconceivable
> that a white soldier could have been shot for the same reasons, or
> that wanton slayings of white personnel would be ignored by the
> federal government as they have been ignored in the case of Negro
> troops.

In an address to a group of black lawyers in November 1943,
Attorney General Francis Biddle blamed the racial unrest in the
country on "the poor treatment of black servicemen, and the contradiction between our profession of faith in democracy and our
acts." A year later he warned President Roosevelt: "The situation
among the Negro voters is still serious. The greatest resentment
comes from Negroes in the armed forces, particularly those who
have been in southern camps, and they are writing home about it."

The War Department was slow to acknowledge the low morale
of black troops, but it could not ignore the events of the summer
of 1943. It issued a directive urging all white officers to treat black
troops with the utmost care and diplomacy. Although there was
an attempt to conceal evidence of black resistance by calling deaths
that resulted from racial battles either combat fatalities or "motor
vehicle accidents," army statisticians were compelled to report an
unusually high number of casualties among white officers of black
troops. In spite of this, the war was almost over before the War
Department called upon Congress, unsuccessfully, to make it a
federal offense to attack or assault men in uniform.

Judge Hastie resigned in January 1943 as civilian aide to the Secretary of War to protest over-all War Department policies and specifically "the reactionary policies of the Army Air Forces in matters affecting Negroes." The effectiveness of his office had been seriously weakened by failure to consult him on policy matters until after they had been developed and formulated. Indeed, it became clear early in his tenure that, as the Chicago *Defender* put it, "Mr. Hastie, though a very capable man, has no appreciable authority and scarcely any influence with the bigwigs of the War Department." "The truth of the matter," said *The Crisis*, "is that Hastie has been unable to do little or nothing to correct the obvious and glaring mistreatment of Negroes in the Army."

At a press conference when he left office at the end of January, Hastie said: "It is difficult to see how a Negro in this position, with all his superiors maintaining or inaugurating racial segregation, can accomplish anything of value."

Hastie's resignation produced several changes in the army's racial policy. Plans for a segregated Air Force school were abandoned. Training in aviation medicine was made available to black doctors. Opportunities for black troops to obtain technical training in the Air Force were broadened. Over a year later, in February 1944, the War Department issued a pamphlet entitled "Command of Negro Troops," in which it refuted the notion of racial superiority or inferiority and acknowledged the right of blacks to the same military opportunities accorded any other soldier. The army also made the film *The Negro Soldier* detailing the contributions made by blacks in wars past and current. The film was shown in training camps and commercial theaters in this country and overseas. The general response of both black and white soldiers was quite favorable; nine-tenths of the blacks and two-thirds of the whites questioned said they "liked it very much."

In the summer of 1944 a directive was issued that presumably banned segregation in theaters, post exchanges, and buses operating within army camps. But the desegregation order had no significant effect. Most post commandants continued their segregation practices, but with subtle variations. The Colored Service Club was now designated "Service Club No. 2," and the Colored Area Exchange now received a branch number or a named area designation. Camps that had only one theater often set aside sections of seats for different units. Black soldiers who demanded equal treatment in compliance with the order were denied service in post exchanges and theaters. An Assistant Secretary of War's ruling that the language of the antisegregation order must be construed to include officers' clubs was almost totally disregarded.

One historian argues that many of the changes in 1944 were influenced by the imminence of the Presidential election. In June 1944 representatives of twenty-five black organizations met in New York and resolved that the support of parties and candidates by black voters would be determined by the candidates' stand on the issue of discrimination and segregation in the armed forces. In the same month, the Republican Party pledged in its campaign platform an immediate Congressional inquiry to determine whether "mistreatment, segregation and discrimination against Negroes in the armed forces are impairing morale and efficiency" and to consider the adoption of corrective legislation. The Roosevelt Administration hoped that its reform measures would have an effect on black voters. In September the President acted to amend War Department plans for segregated rest centers for returning combat veterans.

In response to the urgent need for service troops abroad, the number of black troops overseas had been rapidly increased beginning in the summer of 1943, and several black combat units were transferred to service duties; overseas commanders were more willing to accept black service troops than black combat troops. For example, the 2d Cavalry Division, which included among its regiments "the old and revered 9th and 10th Cavalry," was shipped to North Africa after two years of combat training. The men were informed that after further training in North Africa they would be sent into action. The division landed in North Africa early in 1944 and was immediately broken up into various service units. Instead of further training for combat, the men were assigned to "unloading ships, repairing roads, and driving trucks." To make matters worse, the switch was shrouded in secrecy; the men were forbidden to write home about it, and censorship of mail enforced the order. Nevertheless, the news reached the United States and provoked indignant protest in the black community, which charged that a deliberate policy had been instituted of barring blacks from combat. The *Christian Century* noted that "there is a widespread resentment throughout the Negro community at the belief . . . that Negro troops which have been trained for front-line service have been denied such service and shunted into labor battalions."

The breaking up of the division also strengthened the suspicion among black soldiers that the army meant to keep them "from reaching any of the front lines where they may gain glory and prestige for themselves and their race." One member of the division declared that the black combat unit had been activated because

> someone had to be a stevedore, longshoreman, etc. It was a simple matter—give it to the colored man. After the war is over demands couldn't be so great, didn't his white brother (?) die on the front line, while he was comparatively safe in the rear echelon; that's right, isn't it?

It was about this time that General Davis bluntly told the Advisory Committee on Negro Troop Policy, headed by Assistant Secretary of Defense John J. McCloy: "The colored soldier had lost confidence in the fairness of the Army to Negro troops."

When Secretary of War Stimson admitted to a Congressman that black units had indeed been converted into service troops, the controversy worsened. He insisted, however, that efficiency, not race, had determined the War Department's selection of units for conversion: "It so happens that a relatively large percentage of the Negroes inducted in the Army have fallen within the lower educational classifications, and many of the Negro units accordingly have been unable to master efficiently the techniques of modern weapons." Publication of this letter raised a new storm of protest. The black press angrily accused Stimson of saying that blacks were "too dumb to master modern weapons of war" and called for his immediate resignation. Republican political workers immediately undertook to make capital of this issue by convincing black voters that the Roosevelt Administration was responsible for army policy. Democrats, on the other hand, blamed the army and the War Department. Representative William L. Dawson of Chicago, the only black member of the House, told a group of black Democrats that "the failure to use Negro Americans to the fullest in this war is the diabolical work of a reactionary and prejudiced clique within the Military Establishment."

Responding to the public and political reaction to this issue, the General Staff decided early in 1944 to commit the black 92d Division and elements of the black 93d Division to combat. Shortly thereafter John J. McCloy declared in a newspaper interview that, although the army had not found it easy to make blacks "into efficient combat troops" because of their educational handicaps, it would give the black soldiers every opportunity "to make good on the field of battle." He urged black leaders to cooperate in the army's efforts to improve the morale of black troops: "It is a pity . . . that complete equality in the Army has taken such a hold of the Negro mind as to become their predominating thought. For our first aim, whether Negro or white, should be the winning of the war."

A year later, another statement by a War Department official evoked a new public controversy over "the army's Negro policy." In March 1945 Truman Gibson, Jr., who had replaced Judge Hastie as black civilian aide to the Secretary of War, spoke of the controversial combat record of the 92d Infantry Division—the "Black Buffaloes"—the only large black unit to engage in extensive front-line fighting during World War II. The division had arrived in Italy in June 1944 and had had several successful actions. But counterbalancing the more than 7,000 awards to individual members of the division were reports of "trigger happy" men and of the "melting away" of units under enemy pressure. *Newsweek* magazine commented on "The Luckless 92d": "The most extensive and wholehearted effort by the United States Army to give American Negro troops a role in the war equal to that of white troops has so far been more productive of disappointment and failure than of anything else."

High-ranking officers reported the alleged failures of the black officers and men of the outfit to the War Department and requested that it be withdrawn from further front-line action. When Gibson went to Italy to investigate these reports, he discovered alarmingly low morale among the division's blacks. White officers, he decided, were quick to blame the black division's lack of combat success on supposed racial deficiencies, despite the contradictory evidence of many individual acts of bravery as well as the number of casualties suffered by blacks in the division. He concluded that the underlying reasons for the division's poor performance included the frequency with which black officers were bypassed for promotion by white officers, the "whites-only" officers' clubs that abounded throughout the division, and the instances in which black company commanders had been arbitrarily removed from command and replaced by whites. He found a widespread feeling among black enlisted men that the division's white officers were totally indifferent to the success or failure of the unit and were preoccupied with vilifying the black officers and men. Finally, he found that the situation was aggravated by the presence in the division of an unusually high percentage of uneducated and illiterate men in AGCT grades IV and V (43.7 and 29.4 per cent, respectively), although military authorities had already determined that operational efficiency was unlikely in any unit with more than 10 per cent of grade V men. Gibson left more convinced than ever that segregation led inevitably to unsatisfactory military results.

When Gibson presented these views at a press conference, the correspondents' dispatches emphasized his acceptance of the reports that some black units had "melted away" in battle and his admission that most of the black troops were low in literacy. Milton Bracker of the *New York Times* said that Gibson's judgment "must be taken most seriously because he is the official representative of the War Department and is a Negro." He added: "To understand the situation it must be realized that the generalization that 'Negro troops can't fight' has been depressingly prevalent on and behind the Italian front virtually since the 92d Division arrived."

These press reports aroused vociferous protest from black leaders. Gibson was accused of providing support for those in and out of the armed services who had long contended that blacks were suited only for labor units. "It is enough our boys have to fight Nazis and Dixie race hunters," said the Chicago *Defender*, "without having to face the venom and scorn of 'Uncle Toms.'"

Whatever the conditions in Italy, on the Western Front the demand for infantry replacements sharply increased following the Battle of the Bulge. It was therefore decided to draw men from supply and service units, retrain them as riflemen, and place them in the line. Lieutenant General John C. H. Lee obtained permission from General Eisenhower to allow black enlisted men from service units within his command to volunteer for duty as infantrymen. In his appeal for volunteers, General Lee emphasized that they would serve as individual replacements and would fight along-side whites on a fully integrated basis. However, Eisenhower sub-sequently countermanded Lee's plan when General Walter Bedell Smith, his chief of staff, convinced him that individual integration was contrary to War Department policy and would precipitate trouble. It was then decided that black volunteers would be or-ganized into platoons assigned to white units. "The army," re-ported the Associated Press, "has moved cautiously in breaking its long-established tradition of keeping white and Negro units sepa-rated."

Black enlisted men responded so enthusiastically (many accepted a reduction in grade from noncommissioned officer to private in order to get into the fighting) that a limit of 2,500 had to be set. This resulted in the exclusion of thousands of disappointed volun-teers. After six weeks of training, the platoons of black volunteers were assigned to various white units, and black and white platoons fought side by side as they moved across Germany from the end of March to V-E Day. The black volunteers received commendations for their combat performance from General Eisenhower and from their division commanding officers. "I have never seen any soldiers who have performed better in combat than you," Brigadier General Charles T. Lanham told the volunteers. The War Department added that the blacks had "established themselves as fighting men no less courageous or aggressive than their white comrades."

An experiment conducted by the Army Research Bureau re-vealed that white soldiers with whom the blacks had served in combat had undergone a significant change in their radical atti-tudes. The majority of soldiers in previously all-white combat units had at first resented the plan and seriously doubted whether it would work. After serving with blacks, however, most of those who had been skeptical agreed that the 2,500 black volunteers had fought "very well." Three out of every four of the white soldiers also confirmed that, as a result of their common experience in com-bat, "their regard and respect for the Negro had risen." However, the results of this survey were not made public. Nor were the black volunteers, who had been given to understand that they would remain with the divisions to which they were assigned, permitted to do so. Instead, "as soon as the war in Europe came to an end," one historian reported, "the Negro platoons were unceremoniously detached from their white units and either returned to all-Negro service units or discharged."

Outside the infantry, many other black units "made an indisputable contribution to the war effort." Black artillery, anti-aircraft, and armored units fought in the Pacific as well as in Europe and achieved good combat records and commendations. Major General John P. Lucas, commanding general of the III Corps, Italian Theater, commended the black soldiers of an anti-aircraft unit for capturing a German patrol on its way to blow up a bridge and for shooting down two German planes: "I recommend the whole crew for a Legion of Merit and hope they get it. . . . I have never seen greater enthusiasm and excitement than was evidenced by my colored gun crew. Their chests stuck out at least four feet, their eyes were shining, and they looked the part of the heroes they were."

The 600 Airmen trained at Tuskegee as pilots carried the war from Africa to France, Italy, Poland, Rumania, and Germany. The two major black combat air units overseas were the 99th Pursuit Squadron, the first all-black flying unit, and the 332d Fighter Group, both of which saw combat over Europe, escorting bombers and flying strafing and other missions. In more than 200 missions in the European theater not one U.S. bomber escorted by the "Black 99th" was lost to enemy fighters. The black flying units, together with the 447th Bomber Group, were credited with destroying 111 enemy planes in the air and 150 others on the ground while flying a total of 15,533 sorties.

Black service and supply outfits, particularly the engineer and quartermaster units, provided invaluable support for the Allied armies. In every part of the globe, black soldiers built roads, unloaded ships, drove supply trucks to the front lines, and performed innumerable other vital tasks. The "Red Ball Express," manned mostly by 1,500 black truck drivers provided the supply backbone for the Normandy drive in 1944. Black troops made up 60 per cent of the 15,000 American soldiers who carved the Ledo Road out of "some of the world's densest jungle," and then drove convoys across it to China. Some 3,700 black soldiers—one-third of the GIs sent to Alaska—also helped build and service the Alcan Highway. Press accounts about the linking of the white engineers building from the south with the black engineers from the north stirred the nation in the fall of 1942. Yank, the Army weekly, viewed the link-up as "symbolic not alone of the completion of the road to Alaska but also of the manner of its construction. The first land route in history linking America with its largest territory has been a product of black and white troops of the U.S. Army."

Many units received Presidential citations. The 969th Field Artillery won a Distinguished Unit citation for "outstanding courage and resourcefulness and undaunted determination." Five blacks received the Distinguished Service Cross. First Lieutenant Vernon Baker of Cheyenne, Wyoming, won that award for "extraordinary heroism in action" when he knocked out three Nazi machine gun nests and killed or wounded nine Germans. Private Ernest Jenkins of New York City won a Silver Star for knocking out an enemy gun position and capturing fifteen Germans. Black pilots won 88 Distinguished Flying Crosses and 800 Air Medals and clusters. Colonel Benjamin O. Davis, Jr., Commander of the 99th, who flew 60 missions himself, won a Silver Star, Legion of Merit, Distinguished Flying Cross, and Air Medal with four oak leaf clusters. Several black GIs won foreign decorations. Macon H. Johnson was awarded the "Order of the Soviet Union" by a Russian general and William Green won the "Partisan Medal for Heroism" from Marshal Tito's Yugoslav government.

Just as in World War I, however, no black received the Congressional Medal of Honor. The *Crisis* commented bitterly in December 1945 that it was indeed strange that out of a million blacks in the armed services, not one merited the nation's highest award. Two months later, Representative Helen Gahagan Douglas of California paid tribute to the black soldier, who "fought and shed his blood for a freedom which he has not been permitted fully to share":

> Despite the Selective Service and Training Act, which established a basic policy of non-discrimination because of race or color in building up our army, and in spite of improvement during the course of the war, it must not be forgotten that segregation, discrimination, and race prejudice in all of its varied forms placed an added burden on the Negro in the armed forces and dogged his steps from the induction center to the front line.

Mrs. Douglas's evaluation applied with equal accuracy to the experience of black servicewomen during World War II. In their case, however, the discrimination was even more galling than the hardships and frustrations experienced by their black brothers-in-arms, since all the women were volunteers. As Jesse Johnson wrote in his autobiography, *Ebony Brass*, the army had "two types of segregation—race and sex."

The largest of the women's services was the Women's Auxiliary Army Corps (WAAC), later renamed the Women's Army Corps (WAC). From its inception in 1942, it paralleled the army in its treatment of black personnel. When the first officer training center opened at Des Moines, Iowa, thirty-nine of the 440 women enrolled were black. Although all the candidates attended class together, the black women ate at separate tables, were lodged in separate quarters, and had different swimming pool hours. Upon graduation, the black WAAC officers were assigned to command black WAAC troops or to serve in administrative capacities on "colored posts." Two exceptions were Major Charity Adams, who became supervisor of plans and training at the Des Moines training center, and Major Harriet West, who was chief of the planning bureau control division at WAAC headquarters in Washington.

By the summer of 1945 there were 120 black officers and 3,961 black enlisted women on duty with the corps. Thirty black WAC units were assigned to the Army Service Forces, and thirteen to the Army Air Forces. The commanding officer of Fort Huachuca wrote: "These young women are showing marked ability in taking over essential jobs. . . . The performance of the WACs has been very satisfactory in every respect." The commanding officer of Douglas Army Airfield said: "I've found them cooperative at all times, and their enthusiasm, industry, attention to duty and conduct make them a real asset to the post."

However, the black WACs made the same charges of discrimination in assignments as those made by blacks in other branches of the army. In September 1943 the civilian aide to the Secretary of War complained that black women were being sent only to cooks' and bakers' school instead of to higher technical schools, and that "white women were being assigned to field jobs while Negro women were not." At Camp Breckenridge, Kentucky, five black WACs described as "well-educated" were assigned to sweep warehouses, while fifteen others were employed in the service club and thirty in a civilian-operated laundry.

The most highly publicized instance of discrimination against black WACs took place at Lovell General Hospital at Fort Devens, Massachusetts. In March 1945 approximately 100 black WACs stationed at the hospital staged a sit-down strike, charging that only white WACs were assigned to technical duties while they were restricted to kitchen police (KP). They also accused the commanding officer of the hospital, Colonel Walter M. Crandall, of having stated that he did not want black WACs as ambulance drivers or as medical technicians: "They are here to mop walls, scrub floors, and do all the dirty work."

In response to personal pleas from high-ranking military officers, all but four of the WACs involved in the strike returned to work. The four refused to carry out the order of their superior officer because they said it was discriminatory. Roy Wilkins commented: "They did not believe that just because they were black they should have to do all the dirty work. . . . One girl is quoted as saying she'd rather *die* than be treated as she was. She was through, orders or no orders, Army or no Army." The four blacks underwent court-martial on charges of having disobeyed a superior officer, were found guilty, and were sentenced to dishonorable discharge and one year at hard labor. The conviction was reversed by the Judge Advocate General, who ruled that the court had been improperly convened, and the women were released and restored to duty. Colonel Crandall was removed from his post.

The only black WAC unit assigned to overseas duty was the 688th Central Postal Battalion commanded by Major Adams, which landed in England in February 1945. The War Department acceded to the unit's overseas assignment after receiving hundreds of protests from individuals and organizations against the restrictive WAC policy.

The Army Nurse Corps limited its acceptance of blacks; with rare exceptions, black nurses were assigned to hospitals that served only black troops. In July 1944 the army removed all limitations on black nurses, but by V-J Day a total of only 479 black nurses had been accepted by the army, constituting about 1 per cent of the Army Nurse Corps.

Although the navy had opened enlistments for general service to blacks instead of limiting them, as formerly, to the role of mess attendants, the Secretary of the Navy made it clear that these volunteers would receive basic and advanced training in separate camps and schools, would be grouped in separate units, and would not be placed on seagoing combat vessels. Instead, they would be limited in assignment to shore installations and harbor craft, construction crews, and labor battalions based outside the continental United States. White petty officers were to be in command of the black units until black petty officers could be trained. There would be no black commissioned officers. Secretary Knox termed the new policy an experiment.

The actual recruiting of blacks began in June 1942. A separate area with facilities to accommodate 1,000 black recruits per month was set up at the Great Lakes Naval Training Center in Illinois. The recruits, all apprentice seamen, were under the command of Lieutenant Commander Daniel W. Armstrong, a Naval Academy graduate and son of the founder of Hampton Institute. Two other camps—Camps Moffett and Lawrence—were eventually set up at Great Lakes for the exclusive use of black naval recruits. Two segregated advanced training schools were also operated for black seamen at Camp Robert Smalls and at Hampton Institute, Virginia. At these schools black recruits who successfully completed eight weeks of basic training and qualified for advanced instruction were trained as technical specialists. Recruits who did not qualify for naval vocational schools were assigned to sea duty, naval ammunition depots, or the Great Lakes Training Center operating center.

The navy contended that its assignment policy ensured that individual jobs would be filled solely on the basis of rating and ability. But black critics complained that, in practice, race rather than ability was the determining factor in job assignments and other areas as well. They noted that very few blacks held jobs at sea except as stewards. The navy refused to assign blacks to gun crews and battle stations. Advancement for black naval personnel was extremely slow—in most cases nonexistent. Petty officer ratings were systematically withheld from blacks, and blacks were not trained to become commissioned officers. White men from a biracial faculty were commissioned, while the navy passed up equally qualified blacks from the same faculty. There were no black chaplains and no blacks at the Naval Academy, nor had any blacks been admitted to the Naval Aviation branch except as service workers and mess attendants at aviation shore installations. Finally, very few blacks who had successfully completed their courses in the training schools were permitted to work in their specialties.

The navy's policy was to assign almost all blacks to segregated jobs as construction workers or as laborers and stevedores at magazine, ammunition, and supply depots, where they worked in gangs handling ammunition and loading and unloading ships, largely under the supervision of white petty officers. The organization of all-black construction and labor battalions resulted in mass protests over segregation and lack of opportunity. One critic bitterly observed that blacks in the navy had swapped the waiter's apron for the stevedore's hook.

During World War II a number of widely publicized incidents occurred involving black naval personnel who sought "to remedy or to openly resist in one form or another" conditions and treatment that they regarded as unjust. In October 1943 twelve black SeaBees stationed in the West Indies were encouraged by their commanding officer to express themselves freely concerning racial conditions at the base. Assured that the meeting was off the record, they aired their grievances with candor, charging discrimination in camp facilities and in promotions. Although 80 per cent of the battalion was black, not one was rated above second-class petty officer, while all of the remaining 20 per cent, the white personnel in the unit, rated higher in rank. The commanding officer assured the men that similar meetings would be held in the future and that a committee on interracial matters would be formed by the chaplain. But the next day the commanding officer again summoned the men. Upbraiding them for "griping," he announced that he was calling a halt to the meetings. Several days later, the twelve men and seven others were discharged, sixteen as "undesirable" and three for "unfitness." The latter three, upon appeal, were given honorable discharges.

The black press and civilian organization publicized the case of the black SeaBees and agitated for their reinstatement or honorable discharge, but without success. In June 1944 Congress passed the Bill of Rights for Servicemen, which, among other things, established a reviewing procedure for persons discharged from the armed forces. Fifteen of the sixteen men petitioned for a review of their cases. Early in 1945 the Navy Department's Board of Review announced that fourteen of the men had been granted discharges "under honorable conditions." One petitioner was refused because his record prior to discharge was considered bad.

Following a huge ammunition explosion on July 17, 1944, on two ships at the Port Chicago Ammunition Depot in California, in which about 250 black seamen engaged in loading the ships were killed and several hundred were wounded, a detachment of 258 of the survivors, assigned to resume the loading and extremely fearful of a similar disaster, expressed extreme reluctance to return to work, claiming inadequate training and safety provisions for the hazardous job. After repeated urging by the chaplain and other officers, all but forty-four resumed loading. The forty-four, plus six others who balked after working for a few days, were charged with mutiny and tried by court-martial. The fifty "mutineers," were found guilty and sentenced to long prison terms at hard labor and dishonorable discharge. Thurgood Marshall, who acted as an NAACP observer at the trial, commented:

> The men actually didn't know what happened. Had they been given a direct order to load ammunition, and had they refused to obey that order, then the charges would have been legitimate. But they said no direct order to resume loading was issued them. They were asked whether they would load, and they replied that they were afraid. . . . They had no idea that verbal expression of their fear constituted mutiny.

In January 1946, after numerous petitions and appeals for clemency, the conviction was set aside, and the men were restored to duty on probation.

In response to continuing pressure from black organizations and press and mounting protests from black seamen, a number of steps were taken to improve the status of blacks in the navy. These changes were carried forward under the direction of Admiral Randall Jacobs, Chief of Naval Personnel, and later by Admiral Louis Denfield, his successor. The number of blacks to be assigned to naval ammunition depots was limited to 30 per cent of the black enlisted men in the navy. In the early months of 1944 a special training unit for black illiterate recruits was organized at Camp Robert Smalls. Fifteen thousand men successfully passed through this school, an achievement since characterized as "unprecedented and unmatched." On February 2 "A Guide to the Command of

Negro Personnel" was issued by the navy. It stated that individual performance, not race, should be the basis for navy employment. "The Navy accepts no theories of racial differences in inborn ability, but expects that every man wearing its uniform be trained and used in accordance with his maximum individual capacity on the basis of individual performance." Concurrently, the navy took a "timid step away from racial exclusiveness," when it announced that two ships, a destroyer and a patrol craft, would be manned with predominantly black crews under white officers. Experienced white petty officers were to serve as instructors at first. As soon as blacks reached a level of competence at sea, the white petty officers were to be transferred and replaced by qualified blacks. On March 20, 1944, the destroyer escort USS *Mason* was placed in commission with 160 blacks and 44 whites as crew. In April of the same year a 173-foot submarine chaser, USS *PC-1264*, was commissioned with a crew of fifty-three blacks commanded by thirteen whites. The destroyer escort did not complete the first stage of the experiment with the replacement of the white petty officers with blacks, but seven months after commissioning the eight white petty officers on *PC-1264* were replaced by blacks, and the black company was complete.

Meanwhile, in October 1943 it was officially announced that a number of blacks would be selected to be trained for officer commissions. Staff officers—physicians, dentists, chaplains, and so on—were to be chosen from civilian life, and line officers from existing black enlisted personnel. On January 1, 1944, sixteen men selected from the enlisted ranks of 160,000 black men in the navy, began their officer training on a segregated basis at a special class at Great Lakes. At the end of ten weeks of training, twelve of the original sixteen were commissioned as ensigns. The selection of the twelve men seems to have been arbitrary; none of the original sixteen had failed the course. None of the twelve line officers was assigned to duty outside the continental United States. Six were stationed in Boston, New York Harbor, and Treasure Island in San Francisco aboard patrol craft or tug boats, and six remained at Great Lakes performing unimportant jobs in the recruit training section at Camp Robert Smalls. They were kept segregated and strictly forbidden to use the station's officers' club by order of Commander Armstrong, who claimed he feared racial tension if socializing with white officers were permitted. Armstrong did not hesitate to humiliate the black officers in the presence of white officers.

After six months the black officers at Camp Robert Smalls submitted a request for membership in the officers' club. Armstrong rejected the application, contending that he was acting under the order of the base commandant, Commodore Robert R. Emmet. After Armstrong was transferred from the Great Lakes, a request was again submitted to his successor who forwarded it to Emmet, who granted unconditional permission for the black officers and opened the club facilities to them.

In time, other line officers graduated from the Navy's V-12 officer candidate schools, where they were trained in mixed groups. Upon being commissioned they were assigned to the Navy Department in Washington, D.C., and aboard small craft. When integration finally spread to the wardroom of *PC-1264*, the black officer assigned to the ship was Ensign Samuel Gravely, Jr., who in 1971 would be promoted to the rank of rear admiral, the navy's first black flag officer. By September 1945 the number of black male commissioned officers had increased from twelve to fifty-two—fifteen line and thirty-seven staff officers—as compared with more than 70,000 white officers. These black officers, who constituted .0013 per cent of all naval officers, held their commissions in the Naval Reserve Corps and not the regular navy.

All but five of the black officers eventually saw overseas duty. With but one exception, they had no real authority and were given jobs that did not correspond to their experience and training. The exception was Ensign Dennis D. Nelson, who commanded a logistics support unit, including white and black officers at Eniwetok. Promotions for black officers were few and far between. Only one black line reserve officer reached the rank of full lieutenant by the end of the war. And only one black was admitted to the Naval Academy in wartime, two months before the Japanese surrender.

On April 28, 1944, Secretary of the Navy Knox died and was succeeded by James A. Forrestal of New York. Forrestal was aware of the current trends in race relations, and during his administration the pace toward change accelerated. In July 1944 the navy abandoned its segregated advanced training schools for blacks, declaring that it did not "consider practical the establishment of separate facilities and quotas for Negroes who qualified for advanced training." Recruit training, however, remained segregated. One month later, blacks were assigned to twenty-five auxiliary ships on which they were to be integrated with whites but limited to 10 per cent of the total crew. In April 1945 the navy announced that blacks were now to be eligible for assignment to all auxiliary fleet vessels, although the 10 per cent quota for each ship would still be observed. In the spring of 1945 Lester B. Granger of the National Urban League was appointed to provide special advisory service to Secretary Forrestal.

In July 1945 a program of recruit training integration by companies was undertaken by Captain Richard J. Penny at Great Lakes. Two black companies were placed in the same battalion as four white companies. The results were gratifying. In a short time a black company won battalion honors. In August 1945 Penny moved on to racially mixed companies. Eight to ten blacks were assigned to the same company as whites, shared the same barracks and mess, and trained together with them. Not long after the program of complete integration was inaugurated, a mixed company voted a black sailor the honor man at the conclusion of its training program. Just before the end of the war Captain Charles Alonzo Bond, commandant of the service schools, said: "Segregation was an egregious error. It was un-American and inefficient—a waste of money and manpower." On the other hand, one commentator contends, some high navy officials believed that Jim Crow units were a mistake because concentrating blacks in groups of their own facilitated collective action on their part, which "would be less likely if Negroes were mixed in with whites and generally dispersed. Idealism and realism, thus, were joining together to nurture a will to make the Navy jimcrow free." A total of 166,915 blacks saw service in the navy. However, more than 90 per cent of the blacks in the navy were still messmen in 1945.

The blacks who received the Navy Cross and other awards for gallantry during World War II were all members of the messman's branch. On December 7, 1941, the day Pearl Harbor was attacked, Doris "Dorie" Miller, mess attendant second class on the USS *West Virginia*, dashed to the bridge and helped drag the seriously wounded captain out of the direct line of fire to a more sheltered spot. Then, although he had received no battle training and was unfamiliar with heavy weapons, he took a machine gun from a wounded sailor and brought down at least four attacking Japanese planes before the sinking ship had to be abandoned. Miller's identity was not disclosed until several weeks later after much pressure from black and liberal white groups had been brought to bear. And it was not until nearly a year later, upon the stubborn insistence of various civil rights groups, that the navy awarded to the sharecropper's son from Texas the Navy Cross, a historic first for blacks, "for distinguished devotion to duty, extraordinary courage, and disregard for his own personal safety." Concurrently, the navy "promoted" Miller to mess attendant first class. Three years later Dorie Miller, still a messman, was lost at sea when his new ship, the light aircraft carrier *Liscombe Bay*, was attacked by a Japanese submarine and sunk.

On June 1, 1942, the Marine Corps opened its enlistment rolls to blacks but did not begin to accept them until the end of August of that year, when separate training facilities for black recruits were set up at Montford Point, adjacent to Camp Lejeune, North Carolina. Upon completion of basic training, all but those who served as stewards were assigned to all-black service units. One infantry battalion was formed during the war but was used only for training. The majority of the black units served overseas as depot companies and ammunition companies, as part of beach parties in amphibious landings. Their main duty was to unload ammunition onto beaches and to move it inland to the front lines, usually carrying out the wounded as they returned. After the 3d Marine Ammunition Company won high praise for its handling of ammunition during the invasion of Saipan on June 15, 1944, the commander of the corps said: "Negro Marines are no longer on trial. They are Marines." Approximately 17,000 blacks served in the Marine Corps, 12,000 of them overseas, during World War II. In the aviation branch there were 600 stewards but no other blacks. There were no black Marine officers in World War II.

Almost 4,000 blacks served in the Coast Guard during World War II. Most black Coast Guard recruits were trained at Manhattan Beach, Brooklyn, where they studied in the same classes with whites under black and white instructors. The Coast Guard's first black officer, Ensign Joseph C. Jenkins, was commissioned in April 1942 and assigned as an engineering officer in Boston, where he directed a mixed unit of seamen. In September 1945 the Coast Guard had four black commissioned officers.

Approximately 24,000 blacks served in the Merchant Marine

during World War II and worked in every capacity aboard ship. On September 29, 1942, Hugh Mulzac became the first black master of a United States Merchant Marine ship. The SS *Booker T. Washington* had a racially mixed crew, which had volunteered "to demonstrate the feasibility of . . . interracial cooperation." After the war, the purser of the vessel, John Beecher, published a war chronicle entitled *All Brave Sailors*. The black writer, Ralph Ellison, in a review of the book appearing in the *New Republic* under the caption "*The Booker T.*," called it "one of the more interesting war books" and added: "Beecher saw the ship . . . as a symbol of a type of democracy in which value rests not upon skin color but upon human quality, intelligence, and ability, and where black and white men work and play together in harmony."

Unlike the WACs, the WAVEs and the SPARs, the women's contingents of the navy and the Coast Guard, accepted blacks only late in the war, and then in token numbers. When the two contingents were organized in 1942, both excluded black applicants. Pressure for a reversal of this policy came from many black organizations, especially the nonpartisan lobby of the Alpha Kappa Alpha sorority. However, Secretary Knox remained adamant, contending that since the navy "lacked any substantial body of colored men available or qualified for general service at sea" there was no need for women to relieve black sailors on land, which was the primary task of the WAVEs. Asked whether black women might not relieve landlocked navy men of any color in noncombatant jobs, the Secretary simply replied "no." The AKA continued its campaign until in October 1944, just prior to the Presidential election, the WAVEs announced that they would admit black women. On October 20 the Coast Guard declared that it too would accept black women in the SPARs. On November 13 the first two black women reported to Smith College for WAVE officer training, and late the following month the first contingent of forty enlisted WAVEs arrived at Hunter College for basic training. On July 23, 1945, the navy announced that there were two black commissioned officers and fifty-four black enlisted women in the WAVEs, among the enlisted complement of 78,000 and the officer corps of 8,000. In September 1945 there were five black SPARS in the Coast Guard. Although the Marine Women's Reserve, called Marinettes, eventually reached a strength of 19,000, at no time during World War

II did it accept black women. Out of a total of 10,914 nurses in the navy during World War II, there were never more than four black nurses in that service.

All told, the experience of black servicemen and women during World War II—the segregation, discrimination, and mistreatment —gave evidence, even in the course of a struggle presumably fought to wipe out a monstrous racism overseas, of the racism that pervaded the society as a whole. Said James Baldwin in *The Fire Next Time*: "The treatment accorded the Negro during the Second World War marks for me a turning point in the Negro's relation to America: to put it briefly, and somewhat too simply, a certain hope died, a certain respect for white Americans faded."

8

Desegregation of the Armed Forces

During the war black servicemen wondered what postwar America would be like. One black sergeant asked, "Shall we return to a country where every citizen, regardless of race, is afforded equal opportunities for training and education?" The war was hardly over when blacks learned that "their service in the army and navy had intensified prejudice instead of diminishing it." The American Legion, the Veterans of Foreign Wars, and the Disabled American Veterans maintained segregated posts for blacks and "a second-rate type of membership for them." Black veterans had disappointing experiences with the postwar job training program for veterans. They found access to vocational training virtually closed to them "by segregated schools 'for whites only,' by the inadequacy of the on-the-job training available, or by discrimination by unions and employers in the apprentice training program." The National Urban League estimated that in the South, of the 102,200 veterans receiving on-the-job training benefits, only 7,700 were blacks, although black veterans constituted about one-third of all Southern veterans.

Segregation and discrimination in the armed forces continued into the immediate postwar period. During the summer of 1945 the army directed all field commanders to prepare a report on their black units, including recommendations on postwar policy toward blacks. These reports revealed that most commanders clung to stereotyped racist concepts of black troops: "children at heart," "fine on parade but cowards in battle," "afraid of the dark," "won't obey orders." They drew the conclusion that blacks, because of inferior mental aptitudes and peculiar emotional qualities, were uniquely suited for labor duty and that "practical considerations required maintenance of the segregation and quota systems."

In October 1945 a board of officers under the direction of Lieutenant General Alvan C. Gillem, Jr., undertook a study of black participation in the war and in the peacetime army. In April 1946 the board submitted its report, *The Utilization of Negro Manpower in the Postwar Army*. Although it proposed increased opportunities for blacks within the service, it backed a quota system and separate black units. The report recommended the elimination of the all-black army division and the consolidation of smaller black units and white units into composite organizations—black platoons into white companies, black companies into white battalions, and black battalions into white regiments. Blacks would be assigned as individuals to special and overhead units that performed the housekeeping and administrative jobs of the army. This limited integration extended only to duty hours not to off-duty housing. Under the plan, blacks would serve in the postwar army on a ratio of one to ten and would be stationed at localities where community attitudes were most favorable; black officers would be accorded equal opportunities for advancement and assignment.

The War Department adopted the Gillem report and circularized all army commanders to acquaint them with the new regulations. However, it was condemned by most of the black press and some black leaders as a vehicle for continuing many forms of discrimination in the army. "A Negro American soldier is still first a Negro and then a soldier," complained *The Crisis*. Roy Wilkins wrote: "The basic policy is still jim crow units. Instead of having big jim crow units . . . we are to have nothing larger than jim crow regiments."

Although some steps were taken to implement the recommendations of the Gillem Board, most remained largely paper proposals. The sole recommendation that was implemented was the one calling for a quota system. After the war, the regular army initiated a recruiting campaign, offering a choice of branch of service and of theater of occupation to all those who would re-enlist or enlist for a three-year period. Thousands of black soldiers re-enlisted, and black recruits applied for entry into the service in large numbers, constituting within a year of war's end 25 per cent of all re-enlistments. Charles Bolte, writing in the *Survey Graphic*, offered an explanation for this phenomenon:

> The obvious interpretation of the high rate of Negro re-enlistment is not that the individual soldier loves Jim Crow military life more, but Jim Crow civilian America less. Properly understood, these re-enlistment figures are a penetrating comment on America's home-coming welcome to the Negro service man.

To discourage black enlistments, the army banned shipment of black troops to the European theater and, later in 1946, restricted enlistments to blacks who scored 99 on the AGCT, although whites were accepted with a score of 70.

When these restrictions failed to reduce black enlistments, the army in the summer of 1946 halted further enlistments because its black quota had been reached.

The suspension of black enlistments brought a concerted campaign by blacks and white liberals to reopen them. The United Negro and Allied Veterans of America pressed President Truman to rescind the order, and the American Veterans Committee protested that there had been "no quota on the origin of the men who were killed during the war." In 1947, when the proportion of blacks in the army had been reduced to 10 per cent, the discriminatory restrictions were lifted.

Some small improvements occurred in the navy, but most black seamen remained confined to the mess and related services. After V-J Day the Marine Corps announced that it would retain 2,880 blacks to work as anti-aircraft specialists, garrison forces, service troops, and stewards. In early 1947 the corps switched its policy and offered black Marines the choice of transfer to the steward's branch or discharge. During the immediate postwar years, the great majority of black personnel in the armed forces were still "largely excluded from professional and technical careers, and were shunted into unskilled and menial occupations."

Violent racial conflict, often producing bloodshed and death, also extended into the immediate postwar period. The revived Ku Klux Klan and other Southern white groups, confronted with a demand from returning black veterans for the right to register and vote, took steps to maintain rigid segregation. On July 20, 1946,

Macio Snipes, a veteran and the only black to vote in the Georgia primary in his district, was shot and killed as he sat on the porch of his home. Five days later a white mob ambushed and shot fatally two black veterans and their wives at a lonely spot near Monroe, Georgia. Harold Hinton, a *New York Times* reporter, wrote that the Ku Klux Klan had committed the murders to terrorize returning black veterans who "were getting out of their place."

Blacks and white liberals expressed shock and anger at the series of racial murders and at the government's ineffectiveness in dealing with them. In November 1946 many alienated black voters either backed the Republican candidates or neglected to vote, contributing to the off-year election defeat of the Democratic Party. Early in December 1946, not long after this setback, President Truman issued an executive order creating a Presidential civil rights committee to investigate and make recommendations to him on all aspects of racial discrimination. While the Presidential committee deliberated, blacks expressed concern over their status in the program of Universal Military Training then under Congressional consideration. On December 19, 1946, Truman appointed a nine-member Presidential Advisory Commission on Universal Training. Three months later Congress acceded to the Presidential request not to extend the Selective Service Act when it lapsed on March 31. On May 29 Truman's advisory commission submitted its report. The commission strongly endorsed UMT and vigorously opposed all segregation in a citizens' army: "Nothing could be more tragic for the future attitude of our people, and for the unity of our Nation, than a program in which our Federal Government forced our young manhood to live for a period of time in an atmosphere which emphasized or bred class or racial difference." Nevertheless, blacks were excluded from the experimental universal military training unit at Fort Knox.

When the universal military training bill was introduced in the House it did not (in deference to strong army opposition) contain a nonsegregation provision. Black leaders realized that only strong pressure would preclude segregation in any UMT plan enacted by Congress. In November 1947 A. Philip Randolph and Grant Reynolds, a New York State Commissioner of Correction, set up the Committee Against Jim Crow in Military Service and Training. It brought enthusiastic response in the black community. In late October 1947 Truman received the Civil Rights Advisory Commission's report, which strongly denounced discrimination and segregation in the armed forces. "Prejudice in any area is an ugly, undemocratic phenomenon," the report said, "but in the armed services, where all the men run the risk of death, it is especially repugnant." Among the numerous proposals was one calling for appropriate legislation and administrative action "to end immediately all discrimination and segregation based on race, color, or creed in the armed services."

In December 1947 Henry A. Wallace declared his Presidential candidacy on a third-party ticket, jeopardizing Truman's reelection in 1948. A month earlier, a confidential memorandum from a group of administration liberals, dealing with the politics of 1948, had been sent to the President by Special Counsel Clark M. Clifford. Civil Rights was given a prominent place in the proposed strategy, since black votes were deemed crucial to Truman's chances. The memo deemed the South "safely Democratic" and therefore "safely ignored." It advised that "the President go as far as he feels he possibly could go recommending measures to protect the rights of minority groups." "Unless there are new and real efforts," Clifford wrote, "the Negro bloc which . . . *does* hold the balance of power, will go Republican."

Early in 1948 Truman acted on the advice of the Clifford group. In a special message based upon the findings of his Civil Rights Commission, Truman urged Congress to end racial discrimination in a number of areas, and he announced that he had instructed the Secretary of Defense to eliminate discrimination in the armed services as rapidly as possible.

Truman's civil rights message and his instructions to the Secretary of Defense predictably aroused strong Southern resentment. Leading Southerners acted to push the administration in a conservative direction. As the Southern revolt gained strength steps were taken to pacify it. The administration, early in 1948, decided to delay issuance of an executive order against discrimination. Black leaders stridently opposed delay and pressed for immediate action.

On March 17 the President called for a resumption of the draft. Five days later several members of Randolph's committee met with Truman to insist that the draft bill include an antisegregation amendment. Randolph informed the President that blacks were in no mood "to shoulder a gun for democracy abroad so long as they are denied democracy here at home." The President was clearly unhappy with these remarks, and nothing was settled by the interview. Randolph then decided to press the issue before Congress. Testifying before the Senate Armed Services Committee on March 31, 1948, he warned:

> Today I would like to make clear . . . that the passage now of a Jim Crow draft may . . . result in mass civil disobedience. . . . This time Negroes will not take a Jim Crow draft lying down. . . . I personally pledge myself to counsel, aid and abet youth both white and Negro to quarantine any Jim Crow conscription system. . . . I shall call upon all veterans to join this civil disobedience movement.

Randolph's threat was received with mixed feelings in the black community, but both those who supported and those who disavowed civil disobedience agreed that Randolph had accurately described black resentment.

Military leaders responded to Randolph's threat and the angry criticisms emanating from the black community by restating the need for continued segregation. On April 2 General Dwight D. Eisenhower, appearing before the Senate Armed Services Committee, presented the army's position: "There is race prejudice in this country," he said. "When you pass a law to get somebody to like someone, you have trouble."

At the end of April, during a National Defense Conference on Negro Affairs held at the Pentagon, this position was more sharply defined. A delegation of black leaders met with Secretary of Defense Forrestal and armed services representatives to discuss establishment of a black advisory panel on race problems. Speaking for the black conferees, Lester Granger of the National Urban League warned that, unless the armed forces acted quickly to end segregation, "there will be a reaction among our Negro public resulting in irreparable damage to the national welfare." But Army Secretary Kenneth C. Royall informed the group of black leaders, "Any change must be made within the framework of segregation." This policy, he added, did not represent discrimination. The angry members of the black delegation refused to serve as advisers to the Defense Department and warned, "Our group is concerned with elimination of segregation, not its perpetuation."

Randolph and Reynolds set about organizing a civil disobedience campaign. At public meetings in Harlem, Randolph counseled young men to refuse induction into a segregated army. *Newsweek* reported that 71 per cent of black college students polled backed the idea. On June 7 an amendment to the draft bill introduced by Senator Richard Russell of Georgia to allow enlisted men to request service in military units of their own race came up for debate in the Senate. Southern spokesmen applauded the position taken by the army leaders and cited approvingly General Eisenhower's statement against integration in the military. The supporters of the amendment used the occasion to disparage the black soldier. Senator Burnet R. Maybank of South Carolina said: "The wars of this country have been won by white soldiers. . . . Negro soldiers have rendered their greatest service as cooks, drivers, maintenance men, mechanics and such positions for which they are well qualified." The Russell amendment was defeated. A similar fate befell two antisegregation amendments introduced by William Langer of North Dakota. The UMT proposal also went down to defeat. Finally, on June 22 Congress passed a Selective Service bill. As the army desired, it contained no prohibitions of segregation. On June 24 the President signed the bill.

Despite these setbacks, Randolph continued to oppose the segregated draft. On June 26 he announced the formation of a new organization—the League for Nonviolent Civil Disobedience Against Military Segregation, with Bayard Rustin as its executive secretary. Its purpose was to force the President to end segregation in the armed forces. Unless such an order was issued before the new draft law went into effect, the league "would work in the big East Coast cities in behalf of a campaign of civil disobedience, nonregistration and noninduction." Randolph pressed for immediate executive action and advised Truman that otherwise "Negro youth will have no alternative but to resist a law, the inevitable consequences of which would be to expose them to un-American brutality so familiar during the last war."

At their convention in Philadelphia in late June, the Republicans adopted a platform opposed "to the idea of racial segregation in the armed services of the United States." The Democratic Party platform committee meeting in July adopted the party's weak 1944 civil rights plank but did not go as far. A contingent of ADA liberals spearheaded by the young Mayor of Minneapolis, Hubert H. Humphrey, managed to push through on the floor of the convention a stronger plank calling for "equal treatment in the service and defense of our nation."

When the liberals emerged victorious, diehard Southerners bolted the party and formed a Dixiecrat Party, which strongly endorsed segregation. Wallace's Progressive Party adopted a strong civil rights plank, which demanded a "Presidential proclamation ending segregation and all forms of discrimination in the armed services."

Truman's advisers recognized that the Progressives' firm espousal of civil rights appealed strongly to black voters and insisted that action be taken to undercut their appeal. Immediately after the Democratic convention the two Presidential advisers on racial affairs, Phileo Nash and Clifford Ewing, urged Truman to implement the convention's civil rights plank immediately to forestall loss of the black vote. On July 26 he directed implementation "as rapidly as possible" of "equality of treatment and opportunity" in all the armed services without regard to race, color, religion, or national origin. The President's order, which required no Congressional sanction, further established a seven-man Presidential Commission to undertake a study of the rules, procedures, and practices governing the personnel policies of the armed services to determine how they might be altered or improved to implement the Presidential order.

Confusion immediately ensued as to the precise meaning of the executive order. Indeed, on the day the order was made public, the Washington correspondent of the *New York Times* reported that an unnamed federal official sympathetic to the aspirations of blacks had called attention to the fact that the order made no mention of ending segregation but dealt only with discrimination. This official was convinced that integration would be a long time coming to the army, for high-ranking officers were unalterably opposed to it. On the same day, army staff officers were reported to have stated that separate units would be retained since the order did not specifically ban segregation. On the following day, General Omar N. Bradley, Army Chief of Staff, while on an inspection tour of Fort Knox, was reported to have said: "The army is not out to make any social reform. The army will not put men of different races in the same companies. It will change that policy when the nation as a whole changes it."

Others complained that the order was ambiguously phrased and failed to specify precisely what it meant by equality of treatment and opportunity or when this would occur. Henry Wallace declared that the order said nothing, did nothing, and left "segregation intact." Black leaders and the black press shared his sentiment, leaving the suspicion that the order had been a maneuver to blunt Randolph's threat and Wallace's appeal.

At a press conference held three days after the order was issued, the President acted to meet rising criticism. When asked by a reporter, "Does your advocacy of equality of treatment and opportunity in the armed forces envision eventually the end of segregation?" the President replied "Yes."

Randolph remained unconvinced by the Presidential clarification. He continued to maintain that the order was "deliberately calculated to obscure" the issue and urged blacks not to be taken in by it. To dispel his skepticism, Senator J. Howard McGrath, chairman of the Democratic National Committee, met with Randolph and Reynolds and assured them on the President's behalf that it was "unquestionably" the intent of the executive order to eliminate segregation from the armed services and that the seven-man Presidential committee would "initiate its activities and functions on the basis of nonsegregation." Reassured, Randolph and Reynolds called off the civil disobedience campaign. Despite Randolph's objections, Rustin, along with the radical-pacifist wing of the civil disobedience league, decided to continue the campaign in order to press for a law unequivocally stating that "nonsegregation in military services is the national policy." Nevertheless, Donald Dawson, a White House aide, was able to note in a memo to Truman:

> Since your executive order was issued, all important opposition to the draft on the basis of the Army's race policy has disappeared. Philip Randolph and Grant Reynolds have withdrawn from their Committee Against Jim Crow, and only a few COs and other war resisters remain in the movement. . . . The Negro press, which had been conducting a vigorous campaign against the Army's racial policy, has now abandoned it.

In mid-September the President announced the composition of the enforcement commission. It was to be headed by Charles Fahy, a former United States Solicitor General and a native of Georgia, and included two black members, Lester Granger of the Urban League and John H. Sengstacke, editor and publisher of the Chicago *Defender*. This commission, subsequently known as the Fahy Committee, was to start functioning in January 1949, "assuming, of course, that Truman was still in the White House." Black voters went to the polls on Election Day in record numbers and gave Truman his critical margin of victory in California, Illinois, and Ohio.

Early in 1949 the Fahy Committee held the first of a series of hearings with representatives of the armed services who defended the strict separation of black and white units as the most effective way to insure equality of opportunity and facilities for black servicemen. The Air Force reported that it had submitted to the Secretary of Defense a program of integration calling for complete elimination of racial bias in determining personnel selection and allocation. While welcoming the Air Force's initiative toward full integration, the committee pointed out to the spokesmen of that branch that in an accompanying memorandum to the projected policy black commanding officers had been told: "Care should be taken to insure that a reasonably small number of Negro personnel is assigned to any individual white organization."

The committee felt that adherence to an arbitrary quota would inevitably perpetuate discrimination. The navy proudly defended its termination of discrimination and segregation following World War II. But here too committee members noted shortcomings in the implementation of the directive of February 1946. The Marine Corps still held to a policy of rigid segregation and had only one black among its more than 8,000 officers. Blacks made up only 5 per cent of total naval personnel. Some specialists and technicians had been trained and advanced without regard to color, but more than two-thirds of the blacks in the navy were still in the segregated stewards' branch. There were only five black officers on active duty, and the openings available to them were severely limited. Navy spokesmen agreed to make an effort to meet the committee's objections.

Following the initial hearing, a majority of the committee concluded that only an end to segregation would implement the executive order on equal opportunity. But, on the advice of Chairman Fahy, they agreed to await additional information before answer-

ing the army's contention that segregation did not preclude equality of treatment and opportunity. In subsequent testimony, the secretaries of the Navy and Air Force were firm in their opposition to
segregation and supported integration as a matter of policy. But
Secretary of the Army Royall presented a different picture. He argued that the army was not an instrument for social change. Under-
scoring the views of the generals, he argued that an end to segregation would seriously impair military efficiency. He repeated the old
saw that the two world wars had shown black troops to be inca-
pable of effective combat and "peculiarly qualified" for labor duties. He added that, since voluntary segregation prevailed in civilian
society, integration would undermine the army's capacity to
perform.

Despite criticism from committee members Royall insisted that
the army was implementing Presidential requirements of equal opportunity. On the heels of Royall's unyielding stand, the committee decided to challenge the army's contention that segregation
provided both equality of opportunity and efficient use of black
manpower. It initiated an investigation into army personnel practices under the Gillem policy.

While the committee was conducting its inquiry, the new Secretary of Defense, Louis Johnson, issued a directive to the service
secretaries in early April 1949 declaring that the policy of his department was to provide equality of treatment and opportunity
for all persons throughout the armed forces. Although black units
would continue to exist, qualified blacks were to be allowed "to fill
any type of position . . . without regard to race." The three service secretaries were instructed to submit plans for furthering these
objectives. At the same time, the Fahy Committee found that the
army, with its continued quotas and segregation, had barred blacks
from 198 of its 490 job specialties, denied them admission to army
training schools, and maintained black enrollment quotas in all
but 21 of 106 courses. Blacks in headquarter installations were generally confined to unskilled occupations. All this led to the conclusion that quotas and segregation added up to antiblack discrimination.

The army and navy responded to the Defense Secretary's directive with the assertion that army and navy policy already encompassed his proposed policies. The Air Force complied by disband-

ing the all-black 332d Fighter Wing and distributing its 2,000 officers and men among nonsegregated units. It set about breaking up the few small black support units and abandoned the 10 per cent quota on black enlistments. Qualified black personnel were eligible to fill any vacancy in the Air Force.

Secretary Johnson accepted the Air Force proposals but rejected those of the army and navy as inadequate. At this point the Fahy Committee stepped in to advise the two services on measures they might adopt to satisfy the Secretary's requirements. It recommended that the navy increase the number of black officers and the number of black enlisted men outside the stewards' branch. On June 7 Secretary Johnson approved the second reply of the navy, which contained proposals to encourage blacks to apply for NROTC, to permit men to transfer from the stewards' branch, and to eliminate separate Marine and navy basic training. The navy's announcement of its revised racial policy stated that "all personnel will be enlisted or appointed, trained, advanced or promoted, assigned duty and administered in all respects without regard to race."

The committee recommended that the army open all job classifications to qualified blacks, allow blacks to attend all schools, assign all soldiers on the basis of their training regardless of race, and abolish the 10 per cent black quota—proposals tantamount to ending segregation. In its second plan submitted to Johnson the army insisted that its current policies of assignment, segregation, and racial quotas served the best interests of black army personnel and the effectiveness of the army itself, noting that

> there is a growing concern among many senior officers of the Army that we are weakening to a dangerous degree the combat efficiency of the Army. These officers are familiar with the combat performance of Negro troops during war and feel that we have already gone too far in inserting colored organizations in white combat units.

Secretary Johnson rejected this response as unacceptable; there followed a long delay as the army and the committee struggled to develop an acceptable proposal. At that point Royall resigned and was replaced by Gordon Gray. When the army finally replied, it agreed to eliminate racial quotas from its schools and to open the full range of occupational specialties to all those qualified, regard-

less of race. Integrated assignment was limited to overhead posi-
tions or to units experiencing shortages of skilled personnel. The
Secretary of Defense, much to the chagrin of the Fahy Committee,
accepted the army's limited concession, but Gray discovered late in
October a military order rescinding even these changes, and in
November he reissued the original proposal.

By the end of November the army had fully incorporated its
proposals on training and assignment into a new policy for black
troops. But the committee held that opening the schools to blacks
was meaningless unless assignment restrictions were lifted. The
army finally agreed to make assignments solely on the basis of ability and held commanders responsible for enforcement of the order.
The quota system remained intact.

The Washington correspondent of the *New York Times* viewed
this development as "a step toward ending the Army's strict segregation." But A. Philip Randolph, in a letter to the *New York
Times*, disagreed. "Obviously, the Army does not intend to abolish
its racist quota system or its segregation," he said. "Under the order
the only . . . Negroes to be integrated into white units are 'scarce
specialists.' . . . The bitter reality remains that Jim Crow in the
Army is still with us and going strong."

That there was still strong opposition in the army to integration
was made clear early in February when an army board submitted a
report headed "Utilization of Negro Manpower." Like the Gillem
Board, the generals supported on practical grounds the maintenance of segregation and the quota system. However, in the early
spring of 1950 President Truman and Secretary Gray agreed to a
discontinuation of the racial quota, with the understanding that
the army might restore it if a disproportionate number of blacks
were enrolled. Although gaps remained, the Fahy Committee could
point, when it went out of existence in the spring of 1950, to significant gains. Full integration had not been achieved, but the walls
of segregation had been breached.

Time magazine, in an article entitled "Ahead of the Country,"
said that what the committee had accomplished "amounted to the
greatest change in service custom since the abandonment of the
cat-o'-nine-tails." But fuller integration had to await the coming of
the Korean War.

During the first months of the Korean War, which lasted from

June 25, 1950, to July 27, 1953, integration was extended to training units in the United States and combat units in Korea. In both cases integration was effected at the individual level as experience convinced military commanders that black soldiers performed more efficiently in integrated units.

The rate of desegregation accelerated rapidly throughout army units until, by 1954, full integration of black soldiers into previously all-white units was completed, and the last Jim Crow unit had been disbanded. There were several explanations for such a marked departure from previous army policy. The elimination of the quota system in March 1950 encouraged rapid increases in black enlistments. Black units were unable to absorb the new manpower, even as many white units remained below strength. The Personnel Division of the General Staff proposed the creation of new black units, but the Secretary of the Army rejected this proposal "for the moment." In August 1950, at Fort Jackson, South Carolina, the post commander successfully integrated a number of training units to meet the large daily influx of black recruits, and soon gradual integration extended to all army basic training centers.

Simultaneously, black personnel were integrated into white units in Korea. Traditional army policy kept black troops mainly in service units, but such units quickly proved unable to absorb black replacements. Field commanders, confronted with increasing manpower shortages resulting from white battle losses, decided to employ the surplus of black replacements. Some military commanders were also convinced that segregation was undermining military effectiveness and that all-black units were not performing to full efficiency. *Ebony* magazine maintained, "The record of the Negro soldier in Korea is no different than the record of American soldiers generally. Everything good or bad that can be said about U.S. soldiers generally can be said about Negro soldiers specifically." The only difference was that race did not figure as the explanation for the poor performance of white units. It should also be noted that the percentage of blacks drafted was in excess of their percentage in the total population. The army, which received nearly all of the draftees, included 219,128 black conscripts—12.8 per cent of the total. Moreover, the final casualty rate among blacks was twice as high as among whites. A black veteran writing on "The Korean Conflict" noted that, "while blacks and whites fought, slept, and ate together in Korea," unequal and discriminatory treatment of blacks never-theless remained essentially intact. Blacks were largely excluded from the Officer Corps, service schools for advanced training, and other specialized functions, but received the most arduous assign-ments. "Blacks were largely concentrated in front-line combat assignments [i.e., infantry] and services and supply functions. The risks and tasks were heavy, but promotional opportunities were minuscule."

In particular, court-martial actions against black officers and men in Korea continued to disturb blacks. In the Baltimore *Afro-American*, James L. Hicks reported from Tokyo that eleven mem-bers of the all-black 24th Infantry had been convicted of "miscon-duct before the enemy" and sentenced to long terms at hard labor. Hicks said he was not permitted to talk to the men, who were under heavy guard. On November 17, the NAACP announced that a number of convicted black soldiers had applied for legal assis-tance. One soldier urged an investigation into what he termed "mass persecution." "Please give us your assistance," he pleaded. "We are being court-martialed and sentenced to imprisonment for life—not one or two of us, but in groups of fours and fives." Thurgood Mar-shall, special counsel for the NAACP, declared that the number one task of that organization was the defense of black military per-sonnel in Korea.

On January 11, 1951, with permission from General MacArthur, Thurgood Marshall spent five weeks in Japan and Korea investi-gating the courts-martial of black soldiers. In a subsequent article in *The Crisis* entitled "Summary Justice: The Negro GI in Korea," Marshall argued that the convicted black soldier in Korea was "a victim of racial bias." In almost every instance, defense counsel had not had adequate time to prepare his case. Usually the men had been rushed from foxholes to the courts-martial and allowed only fifteen or twenty minutes with the court-appointed lawyers before the trials began. Of four trials in which the men received life sen-tences, he disclosed that one lasted only forty-two minutes, another forty-four minutes, and the other two fifty minutes. As many as four cases were tried in one day. He added: "I have seen many mis-carriages of justice in my capacity as head of the NAACP legal de-partment. But even in Mississippi a Negro will get a trial longer than 42 minutes, if he is fortunate enough to be brought to trial."

Marshall further pointed out that from August to October 1950 sixty black and eight white soldiers had been accused of violating the 75th article of war—misbehavior before the enemy. Of these, thirty-two blacks were convicted and received sentences ranging from death and life imprisonment down to five years, while only two white soldiers were convicted and sentenced to a five-year and a three-year term. He noted that in many instances the officers of the 24th Infantry were white Southerners "who had brought their prejudices with them" when assigned to that all-black unit. Marshall then pointedly asked:

> Was it a coincidence that all the commanding officers who approved charges were white, that the entire staffs of the Inspector General's office and of the trial Judge Advocate's office were 100 per cent white? Was it also purely coincidental that one week before my visit to Korea a Negro was added to each of these two staffs?

Marshall reported that he had found the convicted men in a state of despair that precluded an adequate defense. Even men "with air-tight defenses" made no effort to defend themselves. When asked why they had neglected to do so, he received the uniform response: "It wasn't worth trying. We knew when we went in there we were all going to come out the same way. Each one of us hoped and prayed we would only get life." Marshall finally noted that the NAACP had had sentences reduced in twenty of the thirty-nine cases they had been asked to defend.

In midsummer of 1951 the army announced the integration of all black soldiers in the Far East. This announcement was largely the result of a "new and highly secret operation" conducted in behalf of the army. In March 1951 the Department of the Army asked that the Operations Research Office of Johns Hopkins University study the effects of integration and segregation on the army. With the code name "Project Clear," it involved surveys in Korea and Japan and at ten training stations in the United States. While the army awaited results, General Matthew B. Ridgway, the new Far Eastern Commander, asked, in April 1951, for permission to integrate all blacks throughout his command. Three months later, the General Staff approved Ridgway's request. This measure was favorably received by blacks, but the black press noted that segregation still prevailed outside the Far East. The *New York Times* made the same point:

Equality of treatment, which rules out segregation, has been for three years a policy in our armed forces. It has not been fully carried out. . . . The sooner every soldier is rated solely according to his abilities, qualities, and achievements, the better.

The final report of Project Clear further stimulated integration. In its investigation of troops in Korea, the research team found that integrated black manpower was more effective than segregated units; 85 per cent of the officers reported that blacks in mixed units performed in battle about the same as white soldiers. Where the contact of officers with integrated units was greatest, their attitudes toward blacks was most favorable. The report concluded that integration had been just as successful in the United States. White soldiers accepted integration as the army's way of doing things and justified it in terms of military efficiency. Asked about their preferences in army assignment policy, most blacks said they would prefer assignment without regard to color. Project Clear emphasized that mixed units functioned best with 80 to 85 per cent white and 15 to 20 per cent black personnel. One month after the final report was submitted, the last stage of integration of army units within the United States was put into effect. In October 1951, the personnel of the 24th Regiment were integrated, and several other all-black units were split up during the late summer and early fall of 1951.

By late 1951 integration lagged only among U.S. troops stationed in France and Germany. There, General Thomas C. Handy, a Virginian who commanded the U.S. Army in Europe, and most of his staff were hostile to the change in policy. In March 1952 a correspondent of the Pittsburgh *Courier* reported that all army installations he had visited in Europe were segregated. Finally, in April 1952, in response to Pentagon pressure, Handy issued an order stating: "The Department of the Army has directed this command to initiate a . . . program of racial integration."

All these steps took place without incurring significant vocal opposition from the many influential Southern legislators who held key positions on the Congressional military committees. The legislators remained silent, evidently convinced by the arguments of leading military figures and civilian officials that integration would not only improve military efficiency but also reduce the battlefield casualties among whites.

The issue of desegregation in the armed forces was publicly aired in the Presidential campaign of 1952. President Truman, seeking to aid Adlai E. Stevenson in holding the Northern black vote, delivered a major address in Harlem on October 11, in which he criticized Eisenhower's civil rights record. He declared:

> While the Republican candidate was in uniform, he told the Armed Services Committee of the Senate that a certain amount of segregation is necessary in the army. You and I know that this is morally wrong. And what is more, it's even militarily wrong.

The next day Eisenhower claimed that he had taken the first steps toward integrating the army during the Battle of the Bulge in World War II. "As President, I will see to it that we end all discrimination . . . in the armed forces," he pledged.

In September 1953 Washington announced that desegregation in the army was ahead of schedule, with more than 90 per cent of army blacks serving in mixed units. Official figures showed that the number of all-black units had been reduced from 385 in June 1950 to 88 in August 1953, with the army pledged to integrate the remaining all-black units. In October 1954 the army met its pledges. The Air Force had abolished late in 1952 its last all-black unit, while in mid-1952 the Marine Corps had integrated its last two all-black units.

Navy stewards were still recruited almost solely from among blacks. Of the approximately 23,000 blacks in the navy in March 1953, almost one-half were in the stewards' branch. During a House debate on defense funds in June 1953, Representative Adam Clayton Powell, Jr. blasted the navy for its discriminatory practices. Powell accused the navy of a "modernized, twentieth century form of slavery." He charged:

> One-half of the Negroes now serving in the United States Navy are serving as mess men, nothing more than manservants to the Admiral clique. . . . It is in absolute defiance of the President's orders. . . . Intelligent, ambitious Negroes are boycotting the United States Navy because they are not interested in making the world safe for democracy by shining shoes.

Finally, in March 1954 the navy discontinued its separate recruitment of stewards and opened its specialty groups to all seamen. In the same year Defense Department administrators desegregated civilian facilities at Southern army and navy bases and eliminated segregation in post-operated schools for dependents of military and civilian personnel.

Black military personnel actively pushed the changes, as indicated by the experience of Representative William L. Clay of Missouri. Drafted the day after his graduation from Saint Louis University in 1953, he was stationed at Fort McClellan, near Anniston, Alabama. When Clay and other black soldiers wanted to swim they were told that the two swimming pools were reserved for National Guard training units, although white military personnel on the base used them without interference. When dances were held at the NCO club, it was placed off limits for blacks. Post barbershops denied service to blacks except on Saturdays, when a black barber imported from Anniston gave them haircuts.

Clay organized black soldiers to protest the discrimination and boycott the barbershop. After three months of boycott, the colonel threatened to discipline Clay and ordered him to get a haircut. Clay explains what followed:

> I didn't refuse the order, I merely refused to have a haircut on Saturdays. I went to the barbershop Monday through Friday each day. The colonel, after about a week of this, was more adamant about his intention to court-martial me. At this point I decided to give real grounds for such action.

Clay, together with his wife, his children, and some of their friends, "crashed the gates of the all-white swimming pool and went swimming." Other black soldiers blocked the doors of the NCO club. The black press publicized these events. Although Clay was quickly transferred to another camp, the protest continued until "most of the racial barriers at Fort McClellan came down."

By the end of 1954 segregation had been officially eliminated from the internal structure of the active military forces. The *New York Times* called the racial integration of the armed forces "one of the biggest stories of the twentieth century. *Per se* it warrants no lesser description."

But there remained areas, both on and off military installations, where segregation and discrimination persisted. White servicemen at some Southern bases were allowed to earn supplementary income as clerks, cashiers, and waiters, while blacks were confined to jobs as dishwashers, busboys, and janitors. NCO clubs remained segregated at some posts. White junior hostesses were invited to base dances and transported to installations, while no effort was made to bring in black junior hostesses. Buses enforced a segregated seating pattern immediately upon leaving a military installation. Taxi companies carried white passengers to and from the base and denied the same service to blacks. In response to public pressure, black members were removed from bands, choruses, marching units, or other military groups representing the installation at off-post functions. At some bases, black servicemen were segregated in funeral details. Post facilities were made available to local segregated athletic teams. At some bases no black MPs were assigned to the base gate to avoid provoking local whites. Black soldiers traveling off base were often obliged to eat in military vehicles while whites were served in segregated restaurants.

Military housing was free from racial discrimination but accommodated only a small fraction of married service personnel. In nearly all parts of the country married black servicemen living off the base encountered discrimination in private and public housing. They were compelled to live in dilapidated, expensive housing distant from the post. A *Harper's* magazine article described the plight of a typical black serviceman:

> On his way to the base each morning, Sergeant Smith passes an attractive air-conditioned, FHA-financed housing project. It was built for service families. Its rents are little more than the Smiths pay for their shack. And there are half-a-dozen vacancies, but none for Negroes.

Consistently, the government failed to include nondiscrimination clauses when it leased property for occupancy by servicemen. Generally, military housing referral services were operated "in conformity with the racially restrictive preferences of private landlords." A proposal was made to strike from the Air Force service lists homes that refused to rent to black airmen and officers, just as homes refusing to rent to service families with children were not listed, but the proposal was never approved. According to a navy official, such a course would result in an end to all available off-post housing.

This situation was not confined to the South. The experience of a black pilot stationed at Topsham AFB, Maine, is worthy of notice. With 120 missions in World War II and eighteen years of service, this officer could not find housing for himself and his family in the nearby town of Brunswick. Real estate agents advised him that they could not rent to him. The local newspaper, the *Brunswick Record*, hearing of his plight, ran an editorial about it. After the editorial appeared the officer received fifteen apartment offers, and the editorial was chosen by the New England Weekly Newspaper Association as the best editorial to appear in nearly 100 New England weekly papers during 1961. The newspaper commented: "While the *Record* takes pride in the award, it came with bitter irony during a week when another Negro airman reported he too was turned away from Brunswick living quarters for himself and his family."

Black service families faced problems in educating their children. Since 1954 schools on military bases had been desegregated, but few posts had such schools. As a consequence, the children of most military men, whether living on or off base, were sent to neighboring civilian school systems, which were reimbursed by the Department of Defense. In the South, for years after the Supreme Court decision of 1954, the great majority of the children of black servicemen attended racially segregated schools. Like the housing available to black servicemen, the black schools were frequently substandard, with rundown buildings and equipment, obsolete textbooks, and overcrowding. As it did with housing, the federal government subsidized the construction, maintenance, and operation of all-white schools with federal "impacted area" payments. A Pulaski County, Arkansas, school built with $650,000 of federal funds and attended only by service children refused to admit black children. The 1,613 children of white servicemen stationed at Fort Lee, Virginia, attended the new Prince George County public school, for which the federal government reimbursed the county; the 210 children of black servicemen were transported by bus to black schools in the next county. Federal payments were made for the education of both black and white children of servicemen, but the Prince George County school board in turn paid the school board of the neighboring county for the schooling of the black children.

In March 1962 the Secretary of Health, Education, and Welfare ruled that beginning in September 1963 segregated schools would not be considered "suitable" and would run the risk of losing federal financial assistance. In response to this ruling, fifteen school districts agreed to accept all children of servicemen, black and white, residing on post. By September 1963 only twenty-six of the 242 affected Southern school districts had met the requirements of the HEW ruling. In addition, the ruling benefited only those children of servicemen living on base, who constituted only 10 per cent of all military dependents in the South. In 1963 the federal government was still paying millions of dollars in subsidies to racially segregated schools, and federal funds also paid for the construction of new segregated schools in the South. Many black servicemen sent their families home to avoid penalizing their children.

Black servicemen stationed in the South were denied access to extension courses at nearby white universities, although the same schools received substantial tuition payments for registered white servicemen. Shopping and recreational establishments ringing military institutions in the South and in some parts of the North often refused to accommodate black servicemen. The *Shopper's Guide*, distributed on base, might advertise "white customers only, please." USO clubs often operated on a segregated basis. Black military personnel fared no better when they tried to use public accommodations outside the black sections of off-base communities. Hotels and motels, taverns and restaurants, movies, plays and concerts, bowling alleys, skating rinks, swimming pools, and beaches were closed to black military personnel, their wives, and their families throughout the South and in parts of the North. In one Alabama installation, foreign black military personnel being trained at the base were given "passports" so that they might travel freely throughout surrounding communities without being subjected to exclusionary practices or harassment.

Base commanders generally refused to challenge discriminatory practices inflicted on service personnel in off-post communities. The armed forces maintained relations with communities near bases through committees made up of high-ranking officers and civilian leaders drawn from local government officials, officers of the Chambers of Commerce, and other business representatives. Black community leaders were not represented on the committees, nor did commanders select black personnel to represent the base. The committees rarely discussed problems of discrimination against black servicemen.

In June 1961 the Department of Defense took the first step toward coping with off-post discrimination problems. A directive was issued to all branches of the service instructing commanders to develop integrated off-post facilities for their men and to use their "community relations committees" for this purpose. However, two years later, the Kennedy Committee on Equal Opportunity in the Armed Forces reported:

> The pattern which the Committee has observed is clearly one of inaction in the face of serious discrimination affecting the morale and military efficiency of members of their commands. . . . To all Negroes these community conditions are a constant reminder that the society they are prepared to defend is a society that deprecates their right to full participation as citizens.

In July 1963 Secretary of Defense Robert S. McNamara reacted with a servicewide directive. It made local commanders responsible for fostering equal treatment for servicemen and their dependents both off and on military installations. In extreme cases, businesses or communities discriminating against black servicemen might be "declared off limits" to all servicemen. The Secretary added that this should be done only with the prior approval of the Secretary of the service involved, and he rejected the committee's recommendation that military bases be closed where discrimination was prevalent. Subsequently McNamara asked the services for their plans to combat discrimination and created an Assistant Secretary of Defense for Civil Rights to oversee such programs.

Southern Congressmen reacted angrily, attacking the use of the military to combat segregation as "economic blackmail in its rawest form" and "a direct invasion of local affairs." The House Armed Services Committee threatened an investigation of the Pentagon's race policies. Newspapers in the South and "high-ranking military officers" joined the opposition. Nonetheless, the Department of Defense ordered a nondiscrimination clause included in leases for servicemen's housing and accepted only listings open to all personnel. Another memorandum ordered commanders not to participate in course offerings at segregated schools, and still another denied military units the authority to participate in segregated functions.

Despite all, however, the Southern protests did succeed in "slowing down Mr. McNamara's drive," and the next few years saw little progress toward resolving the problems confronting black servicemen outside the gates.

In its final report, issued in December 1964, the Equal Opportunity Committee, headed by Gerhard Gesell, found that race discrimination in public accommodations and housing near military bases continued in the United States and abroad. It concluded that there was "a spirit of retaliatory hostility among American Negro troops" and urged base commanders to eliminate discrimination affecting soldiers off base.

Equally objectionable to blacks was the difficulty they faced within the service in achieving advancement into the skilled and semiskilled occupations. Few blacks were found in the lower-grade NCO positions and fewer still in the higher NCO and officer ranks. Blacks were underrepresented in the officers corps of all services. In 1962 only 1.2 per cent of the Air Force officers and fewer than 1 per cent of the navy and Marine officers were black. The percentage of black officers in the army was only 3.2. Moreover, most of these were lieutenants and captains. In 1962 the only black general officer was a major general in the Air Force, Benjamin O. Davis, Jr. The highest ranking black officers in the army were six colonels; in the navy, three commanders and seventeen lieutenant commanders; and in the Marines, seven captains. The Gesell Committee noted that the personnel folders reviewed by promotion boards contained photographs of the officers and in some of the services included forms with racial designations, observed that very few black officers served on these boards, and concluded: "So long as promotion selection is made primarily by white officers, questions as to the impartiality of these boards will continue to arise."

Although over 90 per cent of the National Guard's financial support came from the federal government, ten Southern states excluded blacks from its ranks as late as 1962, while other states maintained segregated units. Segregated units were also found in the Armed Forces Reserves of some states. In April 1962 the Under Secretary of Defense directed the abolition of the remaining segregated reserve units. Twelve weeks later, the Pentagon announced: "Such all-Negro units in the reserves as were found to be in existence, for whatever reason, have been integrated." By 1964 most of the states had removed their formal restrictions and provided for at least token integration of their National Guard units. By accepting a limited number of blacks, the Southern states were able to retain federal funding for their Guard units. One author on the subject declared in 1965:

> There is still segregation in the Armed Services of the United States of America; still inequality of treatment and opportunity for Negro servicemen. Negroes still experience unequal treatment and segregation in the National Guard (especially in Alabama and Mississippi, where only token integration exists). And, in addition, much larger opportunities are needed in the Service Academies . . . before they can claim to be free from racial bias.

Significant gains had been made, but the broadening Vietnam War was to place new strains on the military. The lessening of discriminatory practices had not satisfied blacks but rather had raised their expectations.

9

The Vietnam War and Black Servicemen

Since 1954 the history of the relationship of black servicemen to the armed forces follows a clearly distinguishable pattern. As the numbers of black soldiers, sailors, and Marines increased, particularly in the course of this country's heightened involvement in Vietnam, and as growing numbers of black troops demonstrated that they had no intention of passively accepting any forms of racism and discrimination in the services, the military authorities finally realized that a failure on their part to act positively threatened the very functioning of the military machine.

But each time they reacted to a particular outburst or crisis by appointing a commission or issuing a directive, they found their measures frustrated by the failure of lower-level commanders to implement them save in the most mechanical fashion. Repeatedly, the heads of the military establishment and of the government itself acknowledged the need for eliminating discriminatory practices in the services and promulgated orders seeking to achieve this goal, only to find within a year or two that "the more things changed, the more they remained the same."

The Vietnam period has been characterized by black servicemen's recognition that, when discrimination in its more blatant forms ended, it was replaced, just as in society as a whole, by a "new racism . . . more subtle, although no less immoral, than the more overt examples of bigotry, which have become less common in recent years." The persistence of the "new racism," as well as the black serviceman's reaction to it, has frustrated those in the military commands who genuinely seek to make the armed services the democratic institutions that both our times and our society require.

In 1954, 7 per cent of the soldiers in the U.S. Army were black. But during the post-Korean reduction of army strength black personnel declined more rapidly than white. In 1957 and 1958 alone, blacks accounted for more than 40 per cent of the new reduction in army personnel. However, ten years later blacks constituted 12 per cent of total army personnel, which approximated the percentage of blacks in the total population.

As a result of the escalation of the Vietnam War, draft calls began to increase rapidly in 1965. A year later, nearly 400,000 men were inducted. As in the Korean War, blacks were drafted out of proportion to their numbers in the total civilian population. Since 1966 blacks have constituted almost 16 per cent of all draftees. This disproportion existed even though proportionally more blacks, primarily because of their inability to meet the armed forces' minimal educational standards, were rejected for military service than whites.

Almost twice as many whites were rejected for medical reasons as blacks. The Surgeon General attributed this disparity first to the ignorance of lower-class youths of their physical defects, their limited exposure to medical care, and the paucity of medical records on which rejection might be based; and second, to the greater knowledge of middle-class youths about medical deferment requirements.

Understandably a much greater percentage of blacks than whites were drafted. A 1964 study revealed that only 18.8 per cent of eligible whites were drafted, compared with 30.2 per cent of blacks. And in 1967, 64 per cent of eligible blacks were drafted, whereas the figure for whites was only 31 per cent.

The primary cause for this discrepancy was the difficulty blacks had in qualifying for deferment. Deferments were granted to undergraduates, to graduate students until 1968, and to those engaged in critical occupations. In virtually every instance, these criteria benefited whites primarily. Even in hardship and dependency deferments, more than twice as many whites as blacks qualified. Many more white youths than blacks took advantage of reserve and officer training programs and of service in the National Guard in order to avoid the draft. Small wonder, then, that one observer characterized the draft system as one that provided "escape hatches for middle class whites that simply didn't exist for poor whites or blacks."

On several occasions after 1965, the armed forces' educational standards were lowered to induct previously rejected blacks. Late in August 1966 the Pentagon launched Project 100,000 to induct men who had previously been rejected. Defense Secretary McNamara declared that this project was intended to assist educationally and economically deprived young men. Once in the service, these men were to benefit from a special training program to give them an opportunity to learn a trade. Pentagon officials later acknowledged that the program was simply to enlarge the military manpower pool.

Of the small percentage of Selective Service registrants who were conscientious objectors, the overwhelming majority were white. Most of the traditional pacifist churches were white, and there was an almost complete lack of draft-counseling facilities for blacks. Few black students, unlike their white counterparts, had the opportunity to develop the philosophical and procedural sophistication required to gain CO status.

As in World War II, black religious objectors experienced great difficulty in obtaining CO status. The most widely publicized case was that of Muhammad Ali, world heavyweight boxing champion. As a Black Muslim, he contended that army service would violate his religious beliefs. His refusal to be inducted and his subsequent indictment led the World Boxing Association, in April 1967, to withdraw its recognition of him as the heavyweight champion. In June 1967 he was convicted and sentenced to five years in prison and a $10,000 fine for refusing to be inducted into the armed forces.

Blacks were underrepresented on local draft boards. For example, of 17,123 local board members in 1967, only 261, or 1.5 per cent, were black. This represented an increase of 11 in twenty-five years. Not a single black served on a draft board in Alabama, Arkansas, Louisiana, or Mississippi. Efforts to increase the number of black local board members resulted by June 1970 in a rise to 1,265 out of a total of 18,968, or 6.6 per cent. And in December 1970 Selective Service announced the appointment of "the first Negro ever to be appointed a Director of Selective Service in one of the fifty states."

Between 1968 and 1970 occupational, graduate student, under-graduate student, and fatherhood deferments were abolished. None-theless, blacks still constituted 16 per cent of the draftees in 1970.

Once in the service, blacks were assigned to low-skill combat units. As of December 1965 almost 27 per cent of black soldiers were assigned to the infantry, compared to less than 18 per cent of white soldiers. A reporter of the *Baltimore Sun* noted that "the ghetto man's education points him to the rice paddies." Dispropor-tionate black representation in combat units led to correspondingly high casualty rates. In 1967, 20 per cent of all army fatalities were black.

Nonetheless, during the mid-1960's most black military person-nel and civilians had a decidedly favorable opinion of the armed forces. They considered the military establishment the most com-pletely integrated segment of American society and the one that provided the best career opportunity for black men.

One indication of the attraction that a military career held for blacks was their re-enlistment rates, which were at least twice as high as whites in the Air Force, navy, and Marines, and about three times as high in the army. Jack Moscowitz, Deputy Assistant Sec-retary of Defense for Civil Rights, pointed to the high re-enlistment rate for blacks and declared: "That uniform gives prestige and sta-tus to a guy who has been 100 years on the back burner."

But others gave far different reasons for the disproportionately high re-enlistment rate of blacks. It was prompted, they insisted, by economic factors, such as the "re-up" (re-enlistment) bonus, which varied from $900 to $1,400, and the difficulty discharged black servicemen faced in finding civilian employment.

Blacks tended to volunteer for front-line combat duty and other hazardous assignments at a higher rate than whites. They made up more than 25 per cent of high-risk Marine line companies and élite army units, such as the airborne and air cavalry units, which were the first sent to trouble spots. Black participation reached as high as 60 per cent. These units attracted blacks with their extra pay for combat service, the bonus pay of $55 a month given to paratroop-ers, and the greater promotion opportunities. Front-line duty and élite combat service had the further virtue of imparting status, cer-tification of masculinity, and physical toughness. "Prestige units, combat units," wrote one correspondent from Vietnam in 1967, "enable the young Negro soldier to prove to himself and in his mind to others that he is a man among men."

During the first years of large-scale combat involvement in Vietnam, reports repeatedly stressed the outstanding performance of blacks in the field. Those reports were especially significant because of the long-standing military view that blacks were unfit for combat. The *New York Times* reported in May 1966: "Vietnam gives the lie to the official policy of prejudice by the military establishment in two world wars."

This view was not confined to the press. General William C. Westmoreland, the South Carolinian commander of U.S. troops in Vietnam, unstintingly praised the black soldiers under his command. Before South Carolina's General Assembly, he praised the black soldier as "courageous on the battlefield, proficient, and a possessor of technical skills."

Some even viewed the high casualty rate among blacks as a constructive development. When Lieutenant Colonel George Shaffer, one of the highest-ranking black officers in the army, was asked about it, he answered: "I feel good about it. Not that I like bloodshed, but the performance of the Negro in Vietnam tends to offset the fact that the Negro wasn't considered worthy of being a front-line soldier in other wars."

Reporters for newspapers, magazines, and television alike sent back glowing accounts of the harmonious race relations that existed in the integrated fighting forces. Close living and the common sharing of dangers, they claimed, had cemented friendships and mutual respect between whites and blacks. The *New York Times* reported in 1967: "The American ground forces are almost free of racial tension, and most soldiers—Negro and white—appear proud of this." The fact that, once off the battlefield, blacks and whites continued to congregate in separate groups was attributed to personal choice rather than to imposed segregation.

Correspondents reported that they found little resentment among black servicemen over the draft and no feeling that blacks were carrying an undue share of the American load in Vietnam. Rather, they expressed the view that they were there to serve their country, that the war was justified, and that American shortcomings in the area of civil rights should in no way affect their role. "With all the inadequacies and imperfections," a black infantry officer was reported as saying, "the United States still offers more individual rights than any other country. It's still worth dying for." Finally, black servicemen were generally nonviolent on civil rights issues. Moderate rights leaders were said to rate highest with them, while Black Power and black nationalism were "just as universally scorned."

In 1966 the Student Non-Violent Coordinating Committee (SNCC), the Congress of Racial Equality (CORE), and Dr. Martin Luther King's Southern Christian Leadership Conference (SCLC) joined the antiwar movement, denounced the war in Vietnam, and called for its end. Up until his assassination in April 1968, Dr. King spoke out against the war with increasing sharpness. He expressed the sentiments of many black leaders when he wrote in 1967:

> We are taking the young black men who have been crippled by our society and sending them 8,000 miles away to guarantee the liberties in Southeast Asia which they have not found in Southwest Georgia and East Harlem. So we have been repeatedly faced with the cruel irony of watching Negro and white boys on TV screens as they kill and die together for a nation that has been unable to seat them together in the same school. So we watch them in brutal solidarity burning the huts of a poor village, but we realize that they could never live on the same block in Detroit.

Black critics of the war charged that it drained resources desperately needed to cope with the deteriorating situation of blacks at home. "We have to put an end to that war because that war is blowing up our future," said the Reverend Andrew Young, Executive Vice-President of SCLC.

War opponents saw it as an indictment of American society that many young blacks had nowhere but in the military to look for economic security or career and status fulfillment. Finally, they argued that America, not Vietnam, was the black man's battleground. Thomas A. Johnson, a black reporter, wrote in the *New York Times*: "This is the first time in the history of American wars that national Negro figures are not urging black youths to take up arms in support of American policy to improve the lot of the black man in the United States."

Some leaders, like NAACP Executive Director Roy Wilkins, held that foreign policy was not a proper sphere for public criticism. They felt that the involvement of blacks in the antiwar movement would weaken their fight for equal rights at home.

In 1969 a *Newsweek* poll of black opinion found that a majority of blacks no longer believed that the military gave black youth a better break than they could expect in civilian life. Blacks, it reported, now regarded Vietnam "as their own particular incubus— a war that depletes their young manhood and saps the resources available for healing their ills at home."

These fundamental changes in the black protest movement had a far-reaching effect on the armed forces. Suddenly the almost uncritical picture of contented black servicemen and harmonious race relations was drastically altered. Reports by correspondents during the late 1960's stressed the change in attitude among a perceptible number of black servicemen both abroad and at home. *Time* magazine reported: "These men are a new generation of black soldiers. Unlike the veterans of a year or two ago, they are immersed in black awareness and racial pride." Although the military ascribed this development to attitudes blacks brought with them into the service from civilian society, one observer insisted: "Despite command pronouncements to the contrary . . . most of the rise of black consciousness within the armed forces seems to have occurred after service entry rather than as a spillover from civilian-acquired values."

Traditionally blacks had demanded complete equality of treatment within the armed forces—a demand which had been equated with integration and with the idea that blacks should be treated exactly the same as whites. Now, just as this demand seemed close to fulfillment, black servicemen were demanding an official recognition of their distinctive life-style and culture. But, as always, of course, they were simply reflecting changes in the larger black community and its consciousness.

The new dimension reflected itself in self-imposed separation, especially off the job, and in displays of racial pride and solidarity, along with quick reactions to what they felt were racial slights, acts of discrimination, or racist behavior, whether conscious or unconscious. Many black servicemen insisted on the right to wear "Afro" hair styles and to listen to "soul" music in mess halls and clubs. They read militant black literature and articulated views "identifiable with Eldridge Cleaver and Malcolm X." They also took to wearing amulets and medallions symbolizing their pride in their culture and their determination to defend themselves. White pin-ups were replaced by black pinups. Black servicemen greeted each other with an upraised clenched fist, with "fifty-seven varieties of black power handshakes," and with the rhetoric of "brother-me" and "nation-tie." On many posts they formed their own groups, planned strategies to cope with their problems, and registered their complaints in a group. Increasingly, they spoke of their responsibility and loyalty to their black brothers and sisters "in the civilian community who are suffering discrimination." They increasingly dismissed many black military career personnel as "Uncle Toms" or as "oreos"—black outside and white inside. And, most significantly, they increasingly questioned whether they should be fighting in Vietnam at all.

A further reflection of this trend was the severe drop in black re-enlistments, from 66.5 per cent in 1966 to 31.7 per cent in 1967. This decline overshadowed a decrease among white soldiers during the same period from 20 per cent to 12.8 per cent. Re-enlistment rates reached a new low for the black soldier in 1970 when 87.2 per cent of those eligible refused re-enlistment.

A Defense Department spokesman explained this decline by suggesting that soldiers were less eager "to return to a war that was growing larger and more ferocious." But there were other reasons why blacks found a career in the armed forces less attractive.

Black servicemen charged that discrimination pervaded the entire military system. Upon entering the service, each enlisted man received a series of tests to determine his suitability for placement in one of the many military occupational specialties. The racial and cultural biases in these tests, combined with the low educational training and experience of the average black inductee, assured him assignments in the infantry and the low-skilled jobs that the military termed "soft-core"—food service, supply, and transportation—rather than to such "hard-core" technical specialties as communications, intelligence, and the handling of electronic equipment.

Once assigned to a particular "soft-core" specialty, the black virtually had no further opportunity to advance. Lateral movement to another field involved a process known as "cross-training," something military officials were reluctant to approve, especially for blacks. The rate of promotion, however, tended to be much more rapid in the technical fields.

A serviceman looked to his military training to help him find employment after discharge. Most black servicemen found their training in combat specialties totally inapplicable to civilian life, leaving them with small chance of securing any job, let alone a well-paid one.

In addition to discrimination by prejudiced superiors in the allocation of hazardous and unpleasant assignments and in awarding promotions, black servicemen complained of the military's lack of sensitivity to black cultural identity, citing as evidence the facts that black periodicals and books on black history and culture were unavailable in the dayrooms and libraries and that post newspapers rarely published articles of interest to black servicemen and their families. They objected to the prevalence of slogans such as: "In the army we have only one color—OD [olive drab]" and "we don't have any racial problems; all Marines are green." They also resented the absence in post exchanges and commissaries of black-oriented items and the reluctance, if not outright refusal, to play "soul" music. They complained bitterly about superiors who labeled black literature subversive and those who possessed it militants, and who threatened disciplinary action against and withheld long overdue promotions from soldiers who wore Afro hair styles even as they accepted white GIs with long hair.

Similar complaints extended to the military justice system. Despite the reforms adopted after World War II, a soldier who was charged with an offense was still tried not by a jury of his peers but before a court appointed by the officer preferring charges against him. The same officer appointed the prosecutor and defense lawyers, and he reviewed the case if the soldier was convicted. In addition, black servicemen still suffered more courts-martial than whites and received stiffer penalties for the same offenses. A disproportionately large number of blacks ended up in stockades and brigs, where besides outworn facilities and severe overcrowding, food was poor and rations short, sanitation was defective, and inhumane treatment was rampant.

Further grievances centered upon the nonjudicial punishments administered by commanders, specifically pretrial confinement and "Article 15s." A company commander could hold a serviceman in confinement before his trial. There was no time credit if convicted for pretrial confinement. Theoretically, this practice applied only to servicemen awaiting trial whose presence among other soldiers was considered "dangerous," or to insure the presence of the accused at the trial, or because of the seriousness of the offense charged. In the case of blacks, it was charged that pretrial confinement was repeatedly employed as a punishment, no matter how minor the alleged offense. An "Article 15" action permitted a commanding officer to punish minor infractions without recourse to a court-martial and subsequent appeal. Statistics revealed that this action, like pretrial confinement, was generally meted out to more blacks than whites even when charged with identical offenses. The more "Article 15s" a soldier had on his record, the more difficult it was for him to remain in the service and to receive a regular honorable discharge upon leaving the service.

During the Vietnam War administrative discharges were widely used to eliminate servicemen considered unsuitable or undesirable prior to the conclusion of their term of service. A large number of these were blacks. There were two types of such administrative special discharges: for unsuitability and for unfitness. Almost all discharges for unsuitability were classified as general discharges "under honorable conditions," which entitled the recipient to the regular medical, educational, and other veterans' benefits available to those who received honorable discharges. However, a general discharge did not have the designation "honorable" at the top, and as a result it had a distinctly harmful effect on the separatee's chances for employment. Usually, discharges for unfitness were classified as undesirable discharges.

The undesirable discharge was an administrative separation from the service under conditions other than honorable. It was also sometimes called a "less than honorable" or "bad paper" discharge and could be issued to a serviceman who requested discharge in lieu of a trial by court-martial. In order to apply for veterans' benefits, a serviceman receiving an undesirable discharge had to have his case evaluated by the Veterans Administration. He had practically no possibility of obtaining private employment since in the mind of the public the undesirable discharge was virtually indistinguishable from a punitive—bad conduct or dishonorable—discharge. Most employers refused to hire job applicants with less than honorable discharges. As one administratively discharged veteran who unsuccessfully made the rounds put it: "I have friends who've robbed liquor stores who can get jobs easier than I can."

And an observer stated that such persons had to choose between becoming "either welfare cases or stickup cases."

Before a serviceman could receive an undesirable discharge, he had to be given the right to present his case to a discharge board. Unfortunately, in most cases the prospective dischargee was eager to get out of the service as quickly as possible. Unaware of the problems he would confront in civilian life, he generally accepted a UD without availing himself of the opportunity to contest it.

Undesirable discharges were subject to review by an administrative review board, and many blacks were persuaded to accept a less than honorable discharge under the mistaken impression that it would later be upgraded. Actually, during 1970 only 5 per cent of all administrative discharges were upgraded.

Other complaints contended that the military regularly harassed and intimidated black militants and activists. Branded as "troublemakers" or "misfits," they were likely to be either administratively discharged as unfit for military duty or shunted off to the front. "When a 'brother' speaks out against the unequal treatment imposed upon us," wrote one black soldier from Vietnam, "he is most assuredly 'railroaded' to . . . some . . . extremely dangerous area."

White servicemen were accused of acts of discourtesy, repeated use of racial slurs, antiblack graffiti on toilet walls, and the repeated display of Confederate flags, including their use as shoulder patches. One black serviceman observed: "We're here fighting for the United States, not for the Confederacy."

The scarcity of black officers intensified black grievances. In 1969 there were only 116 nonwhite cadets in the service academies, and only 2.1 per cent of all officers in the three services were black. Many of these officers were disheartened by the seemingly "dead-end" assignments they received. Of the 380 combat battalion commanders in Vietnam in 1967, only two were black. One newly promoted black lieutenant colonel felt he was given a newly established desk job to deny him a command assignment. One black graduate of West Point resigned his commission to protest discriminatory practices and the "bigotry of rating officers."

Off-base discrimination had hardly improved at all, nor were conditions in off-post housing any better. Secretary of Defense McNamara admitted that the voluntary program established in 1963 had "failed and failed miserably." It suffered from insufficient leadership from the top down and from providing no "appropriately stiff sanctions for violations of the antidiscrimination policy." In 1967, at the request of the Maryland legislature, the Secretary of Defense declared any multiple-family rental facilities—apartments and trailer courts—within a prescribed radius of four main Maryland bases off limits if they were not equally available to all military personnel. Most landlords agreed to comply, and similar actions were taken shortly thereafter in other Maryland areas with equal success. This in turn led to a "nationwide campaign for voluntary compliance."

Nonetheless, black servicemen of all ranks faced widespread off-post discrimination, while their commanders furnished them with little or no support.

The growing influence of the "black revolution" spilled over into the military as black servicemen engaged in protest and antiwar activities that attracted national attention and caused intense concern to military authorities. In August 1968 more than a hundred black soldiers at Fort Hood, Texas, staged an all-night demonstration to protest being sent to Chicago for possible riot-control duty at the Democratic National Convention. They feared that they might be used to combat Chicago blacks. Many of those involved faced trials by special courts-martial, with a maximum sentence of six months, and those who were considered leaders underwent general courts-martial.

Similarly, an integrated group at Fort Jackson, South Carolina, called the "GIs United Against the War in Vietnam" was denied permission to hold an open meeting to discuss "the legal and moral questions related to the war in Vietnam and to the civil rights of American citizens both within and outside the Armed Forces." Within a few days nine Fort Jackson soldiers who had been active in the organization were confined in the stockade or placed under barracks arrest on charges stemming from their agitation. In a leaflet protesting the arrests, the GIs United charged: "The Ft. Jackson Nine are black, white and Puerto Rican. They are being victimized for exercising their constitutional rights of free speech and assembly—the rights all GIs should have as American citizens."

As unfavorable publicity mounted and several black Congressmen exerted pressure, the army decided to drop the charges against all the Fort Jackson defendants, discharging six of them as undesirable. Subsequently, the army issued guidelines on dissent, which "instructed commanders that servicemen have limited rights to possess written material, attend off-post meetings, join servicemen's unions, publish papers off post, make complaints, and petition for redress of grievances."

In the spring of 1968 incidents of racial turmoil and discontent increased at military installations throughout the world. The assassination of Dr. King in April accentuated racial tension and controversy, particularly in Vietnam. At Que Viet, a navy installation, whites wore makeshift Klan costumes to celebrate the black leader's death, and at Da Nang Confederate flags were raised. On the day of national mourning for Dr. King, whites burned a cross and hoisted a Confederate flag in front of navy headquarters at Cam Ranh Bay.

Because of the growing tension, an order was issued for the removal of all flags carrying the symbol of the Confederacy from above the men's bunks, including state flags with this symbol. The reason given was that the Confederate flag was viewed as a "symbol of racism." However, when Representative Williamson S. Stuckey of Georgia informed the House on May 6 that he was "upset, angry, and indignant" because one of his constituents in Vietnam had been ordered to remove the Georgia flag from his bunk, the Pentagon assured him and other Southern Congressmen that servicemen would be allowed to fly their home-state flags in Vietnam even if they carried the symbol of the Confederacy.

Meanwhile, the commander of American forces in the I Corps area in Vietnam ordered every unit under his command to organize integrated watch committees. He gave assurances that complaints would be heard without fear of retaliation. In April 1969, the *New York Times* correspondent reported from Saigon that many American commanders were working hard to prevent "more violent incidents growing out of the racial situation."

As Vietnam smouldered, racial incidents erupted at many stateside installations. One of the most serious occurred at the Marine base at Camp Lejeune, North Carolina, where 30,000 Marines were stationed, about 70 per cent of them recent Vietnam veterans. A white corporal died from injuries sustained in a clash between white and black Marines.

Many observers, both within and outside the service, attributed the growing racial tension within the military to a spillover from the problems of the civilian community, and much of the trouble was blamed on the young black militants in the service, many of them recent Vietnam veterans. *U.S. News and World Report* declared that blacks returning from Indochina "are more impatient and quicker to violence than their white counterparts when they feel real or imagined racial slights." A special House Armed Services subcommittee denied that the outbreak at Camp Lejeune had resulted from any specific provocation. Instead, the subcommittee said, it "was generated by a few militant blacks who fanned the flames of racism, misconceptions, suspicions, and frustrations." But this opinion was contradicted by the findings of a study conducted at the base three months before the fatal incident, which placed the onus for the deteriorating situation on racist attitudes and discriminatory policies directed against black Marines stationed at Lejeune.

Relations between black and white Marines at the base had been strained for several months, and in April 1969 Major General Edwin B. Wheeler, commander of the 2d Marine Division, set up an *ad hoc* committee to look into the question of equal treatment and opportunity within the division. The committee consisted of seven officers, including two black officers. In its report the committee warned that "an explosive situation of major proportions" had been created and might be expected to get worse. It placed the blame for the tension in large measure on officers and NCOs of the 2d Marine Division. The committee stated bluntly that they had refused to comply with existing Marine Corps racial policies on equal treatment and opportunity. It charged that many white officers and NCOs not only retained their prejudices but openly aired them often in racial jokes, stories, and references. "The major offenders in this regard," the committee stated, "are among the relatively senior officers and enlisted Marines."

General Leonard F. Chapman, the Marine Corps Commandant, publicly acknowledged that a "serious racial problem" existed in the Marine Corps and pledged to take every possible step to eliminate the causes of racial violence. He reported that numerous efforts had been made to wipe out the vestiges of discrimination but added that "we have not been as successful as we thought." In a subsequent message to all Marine commands, General Chapman ordered that all legitimate grievances were to receive "sympathetic consideration and rapid response," promotion procedures were to be reviewed to insure against any errors, and every Marine was to receive proof by actions that the Marine Corps guaranteed equal opportunity and equal protection, without regard to race.

Explaining the order at a Pentagon news conference, the general added that blacks would be allowed to have Afro haircuts and that the corps would not bar the "Black Power" clenched fist salute if used by black Marines to greet each other, not in a manner to suggest defiance of authority. As an example of one complaint, he noted that a number of blacks had protested about the lack of "soul" music in servicemen's clubs on base. "That sounds like a small thing," he added, "but it means something to any black Marine." These concessions failed to erase many of the deep-seated grievances of blacks, either at Camp Lejeune or elsewhere in the corps. Following General Chapman's order, a petition was submitted by a group of black Marines at Lejeune. In it they complained that too many commanders had no appreciation "of the uniqueness" of different ethnic groups but felt that "the only color of a serviceman" was that of his green uniform. They spoke of the "habitual discrimination and overt prejudice that are allowed to flourish both in the military and socially, in the camp and in the surrounding communities." They added: "We feel that those who could initiate meaningful programs and create a better atmosphere and understanding among the servicemen here no longer possess the moral fiber to relate to a modern multiracial service."

Early in February 1970 the results of a survey of the racial attitudes of 1,700 Marines were made public. Sixty-eight per cent of the blacks questioned felt that the Marine Corps "had failed to practice its preachments on racial equality." The survey also found that, the longer a man remained in the Marines, the more prejudiced he became. In April 1970 the Marine Corps initiated a research project to tackle the problem. One result was a program to train Human Relations Instructors; the initial class of seventy-one students began training a year later.

Meanwhile, an investigation by a Department of the Army team in the summer of 1969 confirmed that the army too had "a race problem of serious proportions both in the continental United

States and overseas." The survey team reported a widespread increase in racial tensions and warned of "increased racial confrontations" unless immediate action was taken to identify problem areas at the squad and platoon level. It concluded that "Negro soldiers seem to have lost faith in the Army."

An official of the Department of the Army in January 1970 told the commanders in South Vietnam that

> to take an ostrichlike approach to racial fear, hostility, and misunderstanding is indefensible, especially when the signs can be read in the racial obscenities written by both groups on latrine walls and can be heard from an alarming number of black soldiers who readily complain they suffer injustice in the Army solely because of their race.
>
>   I can verify from my own experience that the cries of the Negro soldiers—enlisted men and even officers—have never been so loud.

Following the instructions of the Army Chief of Staff to the field in November 1969, army posts began a series of interracial or human relations seminars. Two months later Secretary of Defense Melvin H. Laird ordered the creation of an Interservice Task Force on Education in Race Relations to develop an educational program throughout the armed forces. Each of the services was called upon to examine how it could promote better understanding between the races. Laird suggested a number of possible "communication vehicles," including round-table discussions, panels, and human relations councils. Individual commands were allowed latitude as to how they might approach the problem. Officers and enlisted men at the army base at Fort Dix, New Jersey, and the Marine base at Camp Lejeune, North Carolina, where such race relations programs were subsequently stressed, reported a general lessening of racial conflicts and tensions.

Additionally, steps were taken to make the military more attractive to blacks. A concentrated effort was made to provide black periodicals and books on black history and culture and to publish related articles in post newspapers. Both the army and the Air Force published new regulations permitting a modified Afro haircut. In 1970 the Army and Air Force Exchange Service initiated a million-dollar program to train 6,000 barbers and 1,100 beauticians around the world in the technique of cutting and styling black people's hair. The shelves of the 3,300 Army–Air Force retail exchange outlets around the world were stocked with black-oriented products and supplies. "Shopping in the huge base exchange at Westover Air Force Base near Springfield, Mass.," one writer commented in *Ebony* in July 1971, "black airmen and their families now find one product after another that has been ordered with them in mind. There are various conditioners and oil sprays for Afro hair styles; facial cosmetics and colognes, dashikis, greeting cards with 'soul' messages and drawings, magazines, phonograph records and the like." Finally, foods traditionally enjoyed by blacks were prepared in dining halls.

In March 1970 Air Force Colonel Daniel "Chappie" James, Jr., became the fourth black general in the history of the armed forces and the highest-ranking black in the Air Force. He was immediately appointed Deputy Assistant Secretary of Defense for Public Affairs, where, a black journalist observed, "as a black, he could provide a service for the Secretary of Defense that his white counterparts cannot."

The service academies increased their minority group enrollment. For example, forty-five black cadets entered West Point in 1969, compared to nine in 1968. Each new class at the Air Force Academy had an average of twenty-four black cadets, whereas prior to 1963 there were none. The number of blacks also increased at the Naval Academy. In 1971 Annapolis counted fifty black midshipmen, the highest number in its history. The first black Navy ROTC unit was set up at Prairie View A & M College, in Prairie View, Texas, in 1968, and two years later the college graduated its first thirteen black naval officers.

Despite these widely publicized steps, tension and friction did not abate as the authorities had hoped. Instead, the polarization of white and black servicemen deepened. In combat units, there were black bunkers and white bunkers; in mess halls, blacks and whites usually sat at different tables; and at the service clubs, they congregated separately. Outside the bases, blacks assembled in one area and whites in another. There were black bars and clubs and white bars and clubs, and the facilities of one race were declared off limits to the servicemen of the other. Both blacks and whites continued to express their hostilities openly. One black Air Force sergeant complained: "On any military installation you will see white officers, NCO's and airmen displaying on their autos, wall lockers, etc., rebel flags, rebel bumper stickers, rebel auto tags and Wallace-for-President bumper stickers."

Black servicemen reacted by organizing black activist groups, particularly in the Seventh Army, the main United States force in West Germany. Thirteen per cent out of a total of 28,000 men in the Seventh Army were black. On July 4, 1970, a black activist "call for justice" brought close to one thousand black soldiers to the campus of Heidelberg University for a day of protest and planning. From this meeting emerged an announcement of the intention to unite all groups of black servicemen in West Germany, among them The United Black Soldier, The Black Action Group, and The Unsatisfied Black Soldier, and "march as an Army," to protest discrimination in assignments, promotions, military justice, and housing and recreational facilities.

On and off military installations verbal and physical clashes increased. The most numerous and serious incidents erupted in the West German garrison, where they threatened to obstruct military effectiveness. In October 1971 the *Times* of London reported that in the previous eight months "eighteen race riots" at American installations in West Germany required "significant police action." "Race is my problem," said a white NCO in Frankfort, West Germany, "not the Russians, not Vietnam, Jordan, nor maneuvers. I just worry about keeping my troops—black and white—from getting at one another."

In late August 1970 Washington reported that President Nixon was deeply concerned over the increasing number of racial incidents involving servicemen and would shortly send an investigating team to assess at first hand the racial problems at European installations. In mid-September, a racially-mixed fifteen-member Defense Department team of officers, enlisted men, and civilians headed by Frank Render II, recently appointed Deputy Assistant Secretary of Defense for Equal Opportunity, the highest-ranking black in the Pentagon, left the United States to conduct a three-and-one-half-week study of race relations in the European theater. The mission visited six army bases in Germany, naval stations in Spain and Italy, and Air Force bases in Britain and Germany.

Especially in Germany, during sessions that often ran far into the night, the investigating team listened mostly to black soldiers who bitterly denounced intentional and systematic discrimination against blacks by both the military and civilians. They complained of a discriminatory double standard in assignments, promotions, and especially punishments, charging that commanding officers, unable to cope with black demands for equality of opportunity, had turned increasingly to punitive measures. When disturbances with racial overtones took place, they charged, the army saw fit to punish only blacks. They further complained that landlords went unchallenged in their refusal to rent to black servicemen and that club managers and bar and restaurant owners with impunity catered exclusively to white soldiers.

Upon the return of the team high-level policy changes were initiated. An order was issued making it mandatory to publish all Article 15 actions that involved the four lowest enlisted grades. Another set of guidelines called for the commanding officer to order pretrial confinement only in "absolutely essential cases" and for the Staff Judge Advocate to monitor all pretrial confinements. At Nuremberg, an educational program of seminars and dialogues for junior officers and senior noncommissioned officers was instituted. The commanding general of the Berlin Brigade appointed a black special assistant to hear the grievances of enlisted men. And in December 1970 General James H. Polk, Commander-in-Chief of the Army in Europe, placed off limits all places where discrimination was practiced. Housing referral offices were set up to inquire into complaints and to draw up lists of complying landlords.

In mid-December Secretary Laird made the Render report public. The report expressed dismay at finding "such acute frustration and such volatile anger as we found among the blacks." Small groups of alienated blacks had angrily declared that they had no reason to be fighting in a white man's army and a white man's war and that "their place was back in the States . . . where they could fight to liberate and free their black sisters and brothers from the dirty, stinky, teeming ghettos and from all forms of racial bigotry and oppression." Some of the blacks said they wanted guns, ammunition, and grenades because "whitey" understood no approach but violent confrontation. They accused the mission of intending to "brainwash" them.

The team found that the overriding factor in poor race relations was "the failure in too many instances of command leadership to exercise its authority and responsibility" or to provide for and monitor the equal opportunity provisions that were already a part of the regulations and procedures. Almost everywhere, junior officers, NCOs, and, in some cases, majors and lieutenant colonels seemed unable to implement approved racial policy. Blacks assembling in groups of three or four or more were viewed as a threat, and in many cases these groups were dispersed without provocation, although similar groups of whites were considered "to be merely carrying on social conversation." The report noted that during the European tour a communication from one commander to another at a base the team was soon to visit contained this observation: "Mr. Render is a top grade militant. If he were not in the Army, he would be a leader in the Black Panthers."

The mission also found overwhelming discrimination in military justice, the military police, work assignments, promotions, the management of clubs, and housing. Discrimination by club owners frequently resulted from white threats of economic boycott if discriminatory policies were not maintained.

The Render study recommended that an "equal-opportunity or human-relations officer and a human-relations council" be set up in major units. It also asked for "mechanisms" to ensure effective communication of approved policies through the chain of command and development of a "full scale program in education and race relations" affecting military personnel at all levels.

The Defense Department issued in December 1970 a series of directives on racial equality in the armed services. These included a call for "numerical goals and timetables as a means to increase the utilization of minorities in occupations" where they were underrepresented. The removal or reassignment of officers, noncommissioned officers, and civilians who failed to act against discrimination was recommended. Finally, base commanders were given the power without prior Pentagon approval to declare housing within the United States off limits if landlords practiced racial discrimination.

Eight days later, seven black officers and enlisted men petitioned Secretary of the Army Stanley R. Resor for an inquiry into housing discrimination against black troops in West Germany. One of the seven signers, Major Washington C. Hill of the Medical Corps, had already complained in a letter to the *New York Times* of discrimination by West German landlords. Another, Captain Curtis

R. Smothers, the only full-time black army judge in West Germany, had previously noted that, while the military ignored housing discrimination, it was pressuring the Bonn government to force German insurance companies to lower their automobile insurance premiums for American troops. He continued:

> The Army makes a mistake to assume that these disparities escape the black GI. They do not escape him. This is why you hear young black troopers saying, "Do you think I'm going to die for these people? You have to be some kind of a fool to support American policy when they don't give a damn about you."

In January 1971 Roy Wilkins of the NAACP sent three of his staff members to assess black servicemen's problems in West Germany. Reporting on the forthcoming investigation, the *Christian Science Monitor* accurately referred to the organization's "long history of defending black servicemen in military cases." In February 1970 the NAACP had had charges of rioting against four Marines at Wellington Air Force Base in Tennessee reduced to charges of creating a disturbance. In May 1970 the NAACP's intercession on behalf of five enlisted black airmen involved in racial clashes with white servicemen at the Goose Bay Air Force Base in Labrador had resulted in the dropping of court-martial charges.

The NAACP team left for Europe in late January and made a three-week tour of military bases in West Germany, where it held frank discussions on a broad range of subjects with black servicemen at all levels. Most of the lengthy "eyeball-to-eyeball" talks were taken up by black charges of double standards in military justice. The team concluded that most blacks were prepared to work for improvement within the system and expressed optimism about the situation "because of the determination on the part of black GIs."

Even as the NAACP team prepared its report, several policy changes in the area of race relations were being initiated at the highest level of command. In March 1971 Secretary Laird announced a new program of compulsory classes in race relations designed to prevent "racial unrest, tension, or conflict" from impairing "combat readiness and efficiency." A Defense Race Relations Institute (DRRI) was organized to prepare course materials and train 1,400 instructors a year to teach required courses in race relations. The new DRRI program was to be coordinated with the network of race relations councils, which local commanders, in an attempt to resolve racial problems in their units, had been setting up on an *ad hoc* basis during the late 1960's. Such councils, together with billeted equal opportunity officers and NCOs, now existed on most major military installations.

Secretary of the Army Resor announced, also in March, several major changes in army policy. Personnel at home or abroad who desired off-post housing were required to use a housing referral office to guarantee that housing "be open to all soldiers or . . . open to none." Only landlords who agreed to rent without discrimination were to be listed, and commanders were authorized to place other housing units off limits. In addition, soldiers facing "nonjudicial punishment" were guaranteed counsel. Commanders were required to post announcements of such punishment conspicuously on unit bulletin boards to reduce the possibility of harsher punishments against blacks. On the following day, Captain Smothers, who had been summoned from Germany to consult with officials at the Pentagon, stated that the policy changes aimed at ending discrimination would require strict monitoring and the imposition of sanctions if they were to work. He pointed out that most commanders in Europe had not complied with a similar order issued in 1969.

Also in March 1971, Willy Brandt in a radio speech criticized those of his fellow citizens who discriminated against black American soldiers. The West German Chancellor stated that he had heard "about black soldiers running into prejudices in our country that are hardly different from those in their homeland."

Three Defense Department announcements reported the early retirement of General James H. Polk, Commander-in-Chief of the United States Army forces in Europe; the assignment of Captain Smothers to the office of Secretary of Defense General Counsel; and the promotion of Brigadier General Frederick E. Davison, a black officer, to the rank of major general.

On April 2, the results of the NAACP's inquiry were issued in a report titled "The Search for Military Justice: Report of the NAACP Inquiry into the Problems of the Negro Serviceman in West Germany." The report encompassed the problems of black servicemen in the areas of assignments, promotions, judicial administration, housing, public accommodations, and recreation. The team's general conclusions and recommendations for action completed the report. Its tone was set in its introduction, which contained this significant statement:

A principal cover for leadership failure is to characterize those who resist the status quo as "militants." It is important to understand the sweeping effect this label has taken in the military. It covers all aspects of black consciousness, black civil liberties, even the expectation of equal treatment.

The team reported that for both black enlisted men and officers, inequities in career assignments and promotion practices represented "a grave and pervasive problem." Military tests were unfair to blacks because they hinged on educational level, not potential skill for jobs. The largest numbers of black servicemen were anchored in service, supply, and administrative units that offered little future. Among Air Force men with four years' service, 17 per cent of the whites were in technical assignments, compared with only 5 per cent of the blacks. The same held true for occupational assignments in the army, leading to substantial pay grade and promotion disparities between white and black servicemen. Among non–high school graduates who scored between 31 and 40 on the AFQT and who were assigned to the infantry, 30 per cent of the black GIs were found at pay grade E-3 or lower, while only about 14 per cent of white troops were found there. Fewer than 20 per cent of the black soldiers in this group were at a pay grade of E-5 or higher, compared with 27 per cent of white soldiers.

The team found "deep dissatisfaction" among black commissioned officers. Not only were they concentrated in the lowest grades, but too few were given command positions. Even in cases where some black officers were "certified" for command positions, they were nevertheless denied the opportunity to perform as commanding officers by the transfer in of a white "certified" officer of equal rank but with greater seniority. Black servicemen told the team members that if black officers were placed in command positions with white junior officers accountable to them, it would be a major step toward overcoming racial discrimination in the army.

The feeling was also widespread among black troops that the military justice system was "discriminatory and unjust." The scarcity of black judges and the total absence of black military lawyers tended to confirm this feeling. The white Judge Advocate General lawyers assigned to represent accused blacks were regarded as "neither independent of military influence nor free from racist attitudes." In the words of the blacks, these lawyers had "zero credibility." Nor did they have any more confidence in the white civilian counsel available to them in West Germany. Not only were their fees exorbitant, but they were viewed as being no more objective than the white military lawyers. Since there were no black lawyers to whom they could turn, blacks had little choice but to accept the counsel provided them. All this had the effect of denying black servicemen accused of court-martial offenses the right to adequate counsel as provided by the Uniform Code of Military Justice.

The alarming degree to which Article 15 punishment was meted out to black soldiers, as compared to whites, represented another major source of grievance. In Berlin, for example, black soldiers constituted about 15 per cent of the command but received about one-third of the "Article 15s," and in some other locations the percentage of blacks receiving Article 15 nonjudicial punishment was considerably higher. Many black soldiers were convinced that white soldiers escaped disciplinary action for behavior for which they themselves were punished. They insisted that whites faced no consequences for wearing their hair long, while blacks were punished. The committee found that the publicized attempts by the military command to deal with the issue of "Article 15s" and related problems had been generally ineffective, primarily because "most attempts at reform had been unenforced, ignored, or by-passed."

The team found that the percentage of blacks in confinement was far out of proportion to their total percentage in the armed forces. Most of these soldiers were confined in the stockades because of the "arbitrary and inequitable" pretrial confinement of blacks by commanding officers. Sometimes as many as three or four out of five blacks in confinement were so detained. And the fact that up to one-third of the black servicemen in pretrial confinement in West Germany in 1970 were released without ever having formal charges brought against them was cited as proof that pretrial confinement was used unfairly against blacks, and particularly to remove black activists from their units.

The team further reported that "the disturbingly frequent use" of administrative discharges, especially in the areas of unsuitability and unfitness, had an equally detrimental effect on black servicemen. Forty-five per cent of all black discharges were less than honorable. Black servicemen were convinced that there was a deliberate campaign to get rid of them through the mechanism of special discharges. They charged that blacks were frequently goaded into technical violations by unsympathetic white officers; that officers often harassed black soldiers until they signed requests for discharge; and that commanding officers offered to release jailed black servicemen from the stockades in return for their taking a poorly rated discharge. Although 95 per cent of the soldiers who received administrative discharges had waived board consideration of their cases, the team found that the case against most of these soldiers was too weak to stand up against the scrutiny of an objective panel. Because there was an utter lack of "informed and sympathetic black legal counsel," accused black soldiers failed to take advantage of this available alternative.

Discrimination in housing, "more than any other problem, caused blacks to regard Germany as an unfriendly country and to wonder out loud why they should be stationed there." In each of the nine cities visited by the investigators, they found that black servicemen were either denied housing, overcharged by many landlords, or forced to accept accommodations as many as twenty miles away from their bases, while white servicemen found reasonably priced, conveniently located housing. Commanders consistently failed to protect their troops against such discrimination.

Recent reforms aimed at curbing racial discrimination in the use of off-post entertainment and recreational facilities had been equally "innocuous and ineffective." Inns, bars, and other facilities remained closed to blacks through restrictive devices such as "whites only" and "members only" provisions. A few had been declared off limits by commanders, but even in these cases the sanction was rarely enforced. One black GI in Mainz told of how white GIs would taunt the blacks in the barracks by bragging about their escapades in the local "off-limits" bar. In short, the recently announced programs and policy changes were being effectively subverted by lower grade commanders and NCOs. As a result, "an uncomfortable number" of the younger blacks were "disenchanted, alienated, and had lost faith in the capacity of and the will of the Armed Forces to deal honestly with their problems."

Among its recommendations, the NAACP report proposed a revision of career assignment practices, "a dramatic step-up in the rate of promotion," the recruiting of more black officers and the extending of command instead of staff assignments to more black officers, and the recruiting of black civilian lawyers to defend black soldiers facing trial. It further recommended that no person be placed in confinement without a specific charge being preferred against him, and that persons facing Article 15 punishment be offered legal advice and an ample period of time within which to decide whether to request a court-martial. They called for the education of senior, junior grade, and noncommissioned officers in the subjects of culture and race in order to reduce the "disturbingly frequent" use of administrative discharges. They further urged that drastic steps be taken to terminate the practice of discrimination in off-post housing as well as in recreational facilities.

Two specific recommendations of the team read as follows:

> Installations should take on a physical appearance of racial equality by changing the names of those which may be offensive to black personnel, such as Robert E. Lee Barracks.

> All officers and NCOs who have and are demonstrating a calloused insensitivity to racial problems should be removed from their command. Procedures to recall should be instituted.

On April 22, Roy Wilkins presented the report to Secretary Laird. In his statement to the Secretary Wilkins noted:

> In one respect, the report confirms indictments of American society as one characterized by pervasive institutional racism. . . . On the other hand, the report offers considerable hope if we heed its ominous message. In effect, the report transmits a plea by black servicemen for help in making the system work fairly for them. . . . We feel certain that you will share our anxiety about the need to help these young black Americans retain their faith in the system.

That the West German situation was not unique was pointed up one month later in a report submitted to the Secretary about the racial situation in the Pacific Command. In early spring, on instructions from Secretary Laird, a fifteen-member military and civilian group headed by Render visited installations of each of the military services in Japan, Korea, Okinawa, and the Philippines to find out how well the programs of equal opportunity and treatment were being implemented. On May 23 the team submitted a report that warned of a high level of tension prevalent throughout the Pacific Command, an atmosphere "pregnant with potential for serious racial disorders."

Once again black soldiers, sailors, airmen, and Marines charged they were given "the menial and dirty tasks"; that the promotion system functioned in a discriminatory manner; and that military justice was unfairly applied to blacks. The group found that a disproportionate number of blacks were being processed out of the service by way of administrative discharges, and this tool was being improperly used "to railroad them out of the service as either undesirable or unfit." Here again blacks who attempted redress of their grievances or spoke up for their rights were labeled "troublemakers" and subjected to reprisal. Many of the reforms developed at the highest level of command were not transmitted down the chain of command. To the question often raised by white officers and enlisted men as to what precisely it was that the black soldier wanted, the team responded: "The answer is plain. . . . Respect for his personality as a man. Fairness in selection for duty detail. . . . Fairness in promotion. Appreciation of and recognition for meritorious performance." And to the Secretary the team reported: "There is a new breed of blacks in the Armed Forces, born of a new generation demanding full equality—NOW."

In the aftermath of racial violence at Travis Air Force Base in May 1971, an Air Force Human Relations team was dispatched to investigate rising racial tensions at Air Force training bases. The fifteen-member team included seven officers and eight enlisted men. Four members of the team were black and two were Mexican-Americans. On July 26, after a six-week study of fifteen domestic training installations, the group submitted its report.

As reported in the *New York Times*, the findings stated that everyone in the Air Training Command must understand that "there is discrimination and racism in command, and it is ugly." The report specified a long list of inequities:

Unequal treatment is manifested in unequal punishment, offensive and inflammatory language, prejudice in the assignment of details, lack of products for blacks in the BX [base exchange], harassment by security policemen under orders to break up five or more blacks in a group, double standards in enforcement of regulations.

As an example of this double standard, it noted that a white who made advances to a married black waitress was "personally reprimanded for his indiscretion," while a black doing the same thing had charges brought against him. The report went on:

> Security police are often thought of by the black man as the "Mafia" or the "personal bodyguard of the man." They are seldom viewed by blacks as being objectively removed from the establishment policy-makers in order to enforce the law equally and without bias. We must get the SP away from the "pig" and "Gestapo" image.

The team found that the Air Force Equal Opportunity program was "just that . . . a program and not a way of life." "At only three of the fifteen bases visited," it went on, "did we see an enthusiastic, knowledgeable, and concerned individual that was the EO [equal opportunity] officer." Among its specific recommendations, the team urged that all commanders "must assert in the strongest possible terms that abusive language and inflammatory words of any type will not be condoned." It also recommended that "if fair and equal treatment cannot be obtained for all military personnel and their families, then the base should be closed and/or relocated."

Finally, the investigators told the general that "unless all these words are translated into effective action, and everybody in ATC must understand this, the next time there will be fire."

Senior officials in the Pentagon evidently concurred. They suggested to the Air Force that the report be distributed not only to other Air Force commands but also throughout the military service. "We can't fight an enemy," said one officer, "if our troops are fighting among themselves."

In August 1971 the Defense Department announced that Frank Render, its senior civil rights official and the author of two powerful reports written after trips to Europe and Asia, had resigned for personal reasons. However, Render's supporters immediately accused the Pentagon of dismissing him because of his outspoken criticism of armed services racial discrimination. The following day Pentagon officials confirmed that Secretary Laird had asked for Render's resignation. The action had been taken because of high-level dissatisfaction with his performance in office, specifically his failure to produce solutions for the problems he had identified.

Render, however, noted that he had been pointedly told that he had become a "champion of the people" rather than of the military departments. The Baltimore *Afro-American* also was not satisfied with the official explanation. In an editorial, "Meaning of Render Boot," it declared:

> If Defense Secretary Melvin Laird is unhappy with the progress being made in getting rid of racial discrimination in the military, he should retire some of the responsible people rather than no-power civil rights aides like Frank W. Render II.

Meanwhile, additional steps were being taken to defuse racial tensions in the army in West Germany. In late June 1971 General Michael S. Davison, one of the youngest four-star generals at fifty-four, took over as the army's commander in Europe. Not long after, Major General F. E. Davison, the army's highest-ranking black officer, was appointed Chief of Staff for Enlisted Personnel of the Seventh Army. Both Davisons gave top priority to racial and morale problems. Each unit in the command down to brigade level was required to appoint a full-time equal opportunity officer, whose job it was to detect racial discrimination and, if possible, to eliminate it. Commanders were also instructed to initiate positive and imaginative programs to create racial harmony. These programs were to be guided by one black and one white equal opportunity staff officer. Courts-martial were canceled when the evidence was adjudged flimsy or biased or when the accused had been held an unreasonably long time before trial. In some Seventh Army units a soldier could at any time appeal to his battalion commander against an unreasonable order or unfair or discriminatory treatment.

In August 1971 the first successful defense based on racism and discrimination took place in a court-martial case in West Berlin. The case involved two black GIs who had gone AWOL. Sergeant Ronald Bolden, twenty-three, a Vietnam veteran from Cleveland, left his unit in December 1970, and Specialist 4 Samuel Robertson followed a month later. On June 16 Stanley Faulkner, a New York civil liberties attorney, arrived in West Berlin to consult with Bolden and Robertson. The two described to him numerous instances of racism to which they had been subjected. These included extra duties, denial of promotions, recreational restrictions, orders to cut their Afro hair, even when it was regulation length, being repeatedly addressed by officers as "boy," and so on. Finally, they insisted, they had been unable to endure the harassment and discrimination any longer and had gone AWOL. After several days of consultation, the two decided to surrender and face whatever the charges might be.

On the morning of June 18 Bolden and Robertson appeared at the gates of the Berlin Command, accompanied by their civilian lawyer, to turn themselves in. While waiting for the MPs to arrive, the two black GIs issued a statement to the press. In it they said that they had left the army because of racial discrimination, but had decided to return in order to give other GIs an understanding of the situation "so that they can go about changing it." Following their surrender, charges were formally issued against each of them for absence without official leave.

The trial dates were set for August 16 and 17, with Robertson's case scheduled first. When the court convened, Robertson pleaded not guilty to the charges and specifications. The judge then asked Faulkner what possible defense the accused could have to the AWOL charge. The attorney replied that the defense was fear of immediate danger to the life and body of the accused. After lengthy discussions with his clients and with defense witnesses, Faulkner was convinced that proof of racism and discrimination in the Berlin Brigade would be the central issue of the trial. As he subsequently wrote:

> There is a special defense seldom used in courts-martial of coercion or duress. This means that where an accused has committed an act for which he otherwise would be criminally responsible, but feared that there was an immediate danger to his life or person, this defense could be used. It would be justification for the commission of the act.

The members of the special court were a major, two captains—one of whom was black—and a lieutenant. The military evidence was the morning report establishing that Robertson had been absent without authorization from January 4 to June 18, 1971. All of this the defense conceded.

The first defense witness was a white captain who testified that he had had under him a sergeant who had been transferred because of charges of racism. The second witness was a black GI who testified that he knew of three other black soldiers who had been so harassed that they had been sent to hospitals as mental cases. He also related the uninvestigated incident of a black GI who had been found dead in a local canal. Depositions were introduced from a captain confirming the testimony of the first witness, and from a black soldier who provided further evidence of the oppressive conditions confronting black members of the Berlin Brigade.

The last defense witness was Samuel Robertson, the accused. His testimony confirmed and reinforced what had been said by the previous witnesses. He then said that he had left his company because he feared his life was in danger and needed some time to think over his situation and seek legal assistance.

In the summation, the government's trial counsel argued that the only issue was the undisputed fact that the accused had been absent without leave; the other issues of racism and discrimination were not relevant to the question of guilt or innocence. Faulkner, on the other hand, referred to the oppression suffered by black people in civilian life and asserted that the accused had suffered similar oppression in the military. Robertson's decision to leave his unit, he argued, stemmed from experiences both inside and outside the army. It resulted from accumulated discrimination and fear—the fear that he might be the next black GI found floating dead in the canal or confined to a mental hospital. That fear, Faulkner continued, could not be felt by him as a white person, nor could any other white person sitting in the courtroom experience it.

After deliberating for thirty minutes, the court returned and announced a surprising verdict of not guilty. The charges against Sergeant Bolden were then dropped.

After the trial, Faulkner talked with the Staff Judge Advocate, Colonel Salisbury, whom he described as in a state of shock over the not guilty verdict. Faulkner stressed the need for change within the Berlin command to avoid similar incidents. "I wasn't referring to AWOLs," he later reported, "I was referring to racism and discrimination." The problem remained with the white military officers, and until they seriously examined their attitudes toward blacks it would never be solved.

After a long discussion, the colonel opened a writing pad on his desk and asked, with pencil poised in hand: "Tell me, Mr. Faulkner, how are we going to solve the problem?"

Analyzing the significance of the Robertson case, Faulkner subsequently wrote to the editor of the *Harvard Law Review:* "The Robertson case has been the first one in which racism and racial discrimination was established as having sufficient weight to a black soldier to make him have an immediate fear for his life or person. . . . Had this defense of coercion or duress not been raised the accused would have been found guilty of the offense."

On October 22, 1971, the West German command dropped charges against twenty-nine black soldiers who were facing courts-martial for refusing to obey an order following a racial dispute. The fight had taken place in the mess hall of a camp in Darmstadt in July when a group of white soldiers tried to prevent blacks from listening to "soul" music on a jukebox. It was alleged that after the fight a group of black soldiers attempted to prevent the arrest of one of their number. Seventeen of the black GIs involved in the incident elected to accept nonjudicial (Article 15) punishment rather than face a court-martial. The other twenty-nine decided to "face trial rather than accept an administrative way out." They were charged with failure to obey an order to disperse and failure to respect the authority of the military police.

In the flood of publicity that surrounded the case, there were charges of discrimination against blacks in the administration of military justice. Among other organizations and individuals that interceded, the NAACP sent one of its staff attorneys to participate in the defense. Four days before the opening of the first series of courts-martial, General Michael Davison dismissed the charges. In addition, he directed the setting aside of the Article 15 punishment previously meted out to the seventeen black soldiers.

Early in November an interracial group of two hundred officers and men gathered in Berchtesgaden, West Germany, for the Seventh Army's second Equal Opportunity and Human Relations Conference within six months. Among the leading speakers were Nathaniel R. Jones, general counsel for the NAACP, and Harold Sims, executive director of the National Urban League. Both Jones and Sims hit hard at the army for the inequities that still existed in its administration of military justice, in promotions and job assignments, and in increasing discrimination against black soldiers by West German landlords, club managers, and bar and restaurant owners. Both, however, paid tribute to General Davison and his team for launching new programs designed to remedy these inequities.

Also early in November, the thirteen-member Congressional Black Caucus announced plans to probe the extent and causes of racism confronting blacks in the armed forces and to propose specific actions and programs to combat it. The plan was to begin the inquiry on November 15 with a one-day, on-site visit to military installations in the United States. This was to be followed by three days of open *ad hoc* hearings in Washington to be conducted by the caucus's Military Affairs Committee, co-chaired by Representatives Shirley Chisholm of New York and Ronald Dellums of California.

On the night of November 13 racial disturbances erupted at Fort McClellan, Alabama, ending in the arrest of seventy-one black soldiers and sixty-nine black WACs. "Once again," said Representative Dellums, "the army has seen fit to punish only blacks."

On November 15 ten members of the Congressional Black Caucus fanned out to visit military bases across the United States, where they spent the day conducting hearings into charges of discrimination and discussing the racial situation with black GIs. Following these visits the members returned to Washington to open *ad hoc* hearings the next day. Before calling the first witness, Representative Dellums charged that an agreement between the United States and Iceland had limited the number of black troops assigned to American Icelandic bases and announced that he had secret government documents to support his charge. Secretary Laird denied that such an agreement then existed and that any instructions by previous administrations restricting the assignment of black servicemen had been rescinded by the Human Goals Program.

Throughout the next three days, witnesses—black and white, civilian and military—testified that, despite numerous service directives and guidelines, black servicemen were still victims of racism and discrimination throughout their tour of duty.

Nathaniel R. Jones, in discussing the arbitrary manner in which Article 15s were given to black servicemen in West Germany, related:

> So I looked at his file. In his file was a lengthy list of misconducts by white GIs. . . . Nothing was done. One black GI did the same thing. . . . He got an Article 15. . . . Here, gentlemen and ladies, is where I feel the greatest racism comes out. It is in the discretionary use of military justice. When the white soldier commits an offense,

this offense is excused. When the black soldier commits the same
offense he is dealt with harshly. It is these minor punishments . . .
that lead to the discharges.

The local equal opportunity officers who handled complaints of
discrimination, whether black or white, were said to be hand-
picked by the local commander, who soon recognized that his chief
duty was to protect those officers by silencing or eliminating personnel who complained. One black major dismissed equal opportunity officers as "a farce," since their job was "to protect the MAN
and not our rights."

Frank Render charged that both civilian and military leaders
had failed to carry out either the equal opportunity directives or
their human relations responsibilities. "There is blatant racism
within the military," he added, "and people are very reluctant to
make changes." Representative Parren J. Mitchell concurred: "I
think the dimensions, the pervasiveness, the extent of racism in the
military is so deep and so wide and so effective that we cannot
possibly cope with it."

The hearings emphasized that, too often, discriminatory practices followed the black serviceman into civilian life, where he
wound up without meaningful skills and, in many cases, with a
less than honorable discharge, which made his civilian life at least
as difficult as his former military life. An unemployed black veteran
who was administratively discharged commented bitterly: "I am
unfit, unemployed, due to an undesirable discharge from the military in June of last year."

While he was stationed at Fort Riley, he went on, the Red Cross
informed him of his wife's attempted suicide. Unable to get permission to see her, he went AWOL and was picked up and put in
the stockade. After his less than honorable discharge he found
himself among the 14 per cent of black veterans who were unemployed, with no chance whatever of obtaining employment because
of the stigma of his "bad" discharge. Although commanders frequently told servicemen that such discharges could be easily
changed, he said that he found in reality that this was a rare practice. And, he continued:

Somebody is going to change my discharge and not when they feel
like it, but right now. Either change it now, or I will be the most

worse and fearsome dude out on those streets. . . . If it means grabbin' them in the collar, I'm grabbing. If it means hitting them in the head, I'm hitting them, because I am being hurt from now on with this piece of paper.

Time magazine, under the heading "Armed Forces: Black Power-lessness," declared.

For years the military rested comfortably on its largely unfounded reputation as a fastness of racial fair play and equality. Because it beat chopping cotton or pushing brooms, blacks viewed the armed forces as an escape from a hostile world. That, it turns out, was a mistake. . . . It has become increasingly clear that the military too has its full share of racism.

The unhappy facts surfaced last week during *ad hoc* hearings. . . . A succession of witnesses told the committee that racism is so pervasive both in the U.S. and overseas as to make the armed services virtually intolerable for thousands of black Americans. . . . At one point, Mrs. Chisholm was so moved by the angry testimony of one black ex-GI that she averted her eyes from the witness and wept.

On November 19, while the caucus hearings were proceeding, Defense Secretary Laird appointed Donald L. Miller, a black ship-building executive from Brooklyn and a former army major, to re-place Render as Deputy Secretary for Equal Opportunity. Upon assuming his post, Mr. Miller pledged to make his office "more responsive to the needs of black servicemen."

In January 1972 the Defense Race Relations Institute (DRRI) opened its first seven-week formal class at Patrick Air Force Base, Florida. The DRRI staff and faculty included thirty military per-sonnel and nineteen civilians to teach an average class of 275. Each student was given a number of examinations to determine his own attitudes toward various racial groups and ethnic cultures. The edu-cational program for the course was concentrated on minority stud-ies and behavioral science, and the curriculum sought to foster racial harmony by changing individual attitudes.

Among the subjects studied in the Minority Studies Division were black history, the history of the black servicemen, and con-temporary black thought. The Behavioral Science Division sought to provide students with a knowledge of intergroup relations and the social processes that shape opinions, attitudes, and behavior. There was extensive use of exchange role-playing, in which whites and blacks played reverse roles in simulated situations in the military setting that might be expected to produce interracial misunderstandings and embroilments. Students were given an opportunity to "test out" their classroom knowledge during a three-day weekend experience among minority groups in Miami's inner city.

After graduation, the instructors returned to their respective units in the different services, where they conducted discussion seminars and educational programs in race relations. Every man in uniform—from private to general—received eighteen hours of instruction in this area. Comprehensive as this education program in race relations was, some DRRI instructors and other equal opportunity personnel still had private doubts "as to whether they are attacking racism or engaged in a sophisticated 'black pacification' program."

On April 5, 1972, a biracial task force was commissioned by Secretary of Defense Laird to study the administration of military justice in the armed forces. At its head were Nathaniel R. Jones of the NAACP and Lieutenant General C. E. Hutchin, Jr., Commanding General of the First Army, and its membership consisted of five white generals, five black civilians, and four white civilians.

Steps were taken at the highest command level to implement and expand the equal opportunity and human rights programs. Early in 1972 General Robert E. Cushman, Jr., the newly appointed commandant of the Marine Corps, declared: "Black marines should know I have a personal interest in their problems and I care." This commitment was re-emphasized in an interview in March in which the general spoke of the human relations problem as "a challenge to which we have given the highest priority and to which we have directed our full resources." He added, "We are making it clear, in no uncertain terms, that there is no room in the Marine Corps for racism."

In a letter to all generals and commanding officers on July 31, General Cushman ordered an end to racial segregation in the barracks or other living areas under the jurisdiction of the Marine Corps. He also directed that commanders announce the punishment and work assignments of all Marines at daily formations in order to remove the grounds for complaints of discrimination. Commanders were also instructed to be "tough, aggressive, and demanding" in dealing with racially segregated bars, restaurants, or other places frequented by off-duty Marines. Equal treatment for all

Marines must be carried out vigorously and conscientiously at all times, the general emphasized, and he concluded with this warning: "Those individuals who cannot or will not abide by this principle should seek other employment. There is no room for such Marines in our Corps today."

Similar assurances of equal treatment were forthcoming from leaders of the other services as well. In May it was announced from Washington that future officer fitness reports in the army, navy, and Air Force would include ratings on racial attitudes and commitment to equal opportunity and treatment of minorities as well as on traditional leadership categories. This new procedure was subsequently extended to all enlisted supervisors. A poor record in race relations could now lead to denial of promotion or even removal from command. In October the Air Force Chief of Staff, General John D. Ryan, called on major commanders to support the Equal Opportunity Race Relations Education programs "with the same vigor and enthusiasm as that given the flying mission." Officers and enlisted men of all services who were identified with racist practices were to be relieved of their jobs and, if necessary, dismissed from active duty.

The army required minority representation on all officer selection boards. It established an officer candidate school recruiting objective of 15 per cent blacks. The number of blacks attending senior service college rose sharply. The number of black brigade commanders serving in Europe increased from one to four, and the number of black battalion commanders from five to twenty-three. A program to achieve a more equitable distribution of black soldiers in hard skill military occupational specialties was adopted.

The army also adopted a new Racial Awareness Program designed to improve interracial communication through a formal race relations training course.

The cornerstone of the program was the mandatory race relations seminar. Also included were such activities as Black History Week, the observance of significant calendar events, and unit race relations conferences. Colonel Frazier, the army's equal opportunity director, while affirming that much still remained to be done, concluded: "We are bringing the problems out into the open. We are teaching blacks and whites that they can work and live together harmoniously."

In August 1972, for example, Brigadier General Raymond O.

Miller, Commanding General of the Berlin Brigade, invited Stanley Faulkner, the New York attorney who had defended two black GIs, to speak on "Race Relations and Equal Opportunity" in West Berlin. Faulkner accepted and spent three days discussing race relations with command personnel of the Berlin Brigade and with teachers at the Berlin American High School and TAR School. The result, as General Miller noted to Faulkner, had been "a positive effect on the perception of the racial situation by my soldiers," though the general acknowledged that "the relationship between the company commander and the black soldier is not all that it should be." He concluded:

> Race relations training is now conducted during basic training, but considering the relatively short time a soldier spends in basic training, and the total amount of material which he must learn, the major effort in this area must continue to be made after the soldier reaches his permanent duty station.

Faulkner subsequently observed that both the invitation to lecture and General Miller's response indicated "how desperate the military is to alleviate tensions and problems among servicemen." Only this, he wrote, could explain its invitation to the very attorney who had used racism and racial discrimination in the army as the basis for a successful defense "to help them resolve their dilemma in this particular area."

An example of the type of educational material used in the Air Force race relations program was the *Air Force News Service* bulletin, distributed weekly to all Air Force newspaper editors. The issue of January 19, 1973, the week of Martin Luther King's birthday, contained an editorial entitled "A Piece of the Pie," which read in part:

> Many blacks are afraid of the white superiority complex. Many whites are afraid that blacks want a piece of their pie. That's where the problem comes in. Because it's not the whites' pie at all. The pie belongs to everybody in the United States who's willing to work for it. The black man wants an equal share for an equal amount of effort and he hasn't been getting it. . . .
>
> We can't begin to understand what makes each person tick. It's difficult to overcome prejudice, myth, legend, and stereotype, but there's one thing we all can do and that's make the pie bigger. Equal opportunity for blacks means greater opportunity for whites.

Take a moment and learn to know your brother a little better—eat a piece of pie with him. Don't be afraid.

In June 1970 Admiral Elmo R. Zumwalt, Jr., assumed the position of Chief of Naval Operations. At forty-nine, Zumwalt was the youngest CNO in naval history. He later said that, when he took over his post, he was surprised to find "so great a misunderstanding" between the racial groups in the naval service. Aware of a potentially explosive situation, Zumwalt gave top priority to the resolution of racial tensions. He inaugurated programs to improve service life, particularly for enlisted men, both black and white, and at transforming what he called the "lily-white racist navy" into an institution of racial equality and minority opportunity.

The programs designed to achieve these objectives were launched by a series of prominently posted directives widely known as "Z-grams"—personal messages from the admiral to the entire navy. In 1970 these liberalizing directives abolished a number of restrictions on dress and hair style, derisively called "Mickey Mouse" regulations. Enlisted men were permitted to wear beards, sideburns, mustaches, and civilian clothes on post. Other directives sought to open up the navy to more blacks and to ensure that the special needs of minority groups were recognized and provided for.

In November 1970 the Chief of Naval Operations convened a series of study groups. One of them consisted of a representative group of black officers and enlisted men and their wives who met in Washington to discuss various problems and then briefed the Secretary of the Navy, the CNO, and other senior personnel. Zumwalt afterward stated that he had been sensitized to the racial problem in the navy "by the tremendous experience" of listening to this briefing. He added:

> From this group of black navy men and their wives we learned of discrimination of an order that we had no idea existed. . . . We didn't even understand the nature or basis for some of it until we listened to this group. Since then I have seen the transformation not only in myself, but in all those senior personnel who were in the room on that occasion.

One immediate result was the dispatch of a message from Admiral Zumwalt, in December 1970, addressed to all naval personnel and expressing the determination of both the Navy Secretary and the CNO "to maximize our efforts to improve the lot of our minority servicemen." The admiral called upon the entire command "to help seek out and eliminate those demeaning areas of discrimination that plague our minority shipmates." The message concluded with these words: "Ours must be a Navy family that recognizes no artificial barriers of race, color, or religion. There is no black Navy, no white Navy, just one Navy—the United States Navy."

During the next two years, more than two hundred minority and race relations programs were instituted in the navy, and those already begun were further expedited, covering everything from attracting black recruits and promoting blacks already in the service to the establishment of special counseling on minority affairs and making black cosmetics available in the exchanges. Black recruiting specialists were added to each of the navy's thirty-seven recruiting stations across the country. A new recruiting slogan was adopted: "You Can Be Black and Navy Too," as standards were lowered to allow educationally deficient blacks to enter the navy. By 1972 about 12 per cent of new recruits were black. A vigorous campaign was launched for the recruitment of black officers. New naval reserve officer training programs were set up in predominantly black colleges and universities. Thirty-two NROTC programs were also established in high schools with significant minority enrollment. In 1972 there were 150 black midshipmen at the Naval Academy, the largest number in its history. In the same year, four blacks were elected as top officers of the academy's sophomore class.

Another effort at the junior recruitment level was Project BOOST (Broadened Opportunities for Officer Selection and Training), a program to prepare black and other minority enlisted men for college and careers as officers. The candidates were selected on the basis of post-enlistment tests for one to two years of intensive tutoring and counseling so they could compete for admission to universities and colleges for enrollment in NROTC units and, for a few of them, appointment to the Naval Academy. In 1971 seventy minority personnel were enrolled, and a projected minority participation of 200 was aimed for by June 1972.

In April 1971 Captain Samuel L. Gravely, Jr., became the first black admiral in United States naval history. Blacks were also placed in command of twelve of the navy's vessels, and new ships were named in honor of outstanding blacks. A destroyer, for example, was named for Dorie Miller, the mess attendant at Pearl Harbor who won the Navy Cross in World War II.

Commanders were instructed to give special attention to opportunities for minority personnel to get into all of the enlisted ratings and into senior commissioned grades. They were also directed to advise local officials, community leaders, and business groups that future decisions on the closing of bases would take into account local area practices with respect to housing for minority personnel. Black officers and senior petty officers were assigned as special assistants for minority affairs with direct access to commanding officers of ships and shore installations. Black consumer goods were stocked in all exchanges, ship stores, and commissaries. Black barbers and beauticians qualified in hair care for black personnel were employed in barber shops at bases and stations. Literature on black heritage and culture appeared in ships' libraries and soul music in jukeboxes. And Negro History Week was celebrated at various navy commands.

Lieutenant Commander William S. Norman, a black and the Minority Affairs assistant to Admiral Zumwalt, was directed to visit major naval installations and meet with commanding officers and with minority personnel and their dependents. In cases where individuals felt that they were being discriminated against, Norman had the authority to check out and resolve the complaint. Aggrieved individuals were given the opportunity to write directly to their commanding officers or to request captain's mast (a personal interview). If not satisfied with the results, they could write directly to Vice Admiral David Bagley, Assistant Chief of Naval Personnel.

Human Relations or Race Relations Councils were set up as vehicles of communication between the commanders and their men. Minority Naval Informational Messages were issued regularly to all commands. Another important development was the establishment in June 1971 of the Human Resource Project Office with a Race Relations Education Program. This program had as its objective "the elimination of racism from the United States Navy." Race Relations Institute graduates were assigned in teams to provide race relations training to commands. Similar programs were instituted at recruit commands for all recruits, at the Naval Academy, at the Officer Candidate School, and in the Naval ROTC system. Education in race relations was also provided at advanced schools, the new Chief Petty Officer Management School, and the Naval War College.

Early in 1972 Admiral Zumwalt noted that several major problem areas still remained. Off-base housing discrimination persisted. Minority officer procurement continued to lag.

> Furthermore, we've discovered that there are cultural differences that make it more difficult for some minorities to pass certain examinations. In other words, examinations are written for the cultural biases of the white rather than for the minority. We're trying very hard to correct the examination procedures so that every man will have an equal opportunity and there won't be that artificial bias.
>
> We have just got to make certain that everybody has the same chance—not only the same chance for advancement, the same chance for equal treatment in military justice, but also an equal chance for family housing off base.
>
> I am very optimistic about the future.

Despite these optimistic comments, there was considerable evidence that the navy was falling far short of ending discriminatory practices or eliminating tension and mistrust between the races. Admiral Zumwalt began to receive disturbing reports from black officers assigned to report on the effectiveness of the reform measures. They charged that "the programs are not being implemented or executed." Too many navy leaders were paying only lip-service to the liberalizing directives rather than making sure that they were actually carried through at all levels. They pointedly added that the recruiting slogan "You can be black and Navy too" was false advertising.

Specifically, they complained that black officers assigned as race relations advisers were consulted only in high-tension situations, and not on a continuing basis. They deplored the slow rate of promotions for blacks and other minorities; "biased" tests for enlisted men; a disproportionate number of arrests and punitive discharges; and a shortage of ethnic-oriented entertainment and food. The black officers told Zumwalt that tensions were approaching the flash point. Lieutenant Commander Norman, one of the black officers at the meeting, was quoted as saying, "We have created such a powder keg, and it is going to blow this organization apart unless we take some emergency actions. We have to make commanding officers give the same kind of priorities to race relations that they do to keeping their ships from running aground."

Some insight into the new level to which black complaints had escalated is contained in this statement from a navy official:

> The initial complaints dealt with things that were easily reconcilable such as availability of black magazines, soul music in jukeboxes and black-oriented cosmetics in the PX. Well, we've progressed from that point 'til we're dealing with the real nitty gritty now—problems of promotion, assignments, interracial relationships.

Beginning on October 12 and for weeks thereafter, a rash of racial incidents—"the worst in the naval service's history"—dominated the headlines. They focused public attention on Zumwalt's liberalizing reforms and prompted a special House Armed Services subcommittee investigation. Navy Secretary John W. Warner was led to comment: "Race relations have now been elevated to the same top priority as combat readiness."

The young black sailors involved in these incidents were outspoken in their attacks on what they called racism in the navy and the discriminatory practices that resulted from it. Specifically, they insisted that they were assigned the most menial jobs, were held back from promotion because of consistently lower ratings than whites for the same level of work, received more severe punishment than whites, and were administratively discharged as unsuitable or incompetent.

Others, however, insisted that the rash of troubles in the navy was due not to discrimination against blacks but to a poorly conceived minority recruiting program that had led to an influx of ill-educated blacks who were unqualified for responsible assignments and promotion in the highly technical navy. Their inability to achieve desirable assignments and rapid promotion, the argument went, left them bitter and disgruntled, and they found release for their frustrations in violent confrontations.

Still others blamed the racial flare-ups on the inevitable strains resulting from extended sea duty as the navy took over an ever increasing role in the Vietnam War. They pointed out that the men were required to work eighteen to twenty hours a day, to live for long periods in cramped, overheated quarters, and to go for long stretches without weekend passes. The exhausting work load, lack of sleep, and absence of shore leave, it was held, had operated "to shorten tempers and bring pent-up racial tensions to the surface."

Many navy men expressed the view that drug use, known to be heavy in the Seventh Fleet, might have contributed to rising racial tensions. One admiral contended in an interview that drugs were the most significant factor in the outbreaks.

On the other hand, the anti-Zumwalt forces, both in and out of the navy, were quick to attribute the service's racial troubles to "permissiveness." They launched a campaign to get rid of the controversial CNO.

The first of the incidents erupted aboard the aircraft carrier *Kitty Hawk* on the night of October 12–13. According to accounts of the incident later given by black seamen, the disturbance really began the night before when an argument broke out at the enlisted men's club at Subic Bay in the Philippines, where men from the ship were celebrating their last night of liberty before sailing again for North Vietnam. The argument turned into a fight, and a riot squad was summoned. Tear gas was used, the fight intensified, and five black and four white sailors were arrested.

The next morning the ship departed for the coast of North Vietnam. An investigating officer was appointed to inquire into the Subic Bay brawl, and some black sailors were summoned to testify. The blacks got into an argument with the investigating officer and stalked out to join other black sailors who had congregated on a mess deck. The ship's executive officer, who was part black and part Indian, eventually calmed the men. Meanwhile, however, the riot squad had been summoned. It arrived and began to disperse only the blacks, breaking them up into pairs. The blacks resisted, and a melee quickly broke out throughout the decks of the huge carrier.

When asked what the trouble was aboard the *Kitty Hawk*, some of the sailors shouted "racism." "The blacks just got tired of being treated like dogs," one black sailor said. "Every time we pull into port, there's been little conflicts between whites and blacks." Others traced the disturbance to "unhappy blacks venting their spleen on white seamen." In any event, by the time the incident was over forty-six seamen—forty whites and six blacks—had been injured, and twenty-seven, all black, had been arrested.

On October 22 charges of rioting, which were raised in several cases to assault, were brought against the twenty-seven black sailors. No white crewmen were charged. At the same time, the navy announced that disciplinary proceedings would begin early in November aboard the *Kitty Hawk*. Civil rights groups at once protested that the sailors could not receive fair trials at sea. Roy Wilkins called upon President Richard M. Nixon and Navy Secretary Warner to postpone the trials until the men returned to the United States. On November 8 the navy announced that it had agreed to delay the proceedings until after the carrier returned to San Diego, where the black sailors would be able to secure civilian legal counsel. Twenty-one of the black crewmen, those who requested civilian lawyers, were flown to San Diego from the Philippines and placed in the North Island naval brig to await disciplinary proceedings. Six of the twenty-seven blacks did not request such assistance and remained aboard the carrier to await trial at sea.

Hard on the heels of the *Kitty Hawk* disturbance, another racial incident occurred aboard the oiler *Hassayampa*, moored at the Subic Bay naval base in the Philippines. Four white crewmen were injured and eleven—again only blacks—were arrested and put off the ship to stand trial.

The next outburst occurred aboard the aircraft carrier *Constellation* on the night of November 3, while the ship was at sea on training exercises about eighty miles off the California coast. This incident followed a series of shipboard meetings of black crew members to discuss the racist behavior of the ship's officers and to plan ways to bring their complaints to the ship's commander, Captain J. D. Ward, who had taken charge in October 1971.

The ship was then in the process of reducing its complement by 250 men, and the captain directed that certain records be reviewed. Those considered troublemakers, if they qualified for administrative discharge, were to be notified of the ship's intent to process them for such discharges. On November 2 discharge procedures were initiated against six black crew members, who were informed they would be given general discharges with honor. The six were said to have been chosen on the basis of poor test scores and low efficiency ratings. The news that discharge procedures had been initiated against the six blacks led the black seamen to conclude angrily that similar discharges would be given to 250 black crew members. Chief Petty Officer Wilson, chairman of the Constellation's minority affairs committee, was subsequently quoted as saying:

Why should they have to go through all the degradations, the menial jobs, mess cooking, and when it gets time to come out, they can't get a regular discharge? The brothers wanted a confrontation by then. They thought these six were getting screwed, and, if they were, everybody else could get the same shaft.

On the night of November 3 more than 100 blacks staged a sit-down demonstration on the carrier's mess deck to get the captain to hear their grievances. "We wanted to air our views," explained Radarman Third Class Lonnie Brown, "and tell the captain what was actually happening. We had to get the word across to the man who runs the ship."

Captain Ward, however, refused to meet directly with the men. Speaking over the ship's intercom, he said: "Any member of this ship who has a complaint should take it to the Human Relations Council, and I'll meet with them." The protest continued. At one point during the demonstration Marines in riot dress, with fixed bayonets, were rushed to the scene and then withdrawn. Early in the morning, the captain decided to interrupt the training exercises at sea and return to San Diego, where the dissident crewmen would be put ashore as a "temporary beach detachment." At a muster of the entire crew on the flight deck in the morning, after the carrier returned to North Island, its home port, Ward offered counseling on shore to anyone with a problem, and 130 men—122 blacks and 8 whites—left the ship, which then put back to sea.

Over the next several days various naval personnel met with the "beach detachment" in an effort to resolve the grievances. They asked that a higher authority review the nonjudicial punishments and administrative discharges given to blacks for underachievement and that amnesty be granted to those involved in the protest meetings and demonstration aboard the ship.

On November 8 Captain Ward, who had been ordered by the fleet commander to return to port and meet with the group, ordered them to be aboard the carrier early the following day. Once they were on board, he said, prompt attention would be given to their complaints of racial discrimination in work assignments, discipline, and administrative discharges. However, no complete amnesty would be granted. The following morning two black sailors and all eight white sailors returned to the carrier. The remaining 120, accompanied by five civilian attorneys furnished by the Black Servicemen's Caucus of San Diego, reported for dockside duty near the carrier as ordered but refused to board until all their conditions were accepted. Leroy Templeton, spokesman for the protesting sailors, accused the navy of attempting to "lure the men aboard in order to take reprisals," adding: "We fear for our lives unless these matters are settled on shore."

The vigil at dockside ended late in the day when 120 of the protesters were removed from the carrier's rolls and reassigned to nearby air stations, where they were promised that "prompt attention would be given to their complaints." Next came an announcement that the 120 sailors were to be brought before captain's masts on AWOL charges and that the proceedings would be conducted by Captain Robert McKenzie, Commandant of North Island. He arranged for personnel specialists and legal advisers to meet with the men to discuss their grievances.

On the afternoon of November 16 three spokesmen for the black seamen gave an interview to the press that lasted almost three hours. Outlining their complaints, they described racial incidents that they claimed had taken place aboard the *Constellation*. "The want and the need," Radarman Brown said, "is for justice, and to be treated as a man." Asked how serious the situation was, he replied: "It's serious enough for me to put on the line my three years and eight months of an unblemished record and to put on the line the future of my wife and my son and my life as a man." In a separate interview, Captain Ward accused the dissidents of "not seeking to air grievances" but, instead, "trying very hard to create a violent situation."

But this view was not shared by the commander of the Pacific Fleet, who issued a reprimand to the fleet's ship and shore commands. He said that most racial incidents would have been avoided if officers had been more heedful of minority grievances. Admiral Zumwalt reacted even more sternly. The CNO summoned a "flotilla of admirals and generals" to the Pentagon and delivered a blistering lecture to them. Using strong and direct language, he accused his senior commanders and their subordinates of failures in leadership and of ignoring his directives. The navy, he said, had made "unacceptable progress" in the area of equal opportunity; its more than 200 minority programs were not working "effectively." "We have tended," he added, "to fail wherever a real change from hallowed routine was required." While stressing the importance of maintaining good order and discipline, Zumwalt stated: "It is my view that these current racial incidents are not the results of lowered standards, but are clearly due to failure of commands to implement those programs with a whole heart. . . . Equal means exactly that. Equal."

Zumwalt's emphatic statement was followed by new directives aimed at improving race relations. He ordered all commanders to seek out and take action against any violations of the "spirit or the letter" of the navy's equal rights program. He directed the Inspector General's office to police compliance with equal opportunity directives and grade navy commanders on their performance in handling racial problems under their command. One black officer recalled that in the past most navy directives on race relations had been "filed and forgotten" and predicted: "Until everybody gets the message that promotion depends on ability to provide color-blind leadership, the navy is going to have troubles." On November 18, Zumwalt issued a tough warning to all ranks that strict discipline would not be sacrificed to reform.

From the very beginning the more conservative admirals, captains and commanders, both active and retired, had strongly resisted the "liberalizing reforms" initiated by Zumwalt. His blunt declaration that the navy's racial trouble stemmed from commanders who were deficient in leadership was the last straw for them. In private talks with reporters, administration officials, and politicians, these officers angrily charged that the racial flare-ups had actually been caused by a climate of permissiveness and a breakdown in command control and discipline induced by Zumwalt's sweeping and poorly conceived programs. They strongly urged that the CNO be replaced, his liberalizing reforms de-emphasized, and discipline re-emphasized. In an interview with a *Time* reporter, Navy Secretary Warner indicated that he might consider withdrawing some of Zumwalt's more controversial "Z-grams."

Many officers, including senior officers of the Atlantic Command, rallied to the CNO's defense. They denied that the recent racial strife had been sparked by the reforms and insisted that the Z-grams had had a "highly beneficial effect on service morale." And they praised Zumwalt for recognizing that the navy had to change. Vice Admiral Bagley, the navy's manpower chief, asserted: "Admiral Zumwalt, I think, is the first chief of the navy to recognize changes in society which have necessitated changes in the navy." Vice Admiral J. J. Lebourgeois said: 'Perhaps the changes have come too damn fast for some, but they had to come." And a lieutenant commander echoed: "While a much-needed breath of fresh air is sweeping through the navy, many of my colleagues prefer the musty odor of ancient times."

The controversy between Zumwalt and his critics in the navy was reflected outside the service as well. His defenders contended that, if the entire naval officer corps were as committed to equal opportunity as their chief, the recent racial disturbances "might perhaps have been avoided." The Atlanta *World*, a black newspaper, remarked: "We think that the central issue is far greater than Admiral Zumwalt and 'permissiveness.' It is whether the Navy can catch up with the 20th century as we march swiftly toward the 21st."

The charge of "permissiveness" raised by the anti-Zumwalt forces was echoed by the House Armed Services Committee. On November 13 its chairman, F. Edward Hébert of Louisiana, "a hard-line traditionalist," announced that a subcommittee would investigate "alleged racial and disciplinary problems" in the navy. He declared, "I share the concern of many members of Congress over the apparent breakdown of discipline in the United States Navy."

The three-man subcommittee, all white, was headed by Representative Floyd V. Hicks. On the committee with him were Alexander Pirnie, an army colonel during World War II, and W. C. Daniel, a former National Commander of the American Legion. The Congressional Black Caucus asked to have a black congressman sit in on the hearings, but the request was denied.

Beginning on November 20 the subcommittee took seventy-four hours of private testimony on the incidents aboard the aircraft carriers *Kitty Hawk* and *Constellation*. As soon as the inquiry began it became clear that Zumwalt and his reforms were under attack. Representative Hicks, in an opening statement, declared that the panel would "concentrate our greatest efforts" on the question of navy discipline. "We cannot overlook the possibility," he said, "that there may exist at this time an environment of . . . permissiveness." He added that the panel would also investigate the dissidents' complaints of racial discrimination; that all the hearings would be closed to the public; and that no information would be released until disciplinary action against all the men involved in the incidents was completed.

During a hearing break Zumwalt told the press that there was "absolutely" no permissiveness in the navy and that discipline would be maintained. The hearings moved from Washington to San Diego, where, beginning on November 21, a four-day inquiry was held on the difficulties aboard the carrier *Constellation*. Once again, reports leaked out from the closed-door hearings that the committee was "overly concerned with trying to find evidence of permissiveness, rather than discrimination against blacks." One such report read: "The *Constellation*'s officers were all questioned before any of the black sailors appeared, and the congressmen evinced little interest in asking the *Connie*'s brass to address themselves to specific complaints raised by the enlisted men."

One of the black protesters complained: "They didn't seem very much interested when I told them how blacks get the short and dirty end of the stick in job assignments." Another black witness said that the committee did not take up discrimination at all. "The committee is out to get Zumwalt." Captain Ward was reported to have said that the racial troubles aboard the ship could be traced to a comparatively small group of "hard core" dissidents determined to make trouble.

The subcommittee recessed its hearings until December 5, when it returned to San Diego to investigate the mid-October disturbance aboard the carrier *Kitty Hawk*. The commanding officer, Captain Marland W. Townsend, Jr., reportedly told the subcommittee members that there was no evidence of racial discrimination aboard the carrier and that "things are fine just the way they are." The twenty-one accused seamen refused to testify on the advice of their attorneys because of the possibility that their testimony would be used against them in court-martial proceedings. On December 12 the subcommittee finished its closed-door hearings in San Diego. Representatives Daniel and Hicks agreed that "there is less racism in the navy than in civilian life," and Daniel added that in his opinion a few men "did enter the navy, just as any other organization, to foment strife." The subcommittee then returned to Washington to hear Admiral Zumwalt once more and to prepare its final report.

Meanwhile, disciplinary action was being taken against the men of the *Constellation* and the *Kitty Hawk*. The former received light nonjudicial punishment from Captain McKenzie. Sixty-nine were transferred to other ships, none to aircraft carriers. Two of them were hospitalized for medical conditions that had come to light during routine physical examinations. Thirty-four were given honorable discharges, and ten received general discharges under honorable conditions. Five applied for discharges as either hardship cases or conscientious objectors. The eight crewmen who voluntarily returned to their stations escaped punishment.

The twenty-one blacks accused of rioting and assault on the *Kitty Hawk* were ordered tried before special courts-martial consisting of a panel of three to five naval officers and enlisted men. The maximum sentence in a special court-martial was six months at hard labor, reduction in rank, a fine of two-thirds of the prisoner's pay for that period, and a bad-conduct discharge. At the same time the navy ordered all of the accused held without bail. A request by civilian defense attorneys provided by the NAACP and the American Civil Liberties Union to free the men pending trial was denied "due to the seriousness of the charges."

Black sailors angrily protested that, even though Zumwalt himself had placed the blame for the navy's trouble on the failure of the admirals to carry out his orders, punishment was being meted out only to black seamen. They complained that the navy had recently issued a new series of special orders apparently directed specifically at dissident black crewmen. These new rules, they charged, had made shipboard life "tense and strained." On December 25 Earl Caldwell, a black correspondent, wrote to the *New York Times* from San Diego: "While attention has focused on investigations into racial incidents, the Navy in recent weeks has quietly begun a crackdown on dissident black sailors."

Two days later, at a press conference in San Diego held under the auspices of the Black Servicemen's Caucus, four black crewmen from the *Kitty Hawk*, who had been released from the brig through their civilian lawyer's efforts, made public additional charges of discrimination. They said that white officers on the *Kitty Hawk* often called them "boys" or "dogs" and that there were standing orders on the ship to break up any gathering of more than three or four blacks, while white sailors could gather in groups of any size. "Twenty white sailors could sit at a table but four blacks could not," one of the black sailors said angrily. A white sailor returning late to the ship would be excused, but a black sailor would not. If there was a fight between a white sailor and a black, the black would be punished and the white would not. One of the blacks complained of a feeling on the *Kitty Hawk* that blacks were not welcome in the navy. "They don't feel that we are fit to visit other ports," he said.

On January 2, 1973, Chairman Hicks of the House Armed Services subcommittee submitted the report of the panel's findings to Committee Chairman Hébert. The report was made public on January 25. It constituted a sweeping denial of any charges that discrimination was responsible for the racial unrest in the navy. The subcommittee concluded instead that a climate of "permissiveness" leading to a breakdown of discipline had been the real cause for the disturbances aboard the two aircraft carriers. The subcommittee maintained that it had not found a single case of racial discrimination that could have provoked the disorders. It characterized most of the *Kitty Hawk* rioters as young blacks of "below average mental capacity," and it seriously questioned whether they should have been accepted in the first place. The panel also concluded that the sit-in aboard the *Constellation* was "the result of a carefully orchestrated demonstration of passive resistance" after from twenty to twenty-five blacks talked others into believing that white racism was prevalent both aboard the ship and throughout the navy. The navy was urged to screen out "agitators, troublemakers, and all those who do not measure up."

Not everyone was impressed with the subcommittee's explanation of the Navy's racial difficulties. John A. Robinson, a staff reporter for the *Boston Globe*, commented:

> Knowing the history of racial conflict and confrontation in our society, studies implying [that] disruptions are the result of the unruly nature of black people operating in an atmosphere free from the strictures of tough law and order measures are worthy of the highest degree of skepticism.

The degree of skepticism would have been even higher after a reading of the comprehensive four-volume report on the administration of military justice submitted to Secretary Laird on November 30, 1972, by the Pentagon's interracial task force. The result of an eight-month inquiry, its findings differed sharply from those of the House subcommittee. While acknowledging that racial discrimination was basically "a problem of a racist society" and that the military services could not remain unaffected by it, the study found that, despite the strides taken toward equality, there was still intentional and largely systemic discrimination against blacks in all the military services, and this discrimination produced direct and unwholesome effects. Systemic discrimination was said to include those policies and practices that appeared to be neutral in their effect but that actually operated to the disadvantage of minority individuals or groups. Examples cited were the military testing policies, the job assignment policies, the promotion policies, and the human relations and equal opportunity policies.

The task force charged that the human relations and equal opportunity programs were, in many cases, "more rhetorical than real." The race relations education program came in for critical comment. Among the items not included in the curriculum at the DRRI were instruction in the problems of discrimination in the administration of military justice; techniques in handling grievances; conflict management; and problems in communication. Instructors trained at the institute lacked the necessary resources to implement programs. Existing policies and practices of base commanders, especially overseas, were not dealing with the problems of segregated off-post housing. Nor was the situation any better in off-post recreational and leisure facilities, such as clubs and bars. In many areas, these continued to be closed to minority servicemen, especially blacks. And black and Spanish-speaking servicemen throughout the world were convinced that they were being singled out for punishment "by white authority figures" in cases where their white counterparts were not. "There is enough evidence of intentional discrimination by individuals," the report went on, "to convince the Task Force that such selective punishment is in many cases racially motivated."

The task force also examined and discussed the voluminous statistical data concerning incident reports, short-term AWOLs, Article 15 punishments, pretrial confinement, courts-martial, service correctional facilities, and administrative discharges. It found a clearly discernible disparity in punishments imposed on black and white servicemen. "The Task Force believes," it said, "that the administrative discharge has impacted to the detriment of minority group servicemen." It attributed this inequality to a combination of pre-service racism and in-service systemic discrimination.

The report called for sweeping reforms of the military as a whole and of the judicial system in particular. It made significant recommendations concerning nonjudicial punishments and military justice training and selection, and it proposed the addition of a specific punitive article to the Code of Military Justice outlawing discriminatory acts and practices. It further recommended uniform punishment for minor offenses, the recruitment of additional minority lawyers, and the random selection of court-martial juries to eliminate the suspicion of command influence.

Other aspects of military life touched upon by the task force's recommendations included administrative discharge procedure, equal opportunity programs, service aptitude tests, and job assignment procedures. It also called for a revision of racial and ethnic codes to include "Americans of Spanish descent."

In accepting the report, Secretary Laird attempted to head off the anticipated charge that military reforms would lead to permissiveness and a breakdown of discipline. "Justice and discipline are both indispensable," he said at a news conference. The *New York Times*, commenting editorially on the military justice report, pointed out that the testimony of black crewmen from the carrier *Kitty Hawk* paralleled the panel's discovery of "intentional and systemic discrimination" against blacks in the military branches. The study, it felt, gave support to Admiral Zumwalt's determination to enforce reforms throughout the command structure and exposed the "shallowness" of those who argued that "the Navy's troubles can be cured by a simple reversion to old-fashioned iron discipline." "In the military as in civilian life," the editorial concluded, "order cannot be preserved unless the rule of law is enforced with scrupulous impartiality."

On January 7, 1973, the entire country was electrified by a story from New Orleans. From the rooftop of a Howard Johnson motel a sniper had shot six white persons to death and wounded several others. After thirty hours, during which a considerable part of the New Orleans police force was held at bay, the sniper was killed by machine gun fire from a Marine Corps helicopter. He turned out to be James Robert Essex, a young black navy veteran.

In the days following the newspapers set about to discover the background of this tragic episode. The story that developed served to focus national attention once again on the issue of discrimination in the armed services.

Essex emerged from interviews as a young man whose conduct had given no cause for complaint until he joined the navy early in 1969. He was trained in San Diego and was assigned to the installation at Imperial Beach, California, as a dental technician. In 1970 he was court-martialed by the navy for absence without leave, and in February 1971 he received a general discharge "for character and behavior disorders."

Essex's mother told reporters that during his service in the navy her son suffered constant harassment at the hands of "the white establishment." Another black seaman, Fred Allen, told of an occasion when he and Essex were heading to the galley for supper and Essex was attacked in a passageway by two white enlisted men. Essex was brought before a captain's mast, Allen said, but no charges were preferred against the whites who attacked him. C. B. Wilson, a black petty officer third-class, made the same point to reporters and added: 'But what really burned Essex up was the riding he got from petty officers and other officers. They would write him up for the smallest infraction and usually he would get a captain's mast while the white got off scot free. We all had that sort of experience."

The tragic end of the story came when Essex, "hating whites for what the navy had done to him," took matters in his own hands and lashed out from the New Orleans rooftop.

Just two days after Essex's violent death, Secretary Laird responded to the task force report. He directed the military departments to revise their procedures for nonjudicial punishment by making adequate legal advice available to an accused person, by granting him the right to call witnesses and present evidence, and by staying the imposition of punishment pending completion of any appeal. When requested by the accused, nonjudicial punishment proceedings were to be open to the public, except in those instances where military or security requirements could not permit it. The departments were also directed to provide any prospective recipient of a discharge other than honorable with an opportunity to consult a judge advocate at the outset of the discharge process.

The trials of the twenty-one black *Kitty Hawk* sailors began in San Diego late in December 1972 and continued into April 1973. A navy lawyer acknowledged that the service was having difficulty in establishing "a pattern of concerted deliberate action on the part of the black crew members that would meet the uniform military code's definition of a riot." In fact, riot charges could be sustained against only four of the twenty-one blacks originally so charged. Two pleaded guilty to rioting in exchange for promises of lenient sentences, and two others were convicted of rioting after standing trial. The rest were convicted on lesser charges of simple assault, breach of the peace, and insubordination.

Seven black defendants were freed of all charges, including rioting and assault—two by court acquittal, four by the navy's dismissal of charges for lack of evidence, and one whose conviction was set aside on review by the fleet air commanding officer at San Diego. Riot charges were dropped against six others, leaving them to face trial on lesser counts of assault and insubordination. Three others were charged only with assault, and two blacks received minor punishment for assault after nonjudicial hearings held aboard the *Kitty Hawk* before the ship returned to San Diego.

One case that aroused considerable criticism was that of Cleveland Mallory, a black sailor charged with riot and assault. At his trial, held before a military judge, six of the seven eyewitnesses failed to identify Mallory as the man they claimed to have seen assaulting a white sailor. The seventh witness, Michael Laurie, "made positive identification," insisting that he was able to do so because he had spent time with the accused in a Hong Kong bar while both were on liberty. Although Mallory established that he had neither taken liberty nor been in Hong Kong at the time alleged, he was convicted by the judge and given a bad-conduct discharge.

The indignation voiced by Mallory's attorneys helped persuade the NAACP to hire a professional investigator to check on the witness whose testimony, they were convinced, was untrue. After a month's association with Laurie, the investigator presented a set of tape recordings that confirmed the suspicion that the witness had been "inaccurate in his testimony." This evidence was turned over to the navy; the Mallory conviction was rescinded and the bad-conduct discharge withdrawn. However, the navy insisted that it had acted in the normal process of judicial review, and not because of the evidence in the tapes. Laurie was not charged with perjury.

In several of the *Kitty Hawk* trials the navy asked for bad-conduct discharges, but each time this was refused by the court. On March 18 Everett R. Hollis wrote to the *New York Times* from San Diego: "The courts-martial to date have not only failed to bear out the findings of the Navy's own board of inquiry but have also been at variance with the January 25 report of a three-man investigating panel of the House Armed Services Committee."

Throughout the trials, defense attorneys protested against what they called "navy racial justice." Their criticism was echoed by writers and civilian lawyers who observed the proceedings. The question most frequently raised was why, with one exception, charges were brought only against blacks, even though white sailors were also involved and eleven blacks were injured the night of the incident. Milton Silverstein, an attorney from San Diego, said, "There is no doubt that they were out to get these guys. They singled out blacks to prosecute."

The sole exception was a white airman apprentice whose name was added to the list of defendants ten days after the trials began. He was charged with assaulting a black petty officer. A panel of three white officers acquitted him after only twenty-three minutes of deliberation.

The critics were also disturbed by the fact that the accused blacks, even those charged only with assault, were held in pretrial confinement for as long as five months. A young navy lawyer, who said he had been involved in some 250 cases since joining the service and had previously considered the military judicial system fair, now reluctantly concluded that the *Kitty Hawk* blacks simply "were not treated fairly." He maintained that the handling of the cases was "appalling to me as a military lawyer." The black attorneys involved in the cases were even more outspoken. Chief among them was the NAACP's Nathaniel Jones, who stated: "When blacks complain that they can't get an equal break, they're right."

It was learned about this time that, in compliance with a December 26 directive from Admiral Zumwalt, the navy was quietly discharging thousands of those it considered "misfits and malcontents"—large numbers of them black—"to head off further outbreaks of racial rioting." Most were to be given general discharges under honorable conditions. The official certificates, however, would carry code numbers, which were understood by many employers, to indicate that the discharged sailors were "undesirable and unsuitable for re-enlistment."

In addition to its decision "to weed out men found to be a burden," the navy abandoned its policy of relaxed recruitment standards. Emphasis was now placed on "educational and character qualifications." Under a directive that became effective early in March, only high school graduates or those who could pass an equivalency test might enlist in the navy. The navy defended its decision on the ground that it had advanced technologically to the point where "we don't have many positions to give people with no education," but one recruiting officer remarked, "It appears that the Navy only wants those blacks that it can control." Earlier, he noted, when the navy took a wider selection of blacks, it made no effort to do anything for those who did not qualify for schools but sent them out to the fleet "to do the lousy jobs." "Hell, it's no wonder they rebelled," he concluded. "They looked around and saw that the white guys had all the good jobs and they were doing all of the dirty work."

As the Vietnam war came to a close, the American armed forces moved toward an all-volunteer system. The shift was being accompanied by a sharp increase in military pay and improved conditions of military life. To attract black and other minority personnel to the services, the various branches of the armed forces took full-page recruitment ads in a number of black publications. The acceptance of these ads provoked angry letters of protest from black servicemen. Specialist 4 James Fundenberg wrote to *Ebony* from Germany:

> You are telling the brothers to join the Army when almost 50 per cent of the people in jail over here are black. They are serving time for something whites over here get away with every day. . . . Don't

blow our minds by leading us to think you are so untogether that you would want other blacks to go through the same thing.

In an editor's note in the same issue, the magazine justified its action by claiming that the refusal of black publications to carry recruitment advertisements could well result in the new army's being made up "largely and disproportionately of whites." It insisted that blacks who wished to volunteer for the services should have the privilege of doing so, and it went on to state that "in the case of racial demonstrations or other racial disorders the presence of black brothers in uniform could decisively check or temper the excesses that might conceivably result from the deployment of all-white Army contingents."

NAACP Executive Director Roy Wilkins also urged blacks to continue enlisting in America's military services. In an address in Boston early in April, he maintained that "turning down the opportunity of learning to defend your country in uniform is the silliest thing for a black person."

Blacks really did not need this encouragement. Service life continued to attract and retain a greater proportion of blacks than whites. The advent of an all-volunteer force intensified this tendency, since the new military drew heavily on low-income black and other minority personnel. In July 1973, 35 per cent of those who signed up for the volunteer army were black. This was almost three times the black proportion of the population and approximated the rate of unemployment among black teenagers. Professor Charles Moskos enunciated the dilemma that this will pose for the Armed Forces in an article in the March 1973 issue of *Annals*. Analyzing the prospects for harmonious race relations in the emergent military establishment, he came to the conclusion that "structural as well as attitudinal changes are required to eradicate racism—with its concomitant racial strife—in the military setting. More than just confronting the personal biases of individuals, sources of institutional racism must be frontally attacked." Professor Moskos concluded his analysis with these words:

The American military establishment stands at a crucial juncture in its institutional development. In much the manner that it leaped ahead of civilian society with its integration policies of the 1950's, the military must now again take the lead in the contemporary racial climate of the 1970's. . . . If our American society is ever to realize its democratic promise, the direction it ought to take in race relations will most likely have been set by its men and women in military uniform.

On the other hand, it seems equally certain that, as long as racism exists in the rest of the society, the military will not be able to escape its effects.

10

Conclusion

The heroes have been many and generally anonymous. They have fought and been repulsed, only to return to the fight. The military establishment has been compelled to change, not through a sudden change of heart, but through a growing recognition that black manpower is a vital necessity to its survival. The republic out of self-interest has had to give way to the demands and pressure of the black minority.

In the crucible of military training and the years of Korean and Vietnam wars, blacks have sharpened their solidarity and determination to eradicate the vestiges of racism. It would be fallacious to argue that the worst is over. To believe that the last vestiges of racism will be purged in the lifetimes of living humans would be unduly optimistic. But the battle is joined.

Some future day when those yet unborn are seeking to understand the now living and the long dead, they may find answers not only with the historian but with the poet. They may best appreciate the irony inherent in the fate of the black serviceman and woman through most of American history through Paul Lawrence Dunbar's poem, "The Colored Soldier." It reads:

> In the early days you scorned them,
> And with many a flit and flout
> Said, these battles are the white men's
> And the whites will fight them out.
> . . . .

Then you called the Colored Soldiers
And they answered to your call.
. . . .
They were comrades then and brothers,
Are they more or less today?

Bibliographic Essay

Abbreviations Used

AN: *Amsterdam News* (New York)
CSM: *Christian Science Monitor*
JNH: *Journal of Negro History*
LC: Library of Congress
NHB: *Negro History Bulletin*
NR: *New Republic*
NYT: *New York Times*
PC: *Pittsburgh Courier*
USAMHRC: U.S. Army Military History Research Collection

GENERAL SOURCES

Several surveys of black American history provide essential background material for the study of blacks in the armed forces. Especially helpful are: John Hope Franklin, *From Slavery to Freedom, A History of Negro Americans* (New York, 1969); Eric Foner, *America's Black Past* (New York, 1970); and Herbert Aptheker, *A Documentary History of the Negro People of the United States* (New York, 1959–1973). For a general history of the Army the best work in print is Russell F. Weigley, *A History of the United States Army* (New York, 1967). The most complete collection of materials relating to the blacks in the armed forces during the seventeenth, eighteenth, and nineteenth centuries is "The Negro in the Military Services of the United States: A Compilation of Official Records, State Papers, Historical Records, 1639–1886" (National Archives, Washington, D.C., microfilm copy. 5 Rolls.) The October 1973 issue of the *Negro History Bulletin* (Volume 38) contains a most useful collection of articles on "Black Military History." See also John P. Davis, "The Negro in the Armed Forces of America," The American Negro Reference Book (Englewood Cliffs, N.J., 1966).

Students of this subject will also find it indispensable to examine the extensive collection of materials at the National Archives and at the U.S. Army Military History Research Collection, Carlisle Barracks, Pennsylvania, as well as the files of black newspapers and periodicals.

CHAPTER 1

The use of blacks in the Colonial Militia is discussed in Benjamin Quarles, "The Colonial Militia and Negro Manpower," *Mississippi Valley Historical Review*, 45 (March, 1959), and Larry Bowman, "The Use of Blacks in the French and Indian War," *Western Penna. Historical Magazine* (January, 1970). Benjamin Quarles, *The Negro in the American Revolution* (Chapel Hill, 1940), and Sidney Kaplan, *The Black Presence in the Era of the American Revolution 1770–1800* (Greenwich, Conn., 1973), are the best sources on black participation in the American Revolution. The most thorough and useful account of the changing position toward the recruitment of blacks in the Continental Army is to be found in the article by Pete Maslowski, "National Policy Toward the Use of Black Troops in the Revolution," *South Carolina Historical Magazine*, 73 (January, 1972). See also Donald L. Robinson, *Slavery in the Structure of American Politics, 1765–1820* (Ithaca, 1971). For a discussion of the Rhode Island black battalion see Lorenzo Greene, "Some Observations on the Black Regiment of Rhode Island in the American Revolution," *JNH*, 37 (April, 1952). On the participation of blacks from Louisiana against the British, see Ronald C. McConnell, *Negro Troops of Antebellum Louisiana* (Baton Rouge, 1968). Good discussions of the British use of blacks are contained in Benjamin Quarles, "Lord Dunmore as Liberator," *William and Mary Quarterly*, 15 (October, 1958), and Sylvia R. Fry, "The British Soldier in the American Revolution" (unpublished doctoral thesis, Tulane University, 1969.) The story of the blacks in Canada and their settlement in Sierra Leone is covered in Robin W. Winks, *The Blacks in Canada* (New Haven, 1971). The best summary of gradual emancipation in the Northern states is to be found in Arthur Zilversmit's work, *The First Emancipation* (Chicago, 1967). For James Forten's comments on the treatment of black veterans of the American Revolution see James Forten, *A Series of Letters by a Man of Color* (Philadelphia, 1813).

CHAPTER 2

The best discussion on the subject of blacks and the state militia in particular states in the early period of the Republic is contained in the article "Black Men and the Early New Jersey Militia," by Robert J. Gough, *New Jersey History*, 88 (Winter, 1970). See also, Winthrop Jordan, *White Over Black* (Chapel Hill, 1968). For an understanding of the role of blacks in the War of 1812 see William C. Nell, *Colored Americans in the Wars of 1776 and 1812* (Philadelphia, 1902); Frank A. Cassell, "Slaves of the Chesapeake Bay Area and the War of 1812,"

JNH, 57 (April, 1972); and Frank Lawrence Owsley, Jr., "The Role of the South in the British Grand Strategy in the War of 1812," *Tenn. Hist. Quar.* (Spring, 1972). Information on the role of the black battalion of Louisiana in the Battle of New Orleans and its subsequent history can be gleaned from Marcus Christian, *Negro Soldiers in the Battle of New Orleans* (New Orleans, 1965). Leon Litwack, *North of Slavery* (Chicago, 1961), is the best account of free blacks in the North before the Civil War.

The most comprehensive discussion of the role of blacks in the navy in the period after the War of 1812 is to be found in Harold D. Langley's work, *Social Reform in the United States Navy, 1798–1862* (Urbana, 1967), and in his article, "The Negro in the Navy and Merchant Service, 1789–1860," *JNH*, 52 (October, 1967).

An indispensable work on the previously neglected subject of the black Seminoles and the Seminole Wars is Kenneth W. Porter, *The Negro on the American Frontier* (New York, 1971); see also Mary Frances Berry, *Black Resistance to White Law* (New York, 1971).

CHAPTER 3

The best full-length accounts of black participation in the Civil War are Benjamin Quarles, *The Negro in the Civil War* (Boston, 1953), and Dudley Taylor Cornish, *The Sable Arm* (New York, 1956). James M. McPherson's *The Negro's Civil War* (New York, 1965) contains a valuable collection of documents supplemented by a commentary. On the black troops in the various states see the following: Charles E. Heller, "The 54th Massachusetts," *Civil War Times Illustrated*, 11 (April, 1972); Frederick M. Binder, "Pennsylvania's Negro Regiments in the Civil War," *Pennsylvania History*; and Charles H. Wesley, *Ohio Negroes in the Civil War* (Columbus, 1961). There are a number of contemporary reports on the contributions of black soldiers to the Union cause by white officers and enlisted men. Among the best of these are Thomas Wentworth Higginson, *Army Life in a Black Regiment* (New York, 1962), Horace Montgomery, "A Union Officer's Recollections of the Negro as a Soldier," *Pennsylvania History*, 28 (January–October, 1961); Carl E. Hatch, editor, *Dearest Susie: A Civil War Infantryman's Letters to His Sweetheart* (New York, 1971); and "A Yankee Soldier Looks at the Negro," edited by William Cullen Bryant, II, *Civil War History*, 7 (June, 1961).

On black officers, two articles by John W. Blassingame should be read, "Negro Chaplains in the Civil War," *NHB*, 37 (October, 1963), and "The Selection of Officers and Non-commissioned Officers of Negro Troops in the Union Army, 1863–1865," *NHB* 42 (October, 1968). For the role of black sailors in the Union Navy see Herbert Aptheker, "The Negro in the Union Navy," *JNH*, 32 (April, 1947), and Okon Edet Uya, *From Slavery to Public Service: Robert Smalls, 1839–1915* (New York, 1971).

Several sources detail the discrimination against and mistreatment of black soldiers: Philip S. Foner, "The First Negro Meeting in Maryland," *Maryland Historical Magazine*, 46 (Spring, 1971); Fred Harvey Harrington, "The Fort Jackson Mutiny," *JNH*, 27 (October, 1942); Herbert Aptheker, "Negro Casualties in the Civil War," *JNH*, 32 (January, 1947); Surgeon Robert K. Smith to General J. W. Phelps, April 14, 1863, to be found in the John W. Phelps Papers, Negro Collection, Atlanta University, reproduced by permission; and Albert Castel, "The Fort Pillow Massacre," *Civil War History*, 4 (March, 1958).

On the complex story of the black role in the Confederacy, see W. E. B. Du Bois, *Black Reconstruction* (New York, 1935); Bell I. Wiley, *Southern Negroes, 1861–1865* (New Haven, 1938); James H. Brewer, *The Confederate Negro* (Durham, 1969); and Barbara C. Ruby, "General Patrick Cleburne's Proposal to Arm Southern Slaves," *Arkansas Historical Quarterly*, 30 (Autumn, 1971).

CHAPTER 4

The activities of the black regulars are chronicled in the regimental records of the four units in which they served and which are to be found in Record Group 94, National Archives. Several good studies of black soldiers in the regular army have recently been published. Among these the most important are William H. Leckie, *The Buffalo Soldiers: A Narrative of the Negro Cavalry in the West* (Norman, Okla., 1967); Arlen L. Fowler, *The Black Infantry in the West, 1869–1891* (Westport, Conn., 1971); and John M. Carroll, ed., *The Black Military Experience in the American West* (New York, 1971).

In Chapter 7 of my book *The United States Soldier Between Two Wars: Army Life and Reforms, 1865–1898* (New York, 1970), I examined the issue of equality of opportunity within the regular army and presented the pertinent sources covering this aspect of the subject. On the relations between the black soldiers and the local populations of frontier communities, as well as the resistance to discrimination by black regulars, see Thomas D. Phillips, "The Black Regulars," in *The West of the American People*, Allen G. Bogue, Thomas D. Phillips, and James E. Wright, editors (Itasca, Ill., 1970); Frank N. Schubert, "Black Soldiers on the White Frontier," *Phylon*, 32 (Winter, 1971); and "The Suggs Affray," *Western Historical Quarterly*, 4 (January, 1973).

On blacks in the navy during the post–Civil War period, see Peter Karsten, *The Naval Aristocracy* (New York, 1972). For the experience of black cadets and midshipmen at the Military and Naval Academies, see John F. Marszalek, Jr., *Court-Martial: A Black Man in America* (New York, 1972), and R. L. Field, "The Black Midshipmen at the U.S. Naval Academy," *Naval Institute Proceedings*, April, 1973.

The neglected subject of the use of blacks in the Southern state militias is surveyed in Otis A. Singletary, *Negro Militia and Reconstruction* (Austin, 1957). A general account of the deteriorating situation confronting blacks during the last decades of the nineteenth century is provided by Rayford W. Logan, *The Betrayal of the Negro* (New York, 1965).

CHAPTER 5

An excellent account of the black troops during the period examined in this chapter is to be found in Marvin E. Fletcher, "Negro Soldiers and the U.S. Army, 1891–1917" (Unpublished Ph.D. dissertation, University of Wisconsin, 1968.) Also essential reading for anyone who wants to understand the role of the black troops in American expansion at the turn of the century are several recent works by Professor Willard B. Gatewood, Jr., which also contain most useful background material on the general, racial, social, and political climate of the period: "Black Americans and the Quest for Empire, 1898–1903," *JSH*, 38 (November, 1972); "*Smoked Yankees*" *and the Struggle for Empire: Letters from Negro Soldiers, 1898–1902* (Urbana, 1971); "Negro Troops in Florida, 1898," *Florida Historical Quarterly* (July, 1970); "Kansas Negroes and the Spanish-American War," *Kansas Historical Quarterly*, 37 (Autumn, 1971); "North Carolina's Negro Regiment in the Spanish-American War," *North Carolina Historical Review*, 48 (October, 1971); and "Alabama's Negro Soldier Experiment," *JNH*, 57 (October, 1972). Colonel Kent's letter is to be found in the Jacob Kent Papers, U.S. Military Academy Library, West Point, New York. The quotation from Lieutenant Lenihan is to be found in Michael Joseph Lenihan, "I Remember—I Remember," Unpublished reminiscences, mss. in the USAMHRC, Carlyle Barracks, Pennsylvania. See also Daniel B. Schirmer, *Republic or Empire* (Cambridge, Mass., 1917). For the mounting hostility to the black regulars in the immediate post–Spanish War period, see "No Praise For Negro," Washington *Post*, December 27, 1898. For the role of blacks in the United States Navy in the Spanish War and its aftermath see Nicholas H. Campbell, "The Negro in the Navy," *The Colored American Magazine*, 6 (June, 1903); and Cleveland *Gazette*, August 22, 1903. The letters from Presley Holliday and E. J. Scott cited in the text are to be found in the Booker T. Washington Papers, LC.

The following studies are essential readings for clarifying the Brownsville affray, the impact of President Roosevelt's action on the black community, and the 1972 decision of the army to clear the records of the discharged blacks: John D. Weaver, *The Brownsville Raid* (New York, 1970); Anne J. Lane, *The Brownsville Affair: National Crisis and Black Reaction* (Port Washington, 1971); Lewis N. Wynne, "Brownsville: The Reaction of the Negro Press," *Phylon*, 33 (Summer, 1972); and Moorfield Storey, "Athens and Brownsville," *The Crisis*, 1 (1910). See also "The Army Clears the Record," *Newsweek*, October 16, 1972. On the deteriorating status of black soldiers and sailors prior to World War I see Robert B. Rackleff, "The Black Soldier in Popular American Magazines, 1900–1971," *NHB*, 34 (December, 1971); "The Negro in the Navy," *The Horizon*, 4 (November, 1909); *NYT*, May

26, 1913; *CSM*, May 31, 1949; and Robert A. Hatch, *The Great White Fleet* (Boston, 1965).

CHAPTER 6

The best treatment of the black experience during World War I is Arthur Edward Barbeau's splendid study, "The Black American Soldier in World War I" (Unpublished Ph.D. thesis, University of Pittsburgh, 1970.) It contains extremely pertinent information on the racial, social, and political climate of the period as well as a comprehensive bibliography. See also Edward M. Coffman, *The War to End All Wars* (New York, 1968).

Dr. Du Bois's views on the war can be consulted in Henry Lee Moon, *The Emerging Thought of W. E. B. Du Bois: Essays and Editorials from The Crisis* (New York, 1972). The position on the war adopted by the editors of the *Messenger* is well drawn in Jervis Anderson, A. *Philip Randolph: A Biographical Portrait* (New York, 1973), while the campaign to secure an officer training camp for black men figures prominently in B. Joyce Ross, *J. E. Spingarn and the Rise of the NAACP, 1911–1939* (New York, 1972). The Houston tragedy is covered in Martha Gruening, "Houston: An NAACP Investigation," and in Robert V. Haynes, "The Houston Mutiny and Riot of 1917," *Southwestern Historical Quarterly*, 76 (April, 1973). For the operation of the draft during World War I, see Paul T. Murray, "Blacks and the Draft: A History of Institutional Racism," *JBS*, 2 (September, 1971). The discrimination to which blacks were subjected in the armed forces and their battlefield role are covered in Carter G. Woodson, *The Negro in Our History* (Washington, D.C., 1928). See also letter from Walter D. Binger to *CSM*, April 17, 1963. On blacks in the navy during World War I see William R. Mueller, "The Negro in the Navy," *Social Forces*, 27 (October, 1945).

On the "Red Summer" of 1919 as well as the disillusionment of black veterans see William M. Tuttle, Jr., *Race Riot: Chicago in the Red Summer of 1919* (New York, 1970). For the persistence of the World War I stereotype of blacks during the postwar period, see Robert Lee Bullard, *Personalities and Reminiscences of the War* (Garden City, 1925); and Ulysses G. Lee, Jr., *The United States Army in World War II, Special Studies: The Employment of Negro Troops* (Washington, D.C., 1966).

On the status of blacks in the armed forces on the eve of World War II, see "10th Cavalrymen Just Servants," *The Afro-American* (Baltimore), June 28, 1937. Herbert Gregory, "Tells of Navy 'Slaves,'" *PC*, March 13, 1971; and Walter Wilson, "Old Jim Crow in Uniform," *The Crisis*, 46 (February and March, 1939).

CHAPTER 7

The Franklin D. Roosevelt Papers, Franklin D. Roosevelt Library, Hyde Park, New York; the Henry L. Stimson Papers, especially Stimson's diary, Yale University Library, New Haven, Connecticut; and the files of the black press and the NAACP in the Manuscript Division of the Library of Congress are indispensable for a study of black servicemen in World War II. Three impressive studies are also of paramount importance: Ulysses Lee, *Employment of Negro Troops* (cited under Chapter 6); Richard M. Dalfiume, *Desegregation of the U.S. Armed Forces: Fighting on Two Fronts, 1939–1953* (Columbia, Mo., 1969); and a Department of Defense study, Jean Byers, *A Study of the Negro in Military Service* (Washington, D.C., 1950).

The situation of black Americans just prior to the entry of the United States into the war is treated in Joseph Lash, *Eleanor and Franklin* (New York, 1971). See also *The Crisis*, 47 (November, 1940). On the response of the black community to the war, see Harvard Sitkoff, "Racial Militancy and Interracial Violence in the Second World War," *Journal of American History*, 58 (December, 1971).

On the experience of black servicemen during the war, see "Letters from the Jim Crow Army," *Twice A Year*, Fall–Winter 1946–47; NR, 110 (March 13, 1944); Walter White, *A Rising Wind* (Garden City, N.Y., 1945), and *idem*, *A Man Called White* (New York, 1948). On the black officers during the war, see Jesse J. Johnson, *Ebony Brass* (New York, 1967); *The Crisis*, 52 (May, 1945); and PM, April 26, 1945. John P. Lucas, *Memoirs*, vol, 2: *Memoirs of Italy*, mss. in USAMHRC, and NR, 112 (March 5, 1945), contains much information on the performance of black combat and service units. On the blacks in the navy during World War II see Dennis Nelson, *The Integration of the Negro into the U.S. Navy* (New York, 1951); PM, April 3 and 19, 1945; and *Commonweal*, 42 (September 21, 1945). On the role of black women in the armed forces see Ulysses Lee, *Employment of Negro Troops*, and PM, April 3, 1945.

CHAPTER 8

The Papers of Harry S. Truman at the Harry S. Truman Library in Independence, Missouri, contain a wealth of information on the blacks and the armed forces in the post–World War II era. The most comprehensive analysis of the steps leading to the elimination of racial discrimination in the military service is contained in Dalfiume, *Desegregation* (cited under Chapter 7). See also William C. Berman, *The Politics of Civil Rights in the Truman Administration* (Columbus, 1970), and Harvard Sitkoff, "Harry Truman and the Election of 1948," *Journal of Southern History*, 37 (November, 1971). On the postwar violence directed against the blacks, see Walter White, *A Man Called White*.

The Gillem Board Report is contained in "Report of Board of Officers on Utilization of Negro Manpower in the Post-War Army, 17 November, 1945," USAMHRC. See also Roy Wilkins, "Still a Jim Crow Army," *The Crisis*, 53 (April, 1946), and L. D. Reddick, "The Negro Policy of the American Army Since World War II," JNH, 38

(April, 1953). The executive order ending discrimination in the armed forces and the work of the Fahy Committee are treated at length in Dalfiume, *Desegregation,* and in *Quest and Response* by Donald R. Mc-Coy and Richard S. Ruetten (Lawrence, Kansas, 1973). On black involvement in the Korean War see A. J. Mayer and T. F. Hoult, "Social Stratification and Combat Survival," *Social Forces,* 34 (December, 1955); *Ebony,* 25 (August, 1968); and Samuel L. Banks, "The Korean Conflict," *NHB,* 38 (October, 1973).

The charges of mistreatment of black GIs in Korea and the response of the NAACP are to be found in Federated Press Reports in the Alexander Gumby Collection, Columbia University, the NAACP News Reports, November–December, 1950. See also Thurgood Marshall, "Summary Justice: The Negro GI in Korea," *The Crisis,* 40 (May, 1951).

On Project Clear see Lee Nichols, *Breakthrough on the Color Front* (New York, 1954), and Leo Bogart, ed., *Social Research and The Desegregation of the U.S. Army* (Chicago, 1969). The completion of the integration of the armed forces is discussed in Richard J. Stillman, II, *Integration of the Negro in the U.S. Armed Forces* (New York, 1968), and Charles C. Moskos, Jr., "Racial Integration in the Armed Forces," *American Journal of Sociology,* 72 (September, 1966).

On the persistence of discrimination against blacks in the armed services, see Maurice Christopher, *America's Black Congressmen* (New York, 1971); Edward L. King, *The Death of the Army* (New York, 1972); U.S. Commission on Civil Rights, *The Negro in the Armed Forces* (Washington, D.C., 1963); the President's Committee on Equal Opportunity in the Armed Forces, *Initial Report* (June 13, 1963), and *Final Report* (November, 1964); and "Some Progress," Brunswick, Maine, *Record,* May 18, 1961.

CHAPTER 9

On the attitude of blacks and their role in the war in Vietnam during its early phase see *Ebony* (August, 1968); Samuel Vance, *The Courageous and the Proud* (New York, 1970); "The Great Society in Uniform," *Newsweek,* August 22, 1966; Charles C. Moskos, Jr., *The American Enlisted Man* (New York, 1970); and *CSM,* August 22, 1967. Roger W. Little, ed., *Selective Service and American Society* (New York, 1969), discusses blacks and the draft.

On the changing attitude of blacks to the war and the growing discontent and militancy among black servicemen, see the monthly "Letters to the Editor" section of *Ebony,* and "Our Men in Vietnam," section of *Sepia,* 1969–1973; David Parks, *GI Diary* (New York, 1968); Fred Halstead, *GI's Speak Out Against the War* (New York, 1970); and H. Paul Jeffers and Dick Levitan, *See Parris and Die* (New York, 1971). The annual index of the *New York Times* lists innumerable articles relating to the blacks and the armed forces during these years. See especially the series of articles by Thomas A. Johnson, "The Negro in Vietnam," April 29 and 30, May 1, 1968. *The Bond,* "The Service-

men's Newspaper," published in New York City, also contains numerous articles relating to black servicemen. During these years magazines
and periodicals were also replete with articles on this subject. A selected
few are: Steven Morris, "How Blacks Upset the Marine Corps," *Ebony*,
21 (December, 1969); Jack White, "The Angry Black Soldiers," *The
Progressive*, 34 (March, 1970); John Grady, "The 'Less Than Honorable' Discharge," *The Nation*, 216 (February 19, 1973); and Milton
White, "Malcolm X in the Military," *The Black Scholar*, 1 (May,
1970).

On the efforts to confront the grievances of black servicemen and
ease racial tensions in the armed forces, see "The Military Meets the
Afro," *Ebony*, 25 (July, 1970). See also articles during 1969–72 published in *Army Digest*, *Army*, *Army Times*, *Air Force Times*, and *Military Review*. The Air Force News Service, Washington, D.C., had
countless articles on this particular phase.

On the continuing discontent among black servicemen and racial
tension during 1970–71, see Haynes Johnson and George C. Wilson,
Army in Anguish (New York, 1972); *The Times* (London), October
15, 1971; William Stuart Gould, "Racial Conflict in the U.S. Army,"
Race, 15 (July, 1973); and *PC*, May 6 and 8, September 14, 1971. See
also articles by Thomas A. Johnson listed in *New York Times* Index
and "Air Force Racism Charged in Study," *NYT*, August 31, 1971.
The following reports should also be examined: "Memorandum for the
Secretary of Defense, U.S. Military Race Relations in Europe, to November, 1970" (Washington, D.C., 1970); "Report of the Joint OSD-
Military Departments Base Visits Team to PACOM, March–April,
1971" (Washington, D.C., 1971); "A Survey of Progress in Equal Opportunity in the Armed Forces," Office of the Assistant Secretary of
Defense, October 15, 1971; and *The Search for Military Justice: Report of an NAACP Inquiry into the Problems of the Negro Servicemen
in West Germany* (New York, 1971).

On the inquiry conducted by the Black Congressional Caucus, see
"Racism in the Military," *Congressional Record*, 118, 92d Cong., 2d
Sess., October 14, 1972; "Institutional Racism in the Military," *ibid.*,
March 2, 1972; "Black Powerlessness," *Time*, November 29, 1971; "At
Caucus Hearings," *PC*, November 13 and 27, 1971; and "Rapping
with Chappie," *Air University Review*, 23, July, 1972.

On blacks and the armed forces after the caucus hearings, see
Charles C. Moskos, Jr., "The American Dilemma in Uniform: Racism
in the Armed Forces," *The Annals*, 406 (March, 1973); "Military
Racism," *Civil Liberties*, February, 1973; "A Piece of the Pie," Air
Force News Service, January 19, 1973; and Augustus F. Hawkins, "Racism in the Military," *Journal and Guide*, January 1, 1972. See also
issues of *Commanders Digest* for October 28 and November 4, 1971;
January 13 and 20, February 17 and 24, March 9 and 23, and November 19, 1972.

On Admiral Zumwalt's reform program see *Commanders Digest*,

January 13 and 20, 1972. On the incidents aboard the *Kitty Hawk*, *Constellation*, etc., see *Journal and Guide* (Norfolk), January 6, 1973; articles in the *NYT* listed in index, especially those by Earl Caldwell, December 25, 1972, and March 26 and May 23, 1973; and *Report by the Special Subcommittee on Disciplinary Problems in the U.S. Navy of the House Committee on Armed Services, January 2, 1973.* See also *Time*, November 27, 1972; *Newsweek*, December 4, 1972; and *AN*, November 11 and 25, December 2, 1972, January 27, 1973. The report of the task force appointed by Secretary of Defense Laird is contained in *Department of Defense Report on the Task Force on the Administration of Military Justice in the Armed Forces, November 30, 1972.* See also *Commanders Digest*, March 22, 1973. On the story of Mark Essex, see *Time*, January 22, 1973, and *NYT*, January 20, 1973. On the *Kitty Hawk* trials see *NYT*, December 30, 1972; January 11 and 12 and February 4, 6, 12, 13, 15, and 24, 1973, on the discharge of men found to be a "burden to the navy" and the navy's new recruiting policy, see *NYT*, February 2 and 4, 1973, and *AN*, February 10, 1973. "The Volunteer Army: Black Misgivings," *Christian Century*, February 28, 1973, and "Letters to the Editor," *Ebony*, 28, February–May, 1973, discuss blacks and the volunteer army.

Index